Humana Festival 2016
The Complete Plays

About the Humana Foundation

The Humana Foundation was established in 1981 as the philanthropic arm of Humana Inc., one of the nation's leading health and well-being companies. Located in Louisville, KY, the Foundation seeks to improve community health and well-being through support of nonprofit partners that promote healthy behaviors, health education, and access to health services. For more information, visit www.HumanaFoundation.org.

Humana and the Humana Foundation are dedicated to Corporate Social Responsibility. Our goal is to ensure that every business decision we make reflects our commitment to improving the health and well-being of our members, our associates, the communities we serve, and our planet.

Humana Festival 2016
The Complete Plays

Edited by
Amy Wegener and Jenni Page-White

Playscripts
Inc.

New York, NY

Published by Playscripts, Inc.
7 Penn Plaza, Suite 904
New York, New York, 10001
www.playscripts.com

Cover Design by Philip Allgeier
Text Design and Layout by Lizzie Martinez

First Edition: March 2017
10 9 8 7 6 5 4 3 2 1

LCCN: 95650734
ISSN: 1935-4452

ISBN-13: 978-1-68069-038-5

Contents

Acknowledgments

The editors wish to thank the following persons for their invaluable assistance in compiling this volume:

Jennifer Bielstein
Kate Cuellar
Sara Durham
Bryan Howard
James Kennedy
Steve Knight
Lizzie Martinez
Meredith McDonough
Zachary Meicher-Buzzi
Kevin E. Moore
Hannah Rae Montgomery
Nick O'Leary
Helena D. Pennington
Jessica Reese
Jeffrey S. Rodgers
Julie Roberts
Zan Sawyer-Dailey
Emily Tarquin
Paige Vehlewald
Les Waters
Mary Kate Zihar

Beth Blickers
Michael Finkle
Ben Izzo
Jonathan Lomma
Mark Orsini
Bruce Ostler
Olivier Sultan
Rachel Viola
Derek Zasky

Actors Theatre of Louisville Staff
Humana Festival 2016

ARTISTIC DIRECTOR, Les Waters
MANAGING DIRECTOR, Jennifer Bielstein

ARTISTIC

Associate Artistic Director . . . . Meredith McDonough
Associate Director . . . . Zan Sawyer-Dailey
Arts Administration Coordinator . . . . Zachary Meicher-Buzzi
Interim Arts Administration Coordinator . . . . Curtis Conlin
Company Manager . . . . Dot King
Arts Administration Intern . . . . Kyle Hatfield
Directing Interns . . . . .James Kennedy, Nick O'Leary

Literary
Director . . . . Amy Wegener
Literary Manager . . . . Jenni Page-White
Resident Dramaturg . . . . Hannah Rae Montgomery
Literary Associate . . . . Jessica Reese
Dramaturgy/Literary Management Interns . . . . Kate Cuellar,
Helena D. Pennington

Education
Director . . . . Jane B. Jones
Education Manager . . . . .Betsy Anne Huggins
Education Associate . . . . Lexy Leuszler
Teaching Artists . . . . .Justin Dobring, Liz Fentress,
Keith McGill, Talleri McRae,
Letitia Usher, Karin Partin Wells
Education/Teaching Artist Interns . . . . Jes Childress, Jenn Oswald

Apprentice/Intern Company
Director . . . . .Michael Legg
Assistant Director . . . . John Rooney
A/I Administration Intern . . . . .Jonathan Harper Schlieman
Apprentices . . . . Austin Blunk, Lisa Bol, Michael T. Brown,
Glenna Brucken, Michael Fell, Tracey Green,
Mbali Guliwe, Alejandro Hernandez,
Hannah Karpenko, Yaron Lotan, Esaú Mora,
Jayson Speters, Ari Shapiro, Adenike Thomas,
Walls Trimble, Sara Turner, Kyle Whalen,
Addison Williams, Park Williams,
Amelia Windom

ADMINISTRATION

General Manager . . . . Jeffrey S. Rodgers
Human Resources Manager . . . . Marie Tull
Systems Manager . . . . Dottie Krebs
Executive Assistant . . . . Janelle Baker
Administrative & IT Services Coordinator . . . . Alan Meyer

AUDIENCE SERVICES & SALES

Ticket Sales Director . . . . Kim McKercher
Season Tickets Manager . . . . Julie Gallegos
Box Office Managers . . . . Steve Clark, Kristy Kannapell
Customer Service Representatives . . . . Cheryl Anderson,
Catherine Aubrey, LaShana Avery, Matthew Brown,
Kyle Hatfield, Marty Huelsmann, Deva North, Kelly Scott

Volunteer and Audience Relations
Director . . . . Allison Hammons
Senior House Manager . . . . Elizabeth C. Cooley
House Managers . . . . Kayla Boulton, Tiffany Bush,
Mallory Marsh, Katie Sammons, Samantha Watzek
Lobby Manager . . . . Tiffany Walton
Coat Check Supervisor . . . . Tanisha Johnson
Coat Check Attendants . . . . Tia Kelley, Patrick Vaughn

DEVELOPMENT

Director . . . . Julie Roberts
Associate Director of Development . . . . Shannon Kisselbaugh
National Philanthropy Manager . . . . Justin Williamson
Community Philanthropy Manager . . . . Carrie Syberg
Annual Fund Manager . . . . Jacob Freund
Donor Relations Manager . . . . Liz Magee
Development Intern . . . . Elizabeth C. Cooley

FINANCE

Director . . . . Peggy Shake
Accounting Coordinator . . . . Jason Acree
Accounting Assistant . . . . Jillian Innes

MARKETING & COMMUNICATIONS

Director . . . . Steve Knight
Communications Manager . . . . Sara Durham
Marketing Manager . . . . Melissa Hines
Festival & Events Manager . . . . Erin Meiman
Graphic Designer . . . . Mary Kate Zihar
Assistant Graphic Designer . . . . Amie Villiger
Group Sales Manager . . . . Sarah Peters

Group Sales Associate. . . . . Chris O'Leary
Marketing Intern . . . . .Sonia Diaz
Communications Intern . . . . Tia Kelley
Festival Intern . . . . .Cristine Figueiredo

OPERATIONS

Director . . . . Mike Schüssler-Williams
Operations Manager . . . . Barry Witt
Maintenance. . . . . .Ricky Baldon, John Voyles
Building Services. . . . . Joe Spencer
Receptionist . . . . Amanda Marshbanks

PRODUCTION

Production Manager . . . . .Paul Werner
Assistant Production Manager . . . . Michael Whatley
Production Management Intern. . . . . .Katie Sammons
Production Stage Manager . . . . .Paul Mills Holmes
Resident Stage Managers. Stephen Horton, Katie Shade
Resident Assistant Stage Manager . . . . Jessica Kay Potter
Stage Management Interns . . . . .Abbie Betts, Codey Butler,
Anna Neikirk, Olivia Tymon

Scenic

Technical Director. . . . . Justin Hagovsky
Assistant Technical Director . . . . Braden Blauser
Scenic Charge. . . . . Kieran Wathen
Interim Scenic Charge. . . . . .Sabra Crockett
Shop Foreman . . . . Javan Roy-Bachman
Master Carpenter. . . . . .Ashley Crockett Guido
Carpenters . . . . Alexia Hall, Eric Kneller, Winslow Lindsay,
Joen Pallesen, Collin Sage, Libby Stone,
Jacob Turner, Pierre Vendette
Deck Carpenters . . . . Matthew Krell, Peter Regalbuto
Automation Operator . . . . Nick Dent
Scenic Artistry Intern . . . . .Anna Stine

Costumes

Director . . . . Kristopher Castle
Costume Shop Foreman . . . . Tamara Langman
Crafts Master . . . . .Shari Cochran
Wig and Makeup Supervisor. . . . . Jehann Gilman
Wardrobe Supervisors. . . . . .Emily Astorian, Molly Herman
Draper/Tailor . . . . Jeffery Park
First Hand . . . . Natalie Maynard
Stitcher Captain . . . . .Elizabeth Hahn
Stitchers . . . . .Faith Brown, Christine Leidner
Costume Design Journeymen. . . . . Maggie McGrann, Adrienne Nixon
Wig and Makeup Journeyman . . . . .Marissa Kulp

Lighting

Supervisor . . . . Jason E. Weber
Assistant Lighting Supervisor. . . . . Dani Clifford
Master Electrician . . . . John Newman
Pamela Brown Lighting Technician. . . . . Jon Harden
Bingham Lighting Technician . . . . Katie Carr
Swing Lighting Technician . . . . Jacqueline Malenke
Electricians. Aaron Bowling, Ben Carter, Alexa Holloway,
Michael Pettit, Rob Woodall
Lighting Intern . . . . Cheyenne Davis

Sound

Supervisor . . . . Paul Doyle
Assistant Sound Supervisor . . . . Jessica Collins
Sound Technicians. . . . . Russell Goddard,
Rachel Spear, Amanda Werre

Properties

Director . . . . Mark Walston
Properties Master. . . . . Joe Cunningham
Assistant Properties Master . . . . Heather Lindert
Carpenter Artisan . . . . Karl Anderson
Soft Goods Artisan . . . . Jessie Combest
General Artisans . . . . Brad Baute, Noah Johnson
Props Journeyman. . . . . Lucy Briggs

VIDEO

Media Technologist . . . . Philip Allgeier

USHER CAPTAINS

Dolly Adams, Shirley Adkins, Marie Allen, Miranda Atkinson, Katherine Austin, June Blair, Libba & Chuck Bonifer, Tanya Briley, Maleva Chamberlain, Donna Conlon, Terry Conway, Laurie Eiden, Doris Elder, Reese Fisher, Joyce French, Kate Gemperline, Carol Halbleib, Avani Kabra, Sandy Kissling, Nickie Langdon, Barbara Nichols, Cathy Nooning, Teresa Nusz, Judy Pearson, Beth Phipps, Nancy Rankin, Bob Rosedale, Tim Unruh, David Wallace, Megg Ward

Foreword

The Humana Festival of New American Plays celebrated its 40th anniversary this year. For four decades, Actors Theatre of Louisville has been the home of this theatrical giant, which has introduced 450 plays by more than 370 playwrights and ensembles, launching countless subsequent productions around the country and abroad. The festival's impact on the American dramatic repertoire has been profound. Plays first seen in Louisville include successes such as D.L. Coburn's *The Gin Game*, Beth Henley's *Crimes of the Heart*, and Donald Margulies' *Dinner with Friends*, all winners of the Pulitzer Prize, as well as more recent hits like Branden Jacobs-Jenkins' *Appropriate* (2014 Obie Award for Best New American Play), Kimber Lee's *brownsville song (b-side for tray)* (2014 Ruby Prize), and Lucas Hnath's *The Christians* (one of *American Theatre* magazine's top ten most-produced plays of the 2016–2017 season). Humana Festival plays have won many other honors, have been adapted for film and television, and more than 400 have been published, making them available to readers far and wide. This history encompasses hundreds of successful plays and playwrights, far more than can be catalogued in this brief space.

But the Humana Festival's impact on our industry can be measured in more than awards and subsequent productions. It has also helped catapult careers forward. Since the festival began back in 1977, it's been a critical launching pad for a legion of extraordinarily creative playwrights. For some of those writers, the Humana Festival offered them their first professional production; for many more, it introduced their work to a national audience. The festival is also a pivotal training ground for the young artists in Actors Theatre's Professional Training Company (formerly known as the Apprentice/Intern Company). The Artistic, Production, and Administrative Apprentices in this program are immersed in practical, experiential learning at one of the nation's preeminent powerhouses for new play production. That training has jump-started the careers of many distinguished leaders in theatre. Some former PTC members return to Actors Theatre as full-time staff, like my friend and colleague Meredith McDonough, our Associate Artistic Director. And many, many more go on to leadership positions on staff and onstage in theatres nationwide, extending the ripple effect of the Humana Festival's legacy.

Year after year, the Humana Festival brings together a diverse community of artists for a celebration of the great breadth of American playwriting. As we mark this milestone in the history of the festival, it's no surprise that our 40th anniversary lineup includes a wide spectrum of voices, and plays by friends both old and new. Some of the names featured in this collection are familiar to Humana Festival audiences: playwrights like festival alumni Jen Silverman,

Cory Hinkle, Laura Jacqmin, and five-time veteran Steven Dietz (who has participated as both a playwright and director). *For Peter Pan on her 70ᵗʰ birthday*, written by my longtime collaborator Sarah Ruhl, is her first full-length play to premiere at the festival. But this collection also features work by Humana Festival newcomers Tasha Gordon-Solmon, Hansol Jung, Martyna Majok, Meg Miroshnik, Jiehae Park, Brendan Pelsue, and James Kennedy. (Notably, Brendan is an alumnus of the Professional Training Company, and James was in the program when his ten-minute play premiered at the festival). These twelve remarkable playwrights illuminate the world we live in now, and take us to worlds not yet imagined. It's invigorating to be able to showcase such a range of perspectives in one anthology.

Producing the festival each spring requires tremendous energy from our fiercely talented team of artists, staff, and volunteers—but it also gives energy. I'm so thankful to be a part of the history of the Humana Festival and its decades-long commitment to the full production of new plays. As we look to the future, I invite you to help us shape the next era of American theatre by supporting these groundbreaking plays and playwrights.

—Les Waters
Artistic Director
Actors Theatre of Louisville

Editors' Note

As we reflect upon the plays of the 2016 Humana Festival, with four decades of world premieres in Actors Theatre of Louisville's rearview mirror, we can't help but notice in this collection a preoccupation with the slippery, ephemeral nature of experience. Perhaps the fact that the festival turned 40 this year invites such a lens; after all, 40 is a birthday associated with an awareness of mortality, the roads not taken, and the seeming acceleration of time. While we never program a festival slate with a theme in mind, these extraordinary and wildly different theatrical worlds, in retrospect, do seem to point toward the feeling of arriving at a crossroads. Taken as a group, they examine how memory and history tether us (or don't), and the ways in which life's defining moments can be unexpectedly shaped by chance.

This festival's existential stew often contains insights about the impact of humans' fleeting yet powerful connections with strangers. *Residence*, Laura Jacqmin's keenly observed "containment study" of friendships forged at an extended-stay hotel, examines the meaningful influence of the most temporary of bonds. On the other hand, Steven Dietz's funny and poignant *This Random World* challenges us to consider that our winding paths may be defined more by near-misses than serendipitous encounters, that there are lives happening alongside our own that we just can't perceive. And awkwardly missed and misread social cues are taken to comic extremes by Tasha Gordon-Solmon in *Coffee Break*, wherein the shapes in a woman's latte foam spark a one-sided (and very brief) romance with a barista, derailing conversation with a lovelorn friend.

The transitory nature of things is also a concern for more enduring, life-long relationships, such as the familial bonds that Sarah Ruhl draws with great warmth in *For Peter Pan on her 70th birthday*. Here, five aging siblings gather on the occasion of their father's passing, sharing childhood memories, jokes, political arguments, and the wish that they could avoid growing up. An acute consciousness of loved ones' mortality looms large in several of the Humana Festival plays this year, but it's the characters' heightened awareness of their own tenuous existence, the puzzle of how to survive and move forward in the face of inevitable loss, that sparks the real drama.

The strong pull of events long past is a recurring source of both comfort and conflict in these plays, from Ruhl's fondly remembered family stories to the life-altering trauma in Hansol Jung's *Cardboard Piano*. Jung's moving tale concerns the fateful night when a makeshift wedding between teenage girls is tragically interrupted by the violent civil war in Uganda, and depicts the struggle toward closure and forgiveness years later. In a more supernatural vein, *Wondrous Strange*, this year's show commissioned for our company of Acting Apprentices, also looks at how past traumas can haunt us. Drawing inspiration from ghost stories and hauntings from around the city of Louisville and the state of Kentucky, playwrights Martyna Majok, Meg Miroshnik, Jiehae Park, and Jen Silverman explore how traces of past connection, whether to places or to people, just won't let go of us—nor we of them.

What the ghosts of the past want to impart can be murky, though, and even the annals of history don't always offer clear answers. Such is the case in Brendan Pelsue's eerily prescient *Wellesley Girl*, which imagines the state of American politics in 2465—years after an environmental disaster has reduced the country to a small handful of New England towns. Due to gaps in the historical record, these last Americans don't know quite how they landed in this reality—and when potential invaders arrive, their shared terror doesn't mean they can agree upon how they'll face the future. Truth is also subjective in Cory Hinkle's playful, post-apocalyptic *This Quintessence of Dust*, in which a woman narrates her relief that she's finally free of social media, but has to contend with two eager ex-boyfriends with their own versions of the past. And if common understanding is elusive at the end of civilization, it's also hard to come by at the edge of the galaxy: James Kennedy hilariously imagines a crew of bored astronauts whose moral and navigational compass is starting to crack in *Trudy, Carolyn, Martha, and Regina Travel to Outer Space and Have a Pretty Terrible Time There*.

From a spaceship careening through the stars to a church in Uganda, from a squabbling future U.S. Congress to Neverland, the singular worlds of the 2016 Humana Festival of New American Plays feel utterly distinct from one another, conjuring rich visual and emotional landscapes. If there is a cumulative awareness here of human impermanence, of uncertainty about where we've been and where we're going, that sensibility finds its expression through voices that are as wonderfully idiosyncratic as any compilation we can imagine. And perhaps it's a given that theatre—this most immediate, live, and elastic form of storytelling—addresses the ephemeral, by its very nature. But the pleasure of editing this volume has been revisiting these texts and thinking about them in concert as we recall their marvelous Louisville productions. While we can't bottle up our memories, we hope to help facilitate something much better: making the scripts directly accessible, so that these vibrant worlds live on in readers' imaginations—and so that you can draw your own connections.

—*Amy Wegener and Jenni Page-White*

THIS RANDOM WORLD
(THE MYTH OF SERENDIPITY)
by Steven Dietz

ABOUT *THIS RANDOM WORLD*

This article first ran in the Limelight Guide to the 40th Humana Festival of New American Plays, *published by Actors Theatre of Louisville, and is based on conversations with the playwright before rehearsals for the Humana Festival production began.*

Over a decade ago, playwright Steven Dietz and his wife, fellow playwright Allison Gregory, were both flying home to Seattle from different cities on the same day. Because their flights were scheduled to arrive at roughly the same time, they planned to find each other at the airport and catch a cab home together. Dietz's plane landed, and as previously arranged, he called Gregory's cell phone.

> "Where are you?"
> *"I just got off the plane."*
> "Terrific, so did I! What gate are you at?"
> *"B25."*
> Dietz paused. "Huh…I'm at gate B25.
> …Wait—what flight were you on?"
> *"United flight 735."*
> "I was on flight 735. What row were you sitting in?"
> *"16D."*
> "I was in 25A!"

And during this phone conversation, standing at the same gate 30 feet from each other, they realized the extraordinary irony of their journey that day: they'd sat in the same waiting area at their connecting airport, boarded the same plane, and sat fewer than ten rows apart during the entire flight—all without being aware of the other.

The experience stuck with Dietz over the years, and eventually inspired the bittersweet insight at the center of his new comedy, *This Random World*. "If that had happened before Allison and I first met, my life would be completely different," the playwright muses. "And so would hers." Fascinated by all the possibilities we may never perceive, Dietz began writing what he calls an "absence narrative." Rather than emphasizing the myriad ways we find fulfillment or a sense of wholeness in our lives, *This Random World* contemplates the pilgrimage we didn't take, the confrontation we didn't have, and the reconciliation we never achieved.

When the play begins, a feisty but ailing elderly woman named Scottie is planning a trip to the Shimogamo Shrine in Kyoto, Japan—a fact she keeps secret from her adult children, Tim and Beth. Meanwhile, Beth is planning a trip of her own: a dangerous and expensive adventure to Nepal that she believes will help her avoid the fate of her "shut-in" mother. And Tim— well, Tim's life has been off-course for a while, and even a chance encounter with his former soulmate can't seem to put him back on track. As the web of characters expands outward, a portrait emerges of a group of people— thwarted by bad timing and incomplete information—who continue to just miss making meaningful connections with the people around them.

"The near-misses—comedically, those appeal to me enormously," says Dietz. A phone call unanswered, an exit too soon, a prank gone wrong— the missed opportunities pile up as the play hurtles onward, careening past the possibility of an "aha" moment when its characters experience a pivotal flash of enlightenment. Part of Dietz's interest in writing the play lay in the challenge of crafting this kind of absence narrative. As part of his writing process, he made a list of scenes the audience would expect to happen: "You know, those two characters should come together and have a confrontation or a reconciliation," Dietz explains. "And then I didn't let those two characters have a scene together." While that self-imposed limitation sometimes baffled him—"There were funny moments when I was thinking, 'There should be a scene here, but who *can* talk to each other?!'" he quips—the rigor of the experiment offered both unexpected narrative turns and a quiet, underlying sadness.

Though drawn to the inherent humor and delight of upended expectations, Dietz is not interested in offering the moment of saccharine harmony that sometimes appears at the resolution of comedies. What interests him about the journeys of the characters in *This Random World* is that their understanding remains elusive—their pilgrimages are incomplete. "There's the trip you plan and the trip you take," Dietz observes. "I tend to write a lot of plays when I get back from traveling," he reflects, recalling a vacation he took to Ireland with his family that occurred shortly after both he and his wife lost their mothers. "It was a seminal trip for me and led to a play of mine called *Bloomsday* that premiered a few months ago. But it shows up in ways I didn't expect in *This Random World*. The grief, the sense of loss I was feeling in Ireland—it can allow us to reflect on our life as though we are standing just to the side of it."

That gift of perspective hovers just beyond the grasp of the characters in *This Random World*. As its progression of seemingly random encounters accumulate, this play evokes the sense that more often than not, spiritual enlightenment doesn't arrive the way we planned. Though we may contrive a meeting or isolate ourselves in a faraway place in the hope that it will transform us, sometimes it is the reality happening just beyond our attention that offers true transformation—and only in retrospect do we understand the gravity of all we may have missed. That this tale takes its shape in the form of a play seems fitting: what better place than the theatre to inspire wonder at all the possibilities beyond our comprehension?

—Jenni Page-White

BIOGRAPHY

Steven Dietz's thirty-plus plays have been seen at over one hundred regional theatres in the United States, as well as Off-Broadway and in twenty countries internationally. Recent premieres include *Bloomsday* (2016 Steinberg/ATCA New Play Award Citation), *This Random World* (2016 Humana Festival of New American Plays), and *On Clover Road* (National New Play Network rolling world premiere). Mr. Dietz is a two-time winner of the Kennedy Center Fund for New American Plays Award: for *Fiction* (produced Off-Broadway by Roundabout Theatre Company), and *Still Life with Iris*. He received the PEN USA West Award in Drama for *Lonely Planet*; the Edgar Award® for Best Mystery Play for *Sherlock Holmes: The Final Adventure*; and the Yomuiri Shimbun Award (the Japanese "Tony") for his adaptation of Shusaku Endo's *Silence*. Other widely produced plays include *Rancho Mirage, Becky's New Car, Last of the Boys, Yankee Tavern, Inventing van Gogh, Shooting Star, God's Country, Private Eyes*, and *The Nina Variations*. Other popular adaptations include *Dracula* (from Stoker), *Force of Nature* (from Goethe), *Paragon Springs* (from Ibsen), and several of Dan Gutman's baseball card adventures: *Honus & Me*, and *Jackie & Me*. Mr. Dietz and his family divide their time between Seattle and Austin, where he teaches playwriting and directing at the University of Texas.

ACKNOWLEDGMENTS

This Random World premiered at the Humana Festival of New American Plays in March 2016. It was directed by Meredith McDonough with the following cast:

BETH WARD	Brenda Withers
TIM WARD	Nate Miller
SCOTTIE WARD	Beth Dixon
BERNADETTE	Shirine Babb
GARY	Todd Lawson
CLAIRE	Renata Friedman
RHONDA	Deonna Bouye
A MAN	Mark Sawyer-Dailey

and the following production staff:

Scenic Designer	Daniel Zimmerman
Costume Designer	Kathleen Geldard
Lighting Designer	Paul Toben
Sound Designer	Christian Frederickson
Stage Manager	Kathy Preher
Dramaturg	Jenni Page-White
Casting	Calleri Casting
	(James Calleri, Paul Davis, Erica Jensen)
Properties Master	Joe Cunningham
Production Assistant	Jacob Weitzman
Directing Assistant	David Ian Lee
Assistant Dramaturg	Kate Cuellar

This Random World received developmental support from The New Harmony Project (New Harmony, IN); Riverside Theatre (Iowa City, IA); and the Theatre Lab at FAU (Boca Raton, FL).

CHARACTERS

SCOTTIE WARD – a woman in her 70s.

TIM WARD – her son, 29.

BETH WARD – her daughter, 38.

BERNADETTE – her aide, 30s.

RHONDA – Bernadette's younger sister, late 20s.

CLAIRE – Tim's ex-girlfriend, 29.

GARY – Claire's ex-boyfriend, 30s.

A MAN – 60s/flexible. [Not listed in playbill, if possible. Thank you.]

*A multi-ethnic cast is strongly encouraged.

TIME AND PLACE

The present. Late winter and early spring.

An American city. And Kyoto, Japan.

NOTES

A few simple and permanent units should suffice for everything. Transformations between them should be quick and easy.

Beyond that, a world that is warm, mysterious and evocative would be appreciated.

And rain would be good.

Thank you.

"We must unlearn the constellations to see the stars."
—Jack Gilbert, *Tear It Down*

Brenda Withers and Todd Lawson
in *This Random World*

40th Humana Festival of New American Plays
Actors Theatre of Louisville, 2016
Photo by Bill Brymer

THIS RANDOM WORLD
(THE MYTH OF SERENDIPITY)

Tim's Small Apartment. February. Rain.

TIM *sits on the ground, noodling around on his laptop. He is dressed for a lazy day inside.*
BETH, *his older sister, is nicely dressed. She reads from a document.*

BETH. (*gravely.*) "… *Elizabeth Ward – known to all as Beth – was a loving sister and a caring friend. Though she will be missed by many, her laughter, her warmth, and her passion for living will continue to echo within our hearts. Memorial services will be held at—*"

(*brightly, lowering the paper, to* TIM.)

—and here you'll just insert whichever place you have the service for me. I've included two options in my End Of Life papers. All that info is in the same folder as my Will, which as you know is in my safe deposit box. You've got the key to my safe deposit box I gave you, right? *Tim?*

TIM. Oh, to your little box at the bank—

BETH. Safe deposit box.

TIM. (*overlapping.*) —yes, right, of course. Got it. Safe and sound.

BETH. Where is it?

TIM. I know where it is.

BETH. Tell me. Say it out loud.

TIM. Beth, you are not dying!

BETH. No – but when the day comes, I am counting on you.

TIM. You just stop living. I'll take care of everything else.

BETH. There's no backup plan for us, you know. With Dad gone and Scottie ready to follow him, now it's just us. Just you and me.

TIM. It's weird that you call Mom "Scottie." When did you start doing that?

BETH. That's what everyone's always called her.

TIM. Still – it's weird.

BETH. What do you call her?

TIM. (*incredulous.*) I call her … "Mom" …! And I think she's doing okay.

BETH. How would you know that? Have you talked to her? Of course you haven't talked to her. Why don't you talk to her? You're Scottie's favorite.

TIM. No, I am not her—

BETH. Oh my god! You are the golden boy on top of the shining chariot!

TIM. Don't do that. Don't put that "you are the perfect son" pressure on me. No one should have to live up to that.

BETH. Oh, please—

TIM. I've wanted to talk to her – I've been meaning to talk to her.

BETH. But communication is so hard in these days of the Telegraph and the Pony Express.

TIM. Forget it.

BETH. You can call her aide. If you can't reach Mom, sometimes it's good to call her aide.

TIM. Mom has an aide?

BETH. Bernadette. You know this. And Bernie says Mom only gets out once a day. To look at the sunrise.

TIM. The *sunrise* – why?

BETH. I don't know but that's it. That's all she does. She has no friends, from what I can tell – no activities she's interested in – even though the senior center has bridge and bingo and an a cappella group that does those old-timey songs—

TIM. Mom would hate that!

BETH. —yes, okay – but she's got to do something! I thought sure she'd want to travel. They have those package tours for seniors. Remember all the books she had about India, China, Japan?
It's maddening.
Do you have any Kleenex? Anywhere?

TIM. No. Sorry.
Are you crying?

BETH. She's our mom, Tim.

> (*Pause.*)

TIM. But she can't travel. What if something happened?

BETH. Like she met someone? Or had a conversation? Or saw more of the world than the three mile radius she's lived in for the last 50 years?

TIM. But what if she's not—

BETH. Her health is not great – okay – we know that – but her doctor told me if she really wanted to travel she could travel.

TIM. And you'd do nothing but worry about her – call to check up on her—

BETH. That's not true.
That's true.
Does she let you in?

TIM. What?

BETH. She doesn't let me in. Doesn't tell me things. She never calls. And she doesn't seem to want me to call her.

TIM. She doesn't want you to worry.

BETH. I worry because she doesn't want me to call!

TIM. And what would you say if you did? *Hey, Mom: go on a trip so I'll feel better but don't go on a trip because I'll worry about you.*

> (*Pause.*)

BETH. Yes. That's exactly what I'd say.

TIM. Maybe she just wants to stay home and piss off the Travel Nazis.

> (*off* BETH's *look.*)

You know those people! The ones who travel just to shame other people for *not* traveling: "Oh my god – you haven't been to Such-and-Such?! How can you NOT have been to Such-and-Such?! You *have* to go. I mean, you *HAVE* to go."—

BETH. Yes, Tim, I get it—

TIM. (*overlapping.*) —You just know they take those trips so they can *lord it over you later* – when in fact all they are doing is running away from their lives.

> (TIM *goes back to noodling on his laptop.*)

BETH. So, I'm off to Nepal.

> (TIM *turns to her.*)

I told you this – over a year ago. A group expedition.
Dangerous. Expensive.
I told you this. I sent you a link.

TIM. No, you—

BETH. Yes, I did! This Travel Nazi is going on a very expensive and dangerous adventure to Nepal because apparently I need to *run away from my life!*

> (*before* TIM *can respond.*)

And what about you? I am looking at what passes for your life and your apartment and your "career" and – well – I don't see a lot of proof of your existence either!—

TIM. What kind of thing is—

BETH. (*overlapping.*) —I mean – really – do you have any *actual evidence* that you are, in fact, living and breathing and connected in some way to the known world?!

> (*He stares at her, seemingly preparing a really good answer. Then …*
> *He goes back to his laptop, avidly.*)

You should have Kleenex.
Doesn't Marlene ever need Kleenex when she comes over?

Does Marlene still come over?

Okay, what's up with Marlene?

Oh, Tim …

TIM. It's okay. We were done.

BETH. I'm so sorry.

> (*Pause.*)

Maybe it will give you something to write about.

TIM. That's not happening either.

BETH. Since when?

TIM. That has never happened. You know that. Calling me a "writer" is something you and Mom cooked up to keep from calling me a "failure."

BETH. That is not—

> (*HIS LOOK stops her.*)

Okay. That's true.

> (*Pause.*)

What about work?

You had that big freelance project? Those websites? Some kind of programming that I don't understand.

Did you do it?

Did that end?

Did they let you go?

They let you go.

You did something.

You said something.

It ended badly.

Oh jesus, Tim – not again!

TIM. It's okay.

BETH. It doesn't seem okay.

TIM. It's okay.

BETH. You seem sad. Are you sad?

TIM. I'm not sad. I'm—

> (*stops.*)

BETH. What?

TIM. I'm … *composting.*

A lot of shit has happened to me lately – not just Marlene and the jobs – other stuff too – and so I am just … *sitting with it* and letting it *settle the way it needs to …*

> (*he's just making this up now, but doing so earnestly, convincing himself.*)

… letting the – you know – little flies and worms and things sort of buzz and dig all around in it …

BETH. Oh jesus god.

TIM. ... until my shit isn't shit anymore ... until my shit is, like, *nutrients* ... and then my shit will be *awesome* ... my shit will be *good for me.*

> (*Pause.*)

BETH. Any word from Claire?

TIM. Why do you always bring up Claire?

BETH. We all liked Claire. Especially Mom.

TIM. Claire was high school! Claire was a dozen years ago! I haven't heard from Claire in forever.

BETH. Okay. I just—

TIM. I don't bug you about your love life!

BETH. Because I don't have a love life!

TIM. That's not true! – there was that—

BETH. I have NEVER had a love life.

TIM. Because you've never TRIED.

BETH. CAN WE PLEASE JUST TALK ABOUT MY DEATH?

> (TIM *stares at her.*
> BETH *lifts the paper again.*)

Okay, so: right before you post my obit, you'll just add in whichever place ends up being chosen for the memorial service. I've got a springtime choice and a fall-winter choice. It's all written down.

TIM. Why two choices?

BETH. Well it obviously varies because of the light, the weather, seasonal expenses—

TIM. What if you die in the summer?

BETH. I won't die in the summer. I've run the numbers.

TIM. You've *run the numbers?*

BETH. Odds are I die on this trip to Nepal – midwinter, March at the latest – but in case that doesn't kill me, I'll likely die two years from now when I'm skydiving.

> (*off* TIM's *look.*)

For my 40th. You know I'm skydiving for my 40th. I told you. I sent you a link. And anyway that death would be, like, October-November. If I live through both of those, I'll likely live to be 90 or 92 – at least according to my doctor – and in the long recorded history of our family not a single female has died in June, July or August. Apparently, the women of the Ward family *thrive on summer.*

TIM. Do you just sit around and think about this?

BETH. Of course I do. Have you written your obit?

TIM. Have I *what?*

BETH. Things happen, you know.

TIM. Nothing is going to happen! I am not going on a dangerous trip and then jumping out of a perfectly good airplane.

BETH. Take control of your death, Tim Ward. Or somebody else will. And go see Scottie. She misses you.

(*She gathers her things, preparing to leave.*)

I'll try to check in from an airport somewhere. But if it's a couple weeks, don't freak out.

TIM. I won't freak out.

BETH. I mean, you can freak out a little – if too much time passes. This is a very dangerous trip—

TIM. Yes, you keep saying that—

BETH. —we are WAY off the grid over there, but for once in my life I think that's the thing I want. See you in a month.

TIM. If you live.

BETH. Correct. Oh, hey you know something fun I did? I Googled obituaries of people with my same name. Found a whole bunch of dead Beth Wards.

TIM. You did this for fun?

BETH. It's really odd to read your own name and then see another life listed under it. You feel like a … kinship with these people. Strangers. But not really strangers, you know?

(*off his look.*)

What?

TIM. You are such a weirdo.

BETH. Nice final words.

(*She goes.*)

A Park. February. Dawn.

SCOTTIE *is standing behind her walker, wearing a coat. Staring front, into the distance.*

BERNADETTE, *her aide, is standing nearby. She holds SCOTTIE's enormous and somewhat garish purse. She also stares front, into the distance.*

SCOTTIE. Look at that sunrise.

Isn't that something?

BERNADETTE. (*droll, but friendly.*) It's a lot like yesterday.

 (SCOTTIE *turns to her.*)

And the day before.

SCOTTIE. When I interviewed you, Bernadette, I tried to make it clear that I was a kind but impulsive lady of a certain age, and that—

BERNADETTE. —and that you planned to see the sunrise every day.

SCOTTIE. Yes.

BERNADETTE. *Every single day.*

SCOTTIE. And hasn't it been lovely?

BERNADETTE. Four years and seven months.

SCOTTIE. (*a friendly dig.*) But who's counting, yes?

 (BERNADETTE *smiles a bit, patiently.*
 They turn back and view the sunrise.)

Do they really all look the same to you?
I bet I thought that, too. When I was younger.

 (*They view the sunrise.*)

I heard your mother passed.

BERNADETTE. Yes.

SCOTTIE. I'm sorry.
You didn't mention it.

BERNADETTE. No.

SCOTTIE. Well. If there's anything I can do.

 (*Pause.*
 SCOTTIE *needs something from her purse. Before she even turns and asks,*
 BERNADETTE *has produced and handed it to* SCOTTIE.)

SCOTTIE. (*re: the cup.*) Thank you.

 (*It is a small, unadorned* <u>bronze cup</u> *— no handles, about the size of a small tumbler.*
 SCOTTIE *holds the cup in her hands. She is comforted by its feel, its weight.*)

This cup is well-traveled, you know. It came with us last year to Iceland.

BERNADETTE. Yes, it did.

SCOTTIE. Iceland was so nice. I rode my first horse there, remember? In Iceland of all places! And you took all those pictures.

BERNADETTE. I wanted to send some to Beth and Tim.

SCOTTIE. Thank you again for not doing that. I appreciate your discretion.

BERNADETTE. You told me to lie to them!

SCOTTIE. And you've done a wonderful job with that. Thank you.

BERNADETTE. Why won't you tell your kids you take these trips?!

(*Beat.* SCOTTIE *stares at her.*)

SCOTTIE. Have you heard of the Shimogamo Shrine? It is in Kyoto, Japan. The path to the Shimogamo Shrine goes through what is called "The Forest Where Lies Are Revealed." This forest has been left to grow wild. Never planted, never pruned. This I would love to see.

I've booked a trip for us.

You are very quiet.

BERNADETTE. Could my sister go in my place?

(SCOTTIE *says nothing.*)

My younger sister, Rhonda. I'd be so grateful if she could go instead of me – just this one time. Rhonda rarely travels. And things have been hard for her since our mom died. Rhonda's gotten … strange … sort of mystical or something … she's obsessed with this guy at her work named Steve Greene – who sounds like he might be a shaman or a medium or something—

(*before* SCOTTIE *can respond.*)

—and yes I'm feeling guilty because she keeps saying "Bernie, it's not fair! – Bernie, Mom liked you best!" – but since you've asked if there's something you could do, I thought maybe—

SCOTTIE. Absolutely not. You will come with me on this trip – as you always do – because that is why I hired you—

BERNADETTE. Yes, I know, but—

SCOTTIE. (*overlapping.*) —and that is the end of this discussion. We leave a week from Tuesday. I expect the standard discretion.

(*Pause.*)

BERNADETTE. Yes, Mrs. Ward.

SCOTTIE. And don't let people call you Bernie. Your name is Bernadette.

A Not-Great Diner. February. Rain.

After the meal, CLAIRE *sits alone with the dirty plates.*
The check has been paid.
CLAIRE *stares blankly for a long moment.*
GARY *arrives.*
He is carrying a small plastic "take-away" container for leftovers. He sets the container down carefully in front of CLAIRE.
CLAIRE *stares at the container for awhile.*

GARY. Is that big enough? Claire?

(*off her look.*)

Will that hold the rest of your quesadilla?

CLAIRE. I think it's fine.

Thank you, Gary.

GARY. Sure.

CLAIRE. Thank you for going up there and getting this take-away container for me.

I know I stood up and wanted to leave – but you were right to remind me that I still had a four inch section of quesadilla on my plate. And that's wasteful. I should have known better. *"People are hungry in the world, Claire"* – you said that to me, and how right you are—

GARY. Claire, listen—

CLAIRE. (*overlapping.*) —*how right you are, Gary.*

> (GARY *stares at her. Then looks away.*
> *The SOUND OF RAIN continues.*
> *Now:* CLAIRE *uses a few pieces of her silverware to slowly and carefully lift the section of quesadilla from her plate … and set it with great precision inside the take-away container. It's as though she were working with radium.*
> *Before she closes the lid of the take-away container, she looks up at* GARY.)

CLAIRE. Any final words?

GARY. What?

CLAIRE. Before I close the lid. Anything we want to say to this last little bit of quesadilla?

GARY. Jesus, Claire—

CLAIRE. Let's bow our heads, shall we?

> (GARY *stands—*)

GARY. I'm not doing this.

CLAIRE. Oh, I see: you get to have final words but I don't? Isn't that why we came here today? – it sure wasn't for the food – didn't we come here to listen to your final words to me, Gary?

> (GARY *stares at her. Then …*
> GARY *sits back down at the table.*)

And we are bowing our heads …

> (*They do.*)

And we are closing our eyes …

> (*They do.*)

CLAIRE. (*solemn, real.*) Before the closing of this lid – on this rainy day in February – let us mark for one another this moment:

GARY. (*opening his eyes.*) Oh, c'mon—

CLAIRE. (*quickly, eyes still closed.*) Close your eyes, Gary.

> (*And he does.*)

This lone section of quesadilla – these humble four inches of salt and flour and water and cheese … this represents the very last thing that Gary and Claire will ever share in this world.

GARY. (*quietly, eyes closed.*) Please don't do this …

CLAIRE. So let us properly mark the moment here today when Gary told Claire it was over.
And the next moment when Claire asked Gary why.
And the moment after that when Gary said it seemed like Claire could not be "present" – truly present with him—

GARY. (*eyes still closed.*) Those are not the words I used—-

CLAIRE. (*overlapping.*) —because she is filled with what Gary calls "misplaced nostalgias" – because she still talks about high school and childhood and growing up way too much – as though she were stuck in the past—

GARY. Claire, please—

CLAIRE. (*overlapping.*) —and if Claire is already stuck like that, how will she and Gary ever *look to the future! – live the moment! – Carpe The Diem and All That?!*

(*She opens her eyes and looks at* GARY.)

And let the record note that Claire said:
Okay, Gary. Maybe you're right. Give me another chance. Let's give it one more try.

(GARY *has opened his eyes now, too.*)

And Gary said …
And *you* said:
No.
You said: *We've tried for more than a year. It didn't work. I don't think we should try anymore.*

(*Silence.*)

And I said: *Man, it's really raining out there. We're going to get soaked.*
And you didn't say anything.
And I said: *The hell with it – I don't care if I get soaked. I need to go.*
And I stood up.
And here, Gary … here is where I was waiting for you to say something really Great. I was thinking to myself "god he could say something really Great right here – and maybe that would change everything – maybe we'd still work things out."

(*before* GARY *can respond.*)

I know that's unfair. I know there was no way for you to know it was time to come up with the Awesome Thing and Say It – but *right there*, Gary … *that* was the time for you to say *Something Great*.
And you said …

(CLAIRE *looks down at the quesadilla.*)

"You should box that up. There are homeless people around the corner. You should give that food to them."

> (*In silence – and with a kind of reverence:* CLAIRE *slowly closes the lid to the take-away container. It snaps shut with finality.*)

I suck at life, Gary. I suck big time.

GARY. No, don't say—

CLAIRE. Here I am thinking about my little shattered heart when there are people with nothing to eat. Thank you for reminding me of that.

And thank you for bringing me to a shitty restaurant for our break-up. I should have seen it coming. We've walked by this place so many times and we always said: *God, what a pit.* We always joked that people should break up at shitty places they were never gonna want to visit again. Because of the memories …

The way that goodbyes …

The way that endings just … *stick to a place* …

> (*Pause.*)

Will you please go now? Please go – and give the homeless people this food – and leave me alone so I can have a good cry, you asshole.

GARY. *Claire—*

CLAIRE. *Please.*

> (*She hands him the take-away container.*)

CLAIRE. (*re: the container.*) Tell them I'm sorry. Tell them I wish there was more.

> (*He takes the container and leaves.*
> CLAIRE *is alone.*)

Arbor View Memory Gardens. Day.

> RHONDA *is nicely and conservatively dressed. She stands near a simple counter that holds a laptop computer, a pot of coffee, and a box of tissues. Nearby is a large wreath of flowers on a stand.*
> TIM *appears, wearing old jeans and a sweatshirt.*

RHONDA. (*kind, genuine.*) Good morning and welcome to Arbor View Memory Gardens. I'm Rhonda. Would you like a tissue? They're beige.

TIM. Yeah, no, I don't—

RHONDA. It's a comforting color. White tissues are so *strident*, don't you think? But the beige are more suited to our work here at Arbor View. Now, if I may ask:

How did you know the deceased?

TIM. I am the deceased.

(*She stares at him. He smiles a bit.*)

I know – it's weird. My name is Tim Ward. Timothy Ward. My name just *showed up* online.

RHONDA. It must be odd. To see your own name like that.

TIM. Yes! It is very odd, because—

RHONDA. We get young men who are "Juniors" – you know, same name as their dad – and they see the words on the tombstone and oh my gosh there it is – there is their actual name.

TIM. Tim Ward is my actual name. It's there on your site. You can see for yourself: I'm 29. The dead guy is 29.

RHONDA. We don't say "dead." We say "deceased."

TIM. Okay – look – it's a mistake and I'm sorry, but I need you to please correct it.

RHONDA. Correct it?

TIM. Because obviously I'm not dead!—

(*no reaction from* RHONDA.)

—because I'm standing right here!

RHONDA. Yes, I see you …

TIM. Great – okay—

RHONDA. That is remarkable …

TIM. —yeah, pretty weird, right?

RHONDA. (*sincere.*) Steve Greene told me about this. Steve Greene trained me at this job. And he said every now and again they come back – *one final time* – to look at their own casket, check out the flowers and cards, see who came to mourn them and how they were dressed.

TIM. Wait—

RHONDA. Steve Greene told me they'd walk in the door – or maybe *through* the door – I'm not sure, I wish I'd asked him that – and they would find Steve Greene and talk to him. Steve Greene was the only one who could see them – and I think that's why they fired him. But let me tell you this: *No better friend did the dead ever have than the man we knew as Steve Greene.*

TIM. Is there someone else I can talk to?

RHONDA. There was something about Steve Greene that put the deceased at ease: *a quality of mercy*, I guess—

TIM. Okay, listen—

RHONDA. (*overlapping.*) —and Steve Greene told me if I projected a "merciful countenance" … he said maybe one day the deceased would approach me, too. Like you've done.

TIM. I didn't come to see you, Rhonda.

RHONDA. You came for Steve. I know.

TIM. I came because I was Googling obituaries with the same name as me – some ridiculous thing my sister told me to do – and I found some guy named Tim Ward, age 67 *[or age of actor]*, who had just died. And since your site is so porous – I mean it is *seriously non-secure*—

RHONDA. I'm sorry.

TIM. —you should tell your I.T. guys—

RHONDA. I will.

TIM. —since it was so easy to hack into, I thought, just as a joke, that I'd put my own obit on the site, in place of the other Tim Ward. Maybe take a screenshot to show my sister. I thought it was really funny. For about a minute. But then I went to remove it and I couldn't get back "in" – there was some firewall and my obit was stuck there, on your site—

RHONDA. Oh, wow—

TIM. —but *I think you can see for yourself that I am not dead!*

RHONDA. —yes – of course—

TIM. Thank you!

RHONDA. —that's what Steve *said you would say.*

TIM. No – Rhonda—

RHONDA. There's a "period of transition" for the recently deceased—

TIM. —listen—

RHONDA. (*overlapping.*) —and Steve Greene was very adamant that *"this period is not to be rushed!"* I'll get you some coffee.

> (RHONDA *pours* TIM *some coffee, as*—
> TIM *steps away and makes a call on his phone.*)

TIM. (*on his phone.*) Hey Beth – it's Tim. I know you're trying to not check messages while you're gone, but when you get this I just want you to know that – well – there's been a *thing* – and if you happen to see some thing about me online, please don't worry – it was a dumb mistake and I'm sorry and just know that I'm fine. Please don't worry. Safe travels.

> (*He ends the call.* RHONDA *sets the coffee near him.*)

RHONDA. That's a lovely gesture. Telling them not to worry. I wonder why more people don't do that.

TIM. Rhonda …

RHONDA. I bet they save that voicemail forever.

> (*re: the coffee.*)

Cream and sugar?

TIM. … can you please find someone who can help me? I have things to do.

RHONDA. What things?

TIM. Huh?

RHONDA. What are the things you still need to do?

TIM. All sorts of things! I have to – oh god, I don't have to tell you that!—

RHONDA. I'd love to know.

TIM. (*overlapping.*) —it's really none of your—

RHONDA. My mom had things left to do. I know she did. I wish I'd known what they were.

TIM. Look—

RHONDA. It's such a blurry line, don't you think? There you are: dead – but still you have things you need to do—

TIM. Rhonda—

RHONDA. —and here I am: supposedly alive – but could I prove it? Do I have any evidence of it? Have I done anything lately that anyone would ever notice or remember?

TIM. Touch me.
I'll show you that I'm real.
Go ahead.

> (*Tentatively* … RHONDA *places the palm of her hand against* TIM's *chest. She leaves it there.*)

RHONDA. Oh my …

TIM. (*holding her hand to his chest.*) I'm real, Rhonda. I'm real and I'm alive. And so are you.

> (RHONDA *nods, keeping her hand on his chest.*
> TIM *lifts the cup of coffee.*)

And I am drinking this coffee. This actual coffee. Put your fingers on my neck.

RHONDA. What?

TIM. Right here.
Feel me swallow the coffee, Rhonda.

> (*He drinks. She feels it.*)

What does that feel like?

RHONDA. That feels really cool.

TIM. Okay – good …

RHONDA. You are here.

TIM. I am here.

RHONDA. You are not a ghost.

TIM. No I am not.

RHONDA. That's very kind of you. To show me that even now – *even in death*—

TIM. No … Rhonda …

RHONDA. (*overlapping.*) —you are as nice as everyone on your Memory Page says you were.

(RHONDA *indicates the page on her computer.*)

Have you seen your Memory Page? It's a real outpouring on there. Forty-three Memorial messages already. That number is going to grow.

TIM. I am not going to read those.

(TIM *is trying not to look at the screen – as much as he wants to.*)

RHONDA. So many nice words about you. Like this one … from a woman named Claire. Don't you want to see?

(RHONDA's *phone rings/beeps. She looks at the screen.*)

Oh, this is my sister – just a sec.

(*As* RHONDA *turns away to speak into her phone—*
TIM *leans in to look at the screen.*)

RHONDA. (*on phone, sharp.*) What is it Bernie?
My passport? Yes, my passport is current. Why?
Look – it can't be that important – call me tonight.
I'm at work, Bernie!   call me tonight.

(RHONDA *ends the call. She turns back and sees* TIM *reading the Memorial Page.*)

Isn't it nice what they wrote?

(TIM *turns to her.*)

You had an impact on this world, Tim Ward. Do you know how rare that is?

TIM. I need to go home, Rhonda.

RHONDA. Yes. They say it's a *process*. And in the end, maybe we are all just trying to go home.

(TIM *goes, as we see—*)

A Light on Claire.

CLAIRE. Dear Tim.

Hi.

This is hard.

Everyone else is writing "about" you on this Memorial Page.
I don't want to write about you.

I want to write to you.
I've wanted to write to you for a long time, but I haven't.
Because I suck.

I suck at life, Tim.

I went to some pretty dark places after we broke up. I know that was years ago. God, that was a dozen years ago.

And I know it made sense to call it quits since we were going to different colleges. But I hated that everyone said it was no big deal. Everyone said "you're both so young – don't narrow your options. You'll meet so many new people in college and out in the world." Sorry, but they all said I would outgrow you.

I didn't outgrow you.

I miss you.

> (*As* CLAIRE *continues, lights also rise on:*)

Tim's Apartment.

During the following, TIM *opens a beer and sits in front of his laptop. He begins reading online what* CLAIRE *is saying.*

CLAIRE. (*cont'd.*) And I never told you this … but even though we "went our separate ways," I always thought that if things got hard, down the road, if there was no one out there who would ever love me … well … I knew I'd come back. *I'd come running back to you so fast* – saying "Okay, there, we did that – we went out and met people and did stuff – but now I'm done. Please take me back, Tim Ward. Take me back and let's just be … you know … you and me …"

I broke up with a guy named Gary. He was kind to me – but it didn't work. We tried. No, that's not fair. *He did. Gary really tried.* I mainly really tried not to get hurt. And then I got hurt.

I suck at love.

And I think about 9th grade – when we took keyboarding. Remember Ms. Underwood was trying to teach us keyboarding – but even back then you already knew so much more than any of us.

I remember you told us about "dead keys." The keys on our keyboards that don't do anything when you press them on their own. On their own – you said – they don't make anything happen. Things only happen when you press the key beside them.

And I think that's me. I think I'm a Dead Key.

I think unless I was paired with you … unless we were pressed at the same time … I was never worth a damn.

They said the good stuff – the real stuff – was supposed to happen later, when we got older. But all my good stuff happened with you. In fourteen months. Till we said goodbye. And went out into our … *"lives."*

(TIM *lies down now – putting his face very close to his laptop screen.*)
I've come back, Tim Ward.

And I'm too late.

I loved you.

Did I ever say that?

Claire.

P.S. – I know total strangers are gonna read this now, but I don't care.
(*As* TIM *very slowly closes his laptop* …
Lights fade on CLAIRE.
TIM *feels his own chest with his palm.*
He takes another swig of beer and then …
As he swallows, he feels his neck with his fingers.)

A Rugged Wooden Bench. Outside. Somewhere in Nepal. Cold.

Two very bundled-up people sit on the bench, staring front. They've been there awhile. They are not happy.
Perhaps, at first, only their eyes are visible through their huge arctic weather coats and hoods. During the scene, as some coverings are removed, we come to recognize them as BETH *and* GARY.

BETH. I don't want to hear it—

GARY. Well, tough luck for you.

BETH. —I don't want to hear how far you came. I came farther.

GARY. I planned for years. I've been planning—

BETH. I don't want to hear how long you planned. I planned longer. I planned WAY longer than you.

GARY. Do you want to know how much this COST me?—

BETH. I don't care how much this—

GARY. (*overlapping.*) —no – you listen to me – whoever you are *in there* that made us miss the last bus to the village that we were supposed to depart from!—

BETH. You made us miss that bus!

GARY. I did no such thing—

BETH. Whatever you need to tell yourself.

GARY. (*overlapping.*) —and I want you to know this trip cost me EVERYTHING. My job – my girlfriend – my life savings—

BETH. It could have cost you your life.

GARY. No chance of that now, is there?!

BETH. I don't know, *I kind of want to kill you.*

(*They sit.*)

Your phone updates the time, you know. Even way up here.

(*He glares at her. Says nothing.*)

Even in Nepal. Your phone does that on its own. Unless you manage to turn it off somehow. Which you clearly must have found a way to do.

GARY. Gee – that's neat. I had no idea my phone could do something like that.

BETH. I mention that since you were *in charge of the Time*—

GARY. It's especially *neat* since I worked for the company that built this phone. I repped these phones to distributors for years—

BETH. Okay okay okay okay okay—

GARY. (*overlapping.*) —but now – here – finally – on the other side of the world – I get the expertise of a layman, an informed consumer who cares enough to speak to me about the specific uses and features of *this thing I know like the back of my hand.*

(*Pause.*)

BETH. I can't feel my toes.

Can you feel your toes?

(*He looks at her. Then he looks away.*)

You're mad because we went to the wrong place at first.

GARY. That was your fault.

BETH. Yes – but if we had been operating on the correct TIME—

GARY. You—

BETH. (*overlapping.*) —we could have realized our mistake and still found our group.

GARY. YOU are the reason we missed our group. You are the reason we are stuck here.

BETH. Yes – that's what I expected you would say. Men are never wrong. They are only *chronically misinformed.*

(*Pause.*)

GARY. I can feel my toes. Most of them.

BETH. Lucky you.

GARY. But not my fingers.

Can you feel your fingers?

BETH. Did you buy the gloves they recommended?

> (*He says nothing.*)

I bought the gloves they recommended.

GARY. Good for you.

BETH. They weren't cheap.

GARY. But you can feel your fingers.

BETH. No, I can't. Stupid gloves.

I can't feel my fingers. Or my toes. But I am not going to cry. No matter what.

I am not going to cry.

> (*Pause.*
>
> *Then* GARY *slowly lifts his gloved hand … and pats* BETH *on the knee twice, slowly.*
>
> GARY *takes his hand back. They sit there.*)

BETH. I'm Beth.

GARY. Gary.

It's a stupid name.

BETH. It's not a stupid name.

It's a little stupid.

But not bad stupid.

It's not like … Dirk.

> (*Pause.*)

GARY. Dirk is my brother.

> (*off her look.*)

Really.

Okay. Not really.

He's my step-brother.

BETH. (*quickly.*) Stop it!

GARY. They said there'd be a group coming down the mountain in a couple three hours. I guess we ride back to the base with them.

They also said there'd be no refunds.

BETH. I will get a refund.

GARY. They were very clear about—

BETH. *I will get a refund, Gary.* And I will travel somewhere else. Somewhere *warm.*

BETH. Does a "couple three" mean two hours or three?

GARY. Three for sure. Maybe four. If the weather holds.

 (*Pause.*)

BETH. You know any jokes?

GARY. No.

Do you?

 (*Pause.*)

BETH. What do you get when you cross a priest with a microwave?

GARY. I don't know – what?

BETH. (*as though it is the punch line.*) I don't know any jokes either.

 (*Pause.*)

Your job and your girlfriend?

 (*He looks at her.*)

This cost you both?

GARY. The job was ending anyway. I left a few months early – took my severance pay – put it toward this trip. I put everything towards this trip.

BETH. And the girlfriend?

GARY. That was ending too. But neither of us wanted to say it.

BETH. Was she supposed to come with you?

GARY. No. I never told her about this trip. It was going to be my last big bachelor thing. One crazy solo adventure to the other side of the world before I bought the ring – and popped the question – and she and I settled down to raise our family and—

 (*stops, beat.*)

God, how stupid of me.

BETH. Not at all. It was your trip. You wanted to do it on your own. I get that. I'd do that. I'd totally do that. But the problem is, after you dumped her – did you dump her or did she dump you?

 (*before he can respond.*)

You dumped her. I can tell. It is so clear. Anyway – after that, you couldn't really say: "Oh by the way – I'm heading off to Nepal. Have a nice life."

GARY. Right. That is so right.

BETH. She's probably relieved, Gary. I tell my brother this all the time. That girl you broke up with who you think is so bereft – who you think is going to go to all these dark places because you broke her heart in half – the fact is: she's probably *relieved*. She's probably already moved on.

GARY. Really?

BETH. I would. I'd move on right away.

GARY. You've done that?

BETH. Oh, yeah.

GARY. Moved on like that when some guy dumped you?

BETH. Sure, of course.

GARY. Wow, okay—

BETH. I mean, it's been awhile since I was dumped.

GARY. Oh, you're in a long-term relation—

BETH. *She has moved on, Gary.* She'll be fine. And when you get home you can give her a call and tell her how I ruined your trip.

GARY. I wouldn't do that.

BETH. Thank you.

GARY. I can't imagine calling her. Not now. She'd expect me to say Something Great. Whatever that is.

(*They sit.*)

BETH. I thought it would feel different.
I was so eager to be "way off the grid" ... on the other side of the world ... and here we are ...

GARY. You're not off the grid.

BETH. We're on a remote bench in Nepal!

GARY. With phones in our pockets.

(*off her look.*)

You can't be off the grid with a phone in your pocket. If someone can call you, you are still tethered.

BETH. *Tethered? You think I'm tethered.*

GARY. You would never get rid of your phone.

BETH. You don't know that. You don't know anything about me.
I would never get rid of my phone.

(*Pause.*
They sit.)

A little while ago ... when I was really really mad at you ...

GARY. Yeah.

BETH. ... right in the middle of being really really mad at you I realized that I really wanted to kiss you. Maybe because I could pretty much *only see your lips* – but also because I was *feeling things – even in this arctic snowman suit, I was aroused* – and though I was probably just aroused by *what a friggin' idiot you had been and how you had ruined my expensive and dangerous trip to Nepal,* it was still a great feeling, Gary.
I wanted you to know that.

GARY. Thanks.

And now?

BETH. I'm over it. No offense.

GARY. None taken.

(*Pause.*)

BETH. I don't want to kiss people very often. My friend says I'm "Too much of an island. Too self-sufficient and self-contained." I think that's true. I try not to be an island. I try to stay open to being ... you know ... at least ... more of a ... *peninsula* maybe.

But then I think ... why? What am I missing?

I bet I'm not missing anything at all.

GARY. So no men in your life? Or women?

BETH. No. I guess I don't let them in.

I don't let them in.

I haven't made room. For people. Humans. Humans with hearts. And lips. I should make room.

(*Pause.*)

GARY. Well, at least I know how to arouse you.

BETH. I suppose you do.

(*Pause.*)

GARY. (*pushing a little too obviously.*) God, I can't *believe* this! Trip of a lifetime! – down the drain! – and all because of *you!!!*

BETH. (*droll.*) Not gonna work, Gary.

An Airport Concourse. Dawn.

SCOTTIE *stands at her walker, staring front, looking out the large airport windows toward the sunrise.*

RHONDA *stands nearby, holding* SCOTTIE'*s same enormous purse. Near her are two small roller bags.* RHONDA *is also staring front.*

SCOTTIE. And speaking of sisters! – oh my goodness, Rhonda – *my* sister was a life-long pain in the ass! Thankfully she died in the month of May when I have my bad allergies. That made it look like I had cried. I hadn't cried. I had danced a little jig of joy around my kitchen – *which I am not proud of mind you.* But I felt nothing when they put my sister Eunice in the ground. Can you imagine?

(*No response.*)

Don't let that happen to you. Work things out with Bernadette. She's a good person. She convinced me to bring you on this trip to Japan, didn't she?

(looking toward the windows.)

And she booked us this flight at sunrise. Look at that! Not at all like yesterday.

RHONDA. She's doing it out of guilt.

SCOTTIE. Well, maybe, but—

RHONDA. Just guilt. Pure and simple.

SCOTTIE. Oh, there is nothing simple about guilt.

RHONDA. Our mother left everything to Bernie. Made her the executor of the will. Gave her the house, most all the money. Who does something like that?—

SCOTTIE. Bernadette was the eldest – that happens—

RHONDA. *(overlapping.)* —and all Bernie can say is "Sorry, Sis – nothing I can do – I am bound by the terms of the will. I've got to honor Mother's wishes."

SCOTTIE. Well, that's true – she does.

RHONDA. Of course you'd take her side.

I thought she'd come back. I thought my mom would come back one more time.

(Pause.)

SCOTTIE. Yes. I know that feeling.

RHONDA. I thought she'd come back and talk to Steve Greene. If we'd done the service at Arbor View, she could have done that—

SCOTTIE. Rhonda, what are you talking about?

RHONDA. —but Bernie made us have the service at this place across town – and it was all wrong! – nothing Mom would have liked at all – but Bernie kept saying "it's in her papers, Rhonda" – "it's what she wanted, Rhonda" – "it's paid for, Rhonda" – but it was cold and dark and the flowers were wrong *and there was not a quality of mercy – not anywhere.*

(Pause.)

SCOTTIE. You haven't grieved yet.

(RHONDA *says nothing.*)

You've been too busy fighting with your sister. Haven't you?

(RHONDA *says nothing.*)

Forgive me, Rhonda – I don't know you … but when we lose someone we get very sad and very angry. And we know everyone is watching. And so sometimes we pick fights and lash out – we start to *behave our pain* – we start to *perform how bereft and distraught we are.* And we call that feeling "grief."

That is not grief.

Grief doesn't want attention.

Grief is a hand on your chest.
A hand no one can see.

(*Pause.*)

What was your mother's name?

RHONDA. Beatrice. They called her Bea.

SCOTTIE. No – I want to know her full name.

RHONDA. But no one called her by her—

SCOTTIE. Men get all kinds of things added to their names – because, of course, men want to imagine that the things they possess are actually *much longer than they really are.* So men get: "Junior," "the Third," "Esquire" – all that nonsense.

But women? – we just end up with *the name our Daddy called us when we were three.* When our mother gave us a haircut with floppy little bangs – and our father decided we looked like the Scottish terrier next door. Seventy years later: I'm still "Scottie."

I wish to know your mother's full, entire name.

RHONDA. Her "full, entire name" was: Beatrice Anne Mitchell.

SCOTTIE. That's a wonderful name. That name could start a railroad. Claim a continent for the Queen.

(*Pause.*)

RHONDA. Why don't you tell your kids about these trips?

SCOTTIE. (*smiles.*) Oh, yes – what you must think of me. Asking my kids to have lives of their own that don't revolve around me.

RHONDA. Wouldn't they be glad you were traveling?

SCOTTIE. They'd feel obligated to worry and they'd appreciate the excuse.

RHONDA. What excuse?

SCOTTIE. My sister and I took care of our mother. Worried about her, cared for her, wrapped our plans around her plans – *none* of which she needed or asked for, *none* of which she appreciated in the least. But oh boy – it was great for us! It was the best excuse possible for why we managed to risk *nothing* with our own lives! We blamed all our cowardice on her. Oh the great things we could have done, but we needed to "be there for Mom."

Someone should have slapped us.

I am likely my children's worst nightmare, Rhonda.
But I refuse to be their best excuse.

(*Pause.*
        RHONDA *readies the bags, saying—*)

RHONDA. I think we're boarding now.

SCOTTIE. In my bag is a small bronze cup. Will you take it out?

(RHONDA *does.*)

Feel it in your hand. The weight. The substance of it. Do you feel that?

RHONDA. Maybe. I guess.

SCOTTIE. I don't know why, but I feel centered – comforted – when I hold that cup in my hands. I like to imagine that it has a merciful countenance.

RHONDA. Where did you get it?

SCOTTIE. And here is where I should have a good answer … but I have no idea where this came from. When they moved me out of the house and into the senior center, I was throwing away a lot of knickknacks and junk … and I found that cup.

(RHONDA *gives the cup to* SCOTTIE.)

It will be filled about halfway with water. Rainwater if you can find it. Rainwater is best.

You'll place a tiny stone, or pebble inside. Just pick one off the ground that you like. You'll know – *you will know* the right pebble to choose.

And you'll drop it in the cup.

And then you'll say my full, entire name: I am Elizabeth McHenry Ward. I've written it down for you.

(SCOTTIE *hands a piece of paper to* RHONDA.)

As you say my name … you'll set this cup somewhere near the Shimogamo Shrine. Not the main one. It will be too crowded, I'm told. One of the smaller garden shrines. You'll know the one.

You will set this cup there.

And after a few minutes you will leave.

And that will be the end of it.

(RHONDA *is staring – confused – at* SCOTTIE.)

I can't travel with you. I hoped I could. But yesterday my doctor found a little something. A little more of the same something he found last year and the year before. Apparently this little something has taken up residence in me for good.

Bernadette knows. I told her last night. I asked if she wanted to travel with you – in my place … but she said no.

She said: "This is Rhonda's trip. I want this for Rhonda."

RHONDA. And your kids?

SCOTTIE. I'll tell them when the time is right. The doctor thinks I've still got a little time.

RHONDA. How much?

SCOTTIE. He's not sure. I like that about him.

I wish I'd been less sure. If I could do it all over again, Rhonda, I would have *doubted more.* What was I so busy being *certain about?* I chased away most of the wonder from my life by telling myself I already knew good from bad, right from wrong, left from right, and all the rest of it. God, what a *tedious woman* I must have been.

But uncertainty ... doubt ... oh, lord, *doubt is so appealing to me now.*

Doubt is the unmarked door.

>   (SCOTTIE *puts the cup in* RHONDA's *hands.*)

Do this, Rhonda.

Do this for both of us.

The Not-Great Diner. Day. Sunshine.

>   *This is the same booth/table we saw earlier.*
>   TIM *and* CLAIRE *sit across from each other. They each have menus.*
>   TIM *is looking over his menu;* CLAIRE *is just staring at* TIM. *Really staring at him. For a long time.*

CLAIRE. The quesadilla is pretty good.

TIM. Is it?

CLAIRE. Yes.

>   (*Pause.*)

TIM. Do you come here a lot?

CLAIRE. Not too much. No.

It's kind of terrible. This place.

It is really one of the worst places to eat on earth that I know of.

TIM. Why did you want to come here?

CLAIRE. I wanted to change it. Change my memories of it.

I thought maybe we could do that.

TIM. Sure.

How do we do that?

>   (*A long silence.*)

Does anyone ever come wait on us?

CLAIRE. Not really. But it's okay. You won't like the food anyway. Why rush it?

TIM. Oh. Okay.

Claire ...

How are you?

>   (*She just stares at him.*)

Thank you for what you wrote.

On that Memorial Page.

My name and photo didn't belong on there – I'm sorry. But the mortuary gave me your contact info. They weren't supposed to, but there was this woman, Rhonda. She was leaving on a trip – but before she left she got me your number. She was really determined to make everything right for me.

You look good. I think it's eleven years. Twelve, maybe. We were on blankets. After high school – summer before college – on blankets in the sun. Some lake or park. And people were dancing and drinking … and we were … I guess we were lying on blankets and eating red licorice and trying to decide our lives.

We were trying to decide what we were going to be *great at*.

> (*Pause.*)

CLAIRE. I can order for you, if you want.

TIM. Oh, it's okay …

CLAIRE. I used to order for him – because I knew what he liked. He liked french fries and a vanilla milk shake and coffee. But it had to be good coffee. The coffee here is awful but we can pretend. It seems like that's what we're doing – *pretending*. Isn't that what we're doing?

TIM. Claire …

CLAIRE. And Tim – oh god, Tim had the best plans. He was going to freelance in computer design – websites and stuff like that – just to pay the bills. And then after work he was going to sit in coffee shops and write his novels.

TIM. … right, but Claire …

CLAIRE. He was never so happy as when he was sitting with his coffee, noodling on his computer, working on all the novels he was going to write.

TIM. … no – it's me – I'm here …

CLAIRE. (*overlapping.*) And he'd dip his fries in the vanilla shake. He liked the salty-sugary taste. And god – *you remind me of him so much.*

CLAIRE.	TIM.
CLAIRE. I know he'd be older now – and your hair is a little shorter, but other than that – I mean, god, it's creepy. And on the phone you knew so many things about me – things that only Tim would know. So, whoever you are – however you learned this stuff – maybe you talked to his sister, I don't know – but whatever it was, it's creepy as hell for me because I loved Tim Ward and I know that he is dead. I saw the obituary.	**TIM.** Wait – listen— Yes, of course, because— Would you let me explain, please?

TIM. *I wrote that obit.*

> (*Beat.*)

CLAIRE. Why would you say that? His sister would never let you do that.

TIM. You mean his – I mean *my* sister, Beth?

CLAIRE. Yes.

TIM. It was her idea. "Take charge of your death, Tim Ward." And so I was looking at obits of people with my same name – and *god what a terrible idea that is—*

CLAIRE. Stop it – you can't expect me to believe that—

TIM. (*overlapping.*) —but no – please – listen to me – none of it matters because the only thing I wanted – the only thing I *want* – is to *see you.*

> (*Pause. Tears in* CLAIRE's *eyes.*)

I missed you.
Please say something.

> (*Pause. She wipes her eyes.*)

CLAIRE. This is a shitty thing you're doing. To pretend like this—

TIM. No – listen—

CLAIRE. —are you doing this just to hurt me? I don't even know you!

TIM. Claire, please—

CLAIRE. But I hate you.
I hate that you are not him.
You can't be.
Maybe you're another one. Is that it? Maybe you're another Tim Ward who just happens to …
Maybe you are him.
You can't be him, you asshole.
But are you him?
I don't think so.
I don't think you are.
I don't think you're him.
I think.
I think you are.
I think you are him.
You're him.

TIM. Yes.

CLAIRE. Hi.

TIM. Hi.

> (TIM *reaches across the table for her hand, but—*
> CLAIRE *pulls her hand away.*)

CLAIRE. No. Don't. You've got to tell me. Please tell me. Why did you do it? How did it happen?

TIM. Hmm?

CLAIRE. The obit didn't say how you died.

TIM. I didn't—

CLAIRE. Weren't you scared?—

TIM. —no – you're not listening—

CLAIRE. (*overlapping.*) —I think I'd be too scared, you know? Way too scared to do it.

TIM. Claire, for god's sake—

CLAIRE. You must have found a really good way – maybe pills or something? – is that what you did?—

TIM. —no – no—

CLAIRE. (*overlapping.*) —because you still look like you and sound like you and we get to sit here together – not *with* each other, but *beside* each other – like nothing ever happened.

TIM. I didn't do anything like that—

CLAIRE. And that's where I want to be. I just this second understood this. I want to be just *beside* my life. Not away from it – not in some completely different life – just *a little to the side of it.* Because maybe *right beside my life* everything makes sense. Maybe there ... everything connects. Like you hold down the dead key and you press something ... but if you don't want that life, you press something else – you press the key right next to it – *right beside it – and something brand new happens ...*

> (TIM *takes* CLAIRE's *hand and places it against his own chest. Strong. Firm. With intensity.*)

TIM. Listen to me: you're here. And I'm here. And that's it. That's all that matters. Do you see?

> (*She stares at him – really stares at him – for a long moment.*)

CLAIRE. Yes.

TIM. Good.

CLAIRE. I miss him so much.

> (CLAIRE *pulls away and starts off, quickly—*)

TIM. Claire, please—

CLAIRE. Don't you ever do this again.

> (*—and she is gone.*)

A Hospital Waiting Room / A Taxi.

> BERNADETTE *is on her phone in the Waiting Room. Her purse/bag and her coat are nearby.*
> GARY *is on his phone, riding in a taxi.*

BERNADETTE. (*on phone.*) Yes, I understand – but I was told Beth Ward was traveling with you—

GARY. (*on phone.*) She was traveling with me, but—

BERNADETTE. (*overlapping.*) —and I haven't been able to reach her—

GARY. —okay, I'm sorry, but—

BERNADETTE. (*overlapping.*) —but when I told the tour agency it was an emergency they gave me your number. It's urgent that I speak to Beth Ward.

GARY. She's not here! We're not together.

> (*urgent, to unseen taxi driver.*)
> *No – not Providence – it's the other hospital – the one down near Fifth—*

BERNADETTE. What's that?

GARY. Nothing, I'm in a taxi—

BERNADETTE. Do you know when she'll be back?

GARY. No – we're not in Nepal anymore. That trip fell through. I'm home – I'm in a taxi. Beth got a refund – I don't know how she got a refund – but she re-booked for another trip.

BERNADETTE. Do you know where?

GARY. No – she didn't want anyone to know where she was going.

BERNADETTE. Even her family?

GARY. I guess especially her family. Listen, I've got to let you go—

> (*As the conversation continues—*
> CLAIRE *appears in the Waiting Room.* CLAIRE *is in a hospital gown and socks/slippers. She is pushing a rolling I.V. stand that is attached to the tube in her arm.*
> CLAIRE *is weak and pale … but moving steadily.*)

BERNADETTE. No – wait – please – I've been leaving messages on her phone, but—

GARY. (*to the unseen taxi driver.*) *Anywhere near the entrance – doesn't matter—*

BERNADETTE. —but she's not called me back – and it's important – so if you talk to her—

GARY. I won't talk to her! I don't even know her!

BERNADETTE. Yes, but if you hear from her—

GARY. I WON'T HEAR FROM HER. Look – my girlfriend – I just found out my girlfriend is in the hospital – and my phone is about to die – I'm sorry – I wish I could help—

BERNADETTE. No – wait – please—

> (<u>GARY</u> *ends the call. The light on him goes out.*
> BERNADETTE *continues for another moment, thinking he's still on the line*—)

BERNADETTE. *(still on phone.)* —*if for any reason you hear from her … please have her call me as soon as she can … it's about her mother … her mom …*

> (BERNADETTE *holds the phone another moment or two … and then slowly pushes the button to end the call.*
> *She stands very still. She holds the phone out from her body, as though her hand is not a part of her.*
> CLAIRE, *too, stands nearby, also very still. She has heard the preceding.*)

CLAIRE. I'm sorry.

> (BERNADETTE *turns to her.*)

BERNADETTE. Oh. Thank you.
It's not my mom … but still …
It's a woman I … worked for.
I've been trying to reach her daughter.

CLAIRE. That's hard.

> (*Pause.*)

BERNADETTE. She thought she had more time.
I wish her kids could have seen her. She was so peaceful. She told me this was the same hospital she was born in. Can you imagine?
I said to her: See, it's true what they say … there are no accidents.
And she said: *Don't believe it, Bernadette. There are only accidents.*

> (*Pause.*)

CLAIRE. Do you want to sit down? I think you should sit down.

> (BERNADETTE *slowly places the PHONE on a side table near one of the chairs.*
> *Then she sits.*
> *Long silence.*)

I was just looking for a magazine.

> (*Pause.*)

There's nothing good at the Nurse's station down there.

BERNADETTE. I have a magazine in my bag. I always kept one in there for her.
Every trip we went on … she'd say "how are the famous people doing, Bernadette?" And I'd hand her a magazine and she'd read it – cover to cover.

(BERNADETTE *gets the magazine from her bag and hands it to* CLAIRE.)
This one's a little old – sorry.

CLAIRE. I love *People* magazine.

(CLAIRE *pages through it.*)

I love their troubles. The troubles of magazine people. They have such great troubles. Even when there's a happy story – you know all you have to do is wait a couple issues – and then boom, those same exact people who were so young and beautiful and happy, boom, there's some amazing new trouble that's fantastic and sexy and horrible and complicated and worse than anyone ever thought possible.

My troubles are so dumb.

BERNADETTE. Were you in for surgery?

CLAIRE. I was in for something dumb. I took a bunch of pills. As many as I had. Which were not enough. I know that now.

I got real sick.

And my neighbor – my neighbor across the hall – I'd never even met him …
I guess he heard me getting sick and he called someone. And they helped me.
Pumped my stomach. Gave me fluids.

Turns out, I suck at death.

(*Pause.*)

BERNADETTE. That stranger … he was your guardian angel.

CLAIRE. Maybe. I guess it depends, right? On how my life goes now. How things turn out.

Maybe a real angel – maybe a *really good angel* would have just walked away.
It must be hard to be an angel.

What a complicated gig.

How do you know when to intervene?

(*Pause.*)

BERNADETTE. Maybe you should sit down …

CLAIRE. No – they want me in my room.

(*re: the magazine.*)

Can I keep this?

BERNADETTE. Of course.

CLAIRE. Thank you.

(CLAIRE *starts off, walking slowly … and is gone.*
BERNADETTE *sits.*
She looks off in both directions, waiting.
She looks at her watch.
Waits. Then …

She stands and puts on her coat.
She lifts her bag.
And she leaves.
<u>*And she has left her PHONE behind.*</u>
We stare at the empty stage and the abandoned PHONE for a long moment ...
and then the scene is joined by—
A light on BETH, *at a pay phone.*
BETH *holds the receiver of the pay phone. She has dialed and she is waiting.*
After a moment ...
BERNADETTE's PHONE *in the* **Waiting Room** *begins to RING.*
And RING.
And RING.
And RING.
And meanwhile ...
TIM *enters the Waiting Room.*
TIM *looks exhausted and distraught. He just wants to sit down somewhere.*
He carries a small <u>*paper cup of water*</u>. *He does not drink from it until noted.*
He hears – and then sees – the RINGING PHONE.
He looks around. Whose phone is this?
RING.
RING.
BETH *is growing impatient ...*)

BETH. (*on phone, excited but impatient.*) C'mon ... c'mon ... c'mon, Bernie ...
pick up ...

        (*RING.*
        RING.
        RING.
        TIM *lifts and holds the RINGING PHONE.*
        He looks around once more.)

BETH. Bernie ... Bernie, c'mon ...

        (*RING.*
        RING.
        RING.
        And <u>*just as BETH HANGS UP the pay phone*</u>—
        <u>TIM *presses a button and answers the PHONE.*</u>)

TIM. Hello ...?

        (<u>*The LIGHT ON* BETH *has gone out.*</u>)

Hello – is anyone ...?

        (TIM *slowly sets the PHONE back down.*
        TIM *looks around.*
        He sits on the ground.

He sets <u>the cup of water on the ground</u> in front of him – not drinking from it.
He closes his eyes, as—
GARY *enters – agitated, carrying a shopping bag filled with items.*
GARY *sees* TIM. <u>*They do not know each other.*</u>)

GARY. Oh, hey.

> (TIM *looks up.*)

Have any of the nurses come by here?

TIM. Hmm?

GARY. They said they were gonna help me – but now I can't find them – so I thought – I don't know – I thought maybe they were – you sure no one's been here?

TIM. Sorry.

GARY. I tried to give this bag – give these things to someone – but one of the nurses told me she had to check first – but that was – argh – it's so – there's not – you know??? – god, why is it so hard to *do something for someone?!* Sorry. I'm so sorry. But, I mean … you know?! …
That your phone?

TIM. No.
It was there.

GARY. Oh. Okay.

> (GARY *sits.*
> TIM *closes his eyes once again.*)

Sometimes there's a bell. You know – a little bell you can ring.

TIM. Oh, right.

GARY. But there's no bell down there.

TIM. I think the staff is smaller on Sunday.

GARY. It's Sunday?

TIM. Yeah.

GARY. I had no idea. I was on the other side of the world. I think it was Sunday there too.
Maybe I lost a whole week.

> (*Pause. They sit.*
> GARY *begins looking through his grocery bag.*)

I brought her things she likes. That's all I could think to do. Just … god, I don't know … bring her stuff.
How are you supposed to know what to do?
Do you know what to do?

TIM. When?

GARY. Here. When things happen. When people are here.

TIM. No. I don't know what to do.

GARY. Me neither.

So I just … brought stuff. Red licorice. Carrot cake. Peppermint tea. Almonds. *People* magazine.

I even brought "Yahtzee" – you know, the game.

TIM. My mom's good at that game.

My mom is really good at that game.

GARY. Oh yeah?

TIM. She and my ex-girlfriend used to play for hours. Real cutthroat.

It was great.

GARY. Yeah. It's great.

Games of chance.

She won't see me. *She refused to see me.* She gave them – she gave someone my name. She put me on a list. I didn't know you could do that. But she did that. She put me on a list of people she does not want to see.

So I said to them: okay … can you just give her this bag? It's all stuff she likes.

What if she doesn't want it?

Or what if they don't ask her?

What if she thinks no one was here?

I want her to know someone was here.

I would never have known. But I went to her place. To – to apologize, I guess. To … I don't know – not to make up with her – just to – I wanted to …

I wanted to say Something Great.

TIM. I'm sorry.

> (*Pause. They sit.*)

GARY. Family member?

TIM. Hmm?

GARY. In here?

TIM. Oh. My mom.

GARY. I hear it's good. A good hospital. That's what people say. I hope that's true.

> (*Pause.*)

TIM. I was too late. I never saw her.

Her aide called me – left messages for me, but … by the time I got here …

They've already moved the body.

It's weird that all of a sudden they call it a body. I would call it … I would call *her* … Mom. Elizabeth.

Elizabeth McHenry Ward.

Someone else already signed the paper. For the body. I guess my mom's aide did that. I can see her – see the body – in the morning.

And why does nothing change?

Why does the vending machine keep working? Why do the phones still ring? Shouldn't something be different?

> (*A long silence.*
> TIM *finally lifts the* <u>*cup of water*</u> *and drinks. As before,* <u>*he puts his fingers to*</u> <u>*his neck*</u> *... feeling his neck swallow the water.*
> TIM *sets the cup slowly back down in front of him.*
> *Pause.*
> GARY *removes something from the bag.*)

GARY. I have some licorice.

TIM. I need to tell my sister. My sister doesn't know yet. She's overseas – off the grid – on a trip.

GARY. That's hard.

If it were me – and, whatever, you don't know me from Adam – but if it were me, and I was *really far away* ...

I'd rather think everything was fine.

> (TIM *nods. And leaves.*
> GARY *sits. He looks off in the direction of the Nurse's station. He waits. Then* ...
> *He opens the pack of red licorice and eats.*
> *He does this for awhile, and then* ...
> BERNADETTE *arrives. Her coat is on, and she is carrying her bag – as before.*
> <u>*They don't know each other.*</u>)

BERNADETTE. Excuse me, sir?

> (GARY *turns to her.*)

Hi – did you see a phone here? I left—

GARY. Yeah. Right there.

> (GARY *points to the phone.*
> BERNADETTE *picks it up.*)

BERNADETTE. Oh, that's lucky. Thank you so much.

GARY. No problem.

> (*And* BERNADETTE *is gone.*)

Near the Shimogamo Shrine. Kyoto, Japan. Rain.

A FIGURE *stands with their back to us – holding a black umbrella – looking at* a small, modest, stone Shrine *amid the Forest. The umbrella obscures the* FIGURE's *face.*

After a moment … RHONDA enters, opposite. She wears a backpack. She has been hiking to this spot in the rain. It has not been easy. She is wet and muddy and tired. However …

Upon seeing the Shrine, she stops. Almost reflexively, spontaneously, she goes to her knees.

Silence. Stillness. Rain.

RHONDA *opens her backpack and takes out something wrapped in cloth. It is* the small bronze cup *we saw earlier.*

She holds the cup for a moment. Feeling the weight in her hand.

Then she holds the cup out in front of her … and lets it catch the rain water.

She sets the cup on the ground – letting it continue to catch the rain – as she goes in search of a pebble.

RHONDA *starts this process on her feet – walking around – picking them up and discarding them … but eventually she is on her* knees *… crawling all around the area … searching … inspecting … discarding … she has to find the right one. How will she know which is the right one?*

The FIGURE *with the umbrella turns and begins to watch* RHONDA. *We now recognize this figure as* BETH.

BETH. Did you lose something?

    (RHONDA *does not look up – does not stop searching for the pebble.*)

Excuse me? Do you need some help?

RHONDA. I need a pebble. She said I'm supposed to find a pebble.

BETH. Who did?

RHONDA. This woman.

BETH. Oh, okay.

Well – there's lots of pebbles.

RHONDA. Yes, I know that.

    (RHONDA *keeps crawling, searching.*)

BETH. What kind are you looking for?

RHONDA. She said I'd know. That I'd just *know* the right one.

BETH. That was probably not very helpful.

RHONDA. No. It was not.

    (RHONDA *keeps searching.*)

BETH. Can I help you?

(RHONDA *stops – looks up at her.*)
Or would that be weird?

RHONDA. No. Go for it.

(BETH *sets her umbrella aside.*
She joins RHONDA *in searching for the pebble.*)

BETH. So, who is this woman that sent you to find a pebble?

RHONDA. I don't know her well. I met her through my sister. She sent me on this trip.

BETH. Why didn't she come with you?

RHONDA. I can't tell you.

BETH. Oh, okay …

RHONDA. She made me promise not to tell anyone. Even her family.

BETH. Really? – why?

RHONDA. They're not close, I don't think. She and her kids.

BETH. No, I would guess not.

(*They continue their search for the pebble.*)
How big should this pebble be?

RHONDA. We will just "know."

BETH. Oh, right.

RHONDA. It has to fit in that cup over there.

(BETH *is at some distance from the cup. She continues her search for a pebble.*)
How did you hear about the shrine?

BETH. This is a shrine?!

RHONDA. The Shimogamo Shrine. Yes. It's down that path. Through "The Forest Where Lies are Revealed."

BETH. Wow.

RHONDA. Are you visiting with a group?

BETH. Oh, I'm just lost. And I don't have my phone – which felt so fantastic at first. I was on this other trip that sort of fell through, so I called and got them to book me somewhere else. And I felt so … free. *Untethered.* So, on a whim, I just tossed my phone in a trash can at Narita airport. And I never looked back. It felt great.
For about a minute.
Then I panicked – raced back to the trash can – and it was empty. And they were calling my flight.
There's a lesson there.
And I'm pretty sure I have not learned it.

RHONDA. Why Kyoto?

BETH. Warmer than Nepal.

And my mom. My mom used to talk about it. The temples and shrines. How they'd been spared in the war.

RHONDA. Did she ever come visit?

BETH. No. She doesn't travel. I wish she did.

RHONDA. You'll have to call her — tell her you're here.

BETH. I did. Well — I *tried* — I tried to call her aide. Sometimes that's the best way to reach her. And I had to use a *pay phone* … which made me feel like a *pioneer*, or something.

I didn't get an answer.

I'll try again tomorrow.

> (*Silence. Rain.*
> *They search.*)

RHONDA. My mom never traveled either. We didn't have the money. But the last good conversation I had with her — in the hospital — she went on and on about wanting to see Savannah, Georgia.

She told me that she'd wanted to name my older sister Savannah and name me Georgia. Said that way when she called us down to supper it would sound like she was going on a lovely little trip.

BETH. And did she name you that?

RHONDA. No — my dad didn't like those names. And Mom never saw Savannah.

But she held onto that thought till the end.

> (*Pause.*)

Do you have a sister?

BETH. No.

RHONDA. Do you want one? I've got one you can have.

BETH. I'll trade you straight-up for my brother.

RHONDA. Is that a good trade for me?

BETH. Not really. I'll throw in some cash.

RHONDA. Okay. And just to warn you: your new sister was Mom's favorite.

BETH. Just like my brother is.

RHONDA. Why do parents pretend?!

BETH. Amen!

RHONDA. Just say it! You know you have a favorite — especially when they are grown and moved away. Just say it out loud and be done with it!

> (RHONDA *has found what she thinks might be the right pebble.*)

Hey! — maybe this! …

> (*considers it more fully.*)

… no … sorry. Keep looking.

(*They do.*)

BETH. When my mom dies, it is going to devastate my brother. And he has no idea. No idea what it's going to do to him.

RHONDA. What about you?

(*Pause.*)

BETH. I keep thinking I will *know*. That – no matter where I am or what I am doing – I will know when it happens. The moment it happens.

People say there's a feeling you get … something … a shiver.

I think that will be me.

I think I'll just know.

(BETH *picks up a pebble. Certain and simple.*)

This one.

(*She shows it to* RHONDA.)

Don't you think?

(RHONDA *holds it. Looks at it.*)

RHONDA. Yes. That's it.

How do we know that?

BETH. We just do.

(*They stand in the rain, looking at the pebble.*)

RHONDA. Now we put the pebble in that cup.

You can do it if you want. You found it.

(RHONDA *hands the pebble to* BETH.

BETH *approaches the cup.*

BETH *kneels beside the cup. This is done simply – without obvious import or reverence.*

Before BETH *drops the pebble in, she picks up the cup and looks at it.*)

BETH. I had a cup like this. Mine was bigger, I think. Found it in the field behind our house when I was little. I kept like hair bands and plastic rings and pennies in it, I think.

My mom probably threw it away.

(BETH *drops the pebble down into the cup.*

She hands the cup to RHONDA.)

BETH. What now?

RHONDA. I'm supposed to put this cup near the Shrine.

And then I say her full, entire name.

And then it's done.

BETH. This woman you barely know asked you to come here and do all these things?

RHONDA. Yes.

BETH. Why? What is this supposed to do?

> (RHONDA *doesn't know.*
> RHONDA *walks toward the simple, stone Shrine.*
> BETH *retrieves her umbrella, nearby. She approaches and stands near* RHONDA.
> BETH *begins to cover them both with the umbrella. But …* RHONDA *gently takes* BETH'*s arm and lowers it. Saying, in essence: "let it rain on us." They stand in the rain …* BETH *with the open umbrella at her side …* RHONDA *holding out the cup to catch just a little more rain.*
> *Finally …*
> RHONDA *lifts the cup in the air in front of her and says:*)

RHONDA. Beatrice   Anne   Mitchell.

> (RHONDA *carefully sets the cup on or near the Shrine.*
> *Silence. Rain.*)

BETH. That was nice.

> (*There is water on* RHONDA*'s face. She is not moving.*)

Thank you. For letting me help you.

> (*No response.* RHONDA*'s eyes may be closed.*)

I should try to find where I'm staying.

> (RHONDA *nods.*)

Bye, now.

> (BETH *takes her bag … and her umbrella … and leaves.*
> *Silence. Rain.* RHONDA *alone. Then …*
> *From her pocket,* RHONDA *removes the small folded piece of paper we saw earlier.*
> RHONDA *opens the paper. Looks at it. Then she puts the paper away in her pocket.*
> RHONDA *looks around at the ground near her feet.*
> *She reaches down and selects another pebble. Looks at it.*
> *It is the right one. She just knows.*
> RHONDA *carefully drops this pebble into the cup.*
> *Pause. Then …*
> *Once again, she lifts the cup in the air in front of her and says:*)

RHONDA. Elizabeth   McHenry   Ward.

> (RHONDA *slowly sets the cup on the Shrine. Then she lifts her head to the sky … as it continues to rain.*)

Arbor View Memory Gardens. Morning.

A MAN *is standing with his back to us at the counter we saw earlier. Same computer, tissues and coffeepot.*
A new wreath of flowers stands nearby.
The MAN *is looking off and around – impatient – wanting someone to help him.*
No one comes to help him. After a moment …
SCOTTIE *enters. She wears a pastel-colored exercise outfit – pants and jacket – along with brand-new tennis shoes. She moves easily, without a walker.*
SCOTTIE *approaches the counter and the* MAN.

SCOTTIE. Excuse me. Hi. I thought I saw some tissues here.

(*The* MAN *steps away, so* SCOTTIE *can grab a couple tissues.*)

Thank you so much. Are you waiting for Rhonda? She was on a trip to Japan. I'm not sure if she's back yet.

MAN. I'm looking for Steve Greene! He told me to come back and see him if something wasn't right.

SCOTTIE. Oh, I'm sure everything will be fine. They had my service just now in the Sequoia room. Everything went perfectly. Although my son looked so sad.
They'll be heading outside for the burial in a few minutes.

MAN. They should have a bell.

SCOTTIE. I'm sure someone will be here soon. There's free coffee.

MAN. I don't drink coffee. Even though – for some reason – my obituary said I loved it! Said I was *never so happy as when I was in a coffeehouse, noodling away on my computer, working on all the novels I was going to write.*

SCOTTIE. Why would they say that if that's not you?

MAN. They also said I was 29. I'm not 29. I'm 67 *[or age of actor]*. And the photo on the Memory Page was of a completely other person!

SCOTTIE. I'm sure they'll correct that.

(BERNADETTE, *dressed in black, walks past them – carrying a black umbrella.*
She does not see SCOTTIE *or the* MAN.
SCOTTIE *watches her leave …*)

MAN/ANOTHER TIM WARD. Sorry to go on and on. I'm Tim.

(SCOTTIE *turns to him.*)

SCOTTIE. Oh, that's my son's name.

(SCOTTIE *shakes the* MAN's *hand.*)

MAN/ANOTHER TIM WARD. I don't mean to complain – I was no great person – I had a decent life – nothing out of the ordinary – but now that I'm gone and people are reading about me, I want them to know who I really was. You know?

> (BETH *and* TIM *enter, both also dressed in black.* TIM *carries a black umbrella.*
> *They do not see* SCOTTIE *or the* MAN.)

SCOTTIE. (*to* MAN, *re:* TIM.) That's him – right there – that's my son, Tim … he's a writer.

> (TIM *and* BETH *are gone.*)

MAN/ANOTHER TIM WARD. (*looking around, impatient.*) Steve Greene promised me he'd be here.

SCOTTIE. Oh, I'm sure there's—

> (RHONDA, *dressed in black, walks past – carrying a black umbrella of her own.*
> *She does not see* SCOTTIE *or the* MAN.)

Here! – this is Rhonda – she'll help you!

> (*to* RHONDA.)

Hello, Rhonda—

> (*But* RHONDA *keeps walking.*)

—how was the trip? – did you get to the Shrine?

> (RHONDA *is gone.*
> SCOTTIE *is calling after her.*)

Rhonda …?

MAN/ANOTHER TIM WARD. (*looking around.*) I can't wait all day, you know. I've got things to do.

SCOTTIE. What things? – what will you do now?

MAN/ANOTHER TIM WARD. I'm gonna try the offices down the hall.

> (*The* MAN *starts off—*)

SCOTTIE. (*to the* MAN, *as he goes.*) I had planned to see the sunrise.

> (*—and the* MAN *is gone.*)

But I missed it.

> (*SOUND OF RAIN BUILDS, as—*
> BETH, TIM, BERNADETTE *and* RHONDA *are revealed behind* SCOTTIE – *at a distance.*
> *All but* BETH *hold black umbrellas. They stare front, not looking at one another – their faces in shadow.*
> RHONDA *approaches* BETH *and puts her umbrella over the two of them …*)

SCOTTIE. I wonder what else I have missed.
> (*… but* BETH *takes* RHONDA's *hand and gently lowers the umbrella [as* RHONDA *did in Kyoto].*
> *They both lift their faces to the rain.*
> *Lights fade.*)

End of Play

COFFEE BREAK
by Tasha Gordon-Solmon

BIOGRAPHY

Tasha Gordon-Solmon's plays have been developed and produced at Actors Theatre of Louisville, the Perry-Mansfield New Works Festival, Clubbed Thumb, Dixon Place, New Georges, Ars Nova, and The Flea Theater. She is a recipient of the Dramatists Guild Fellowship, a member of the Clubbed Thumb Falcons Writers' Group, a lyricist in the BMI Workshop, a New Georges Affiliated Artist, a member of the Project Y Playwrights Group, and an alumna of Ars Nova's Play Group. Her writing has been published in *The Brooklyn Rail, The Dramatist*, and *The Huffington Post*. As a director, Gordon-Solmon has worked at Ensemble Studio Theatre, The Tank, The Brick, The Flea, The Cell, The Signature Ford Studio, Pipeline Theatre Company, Studio Tisch, Columbia University, the New York Fringe Festival, The Fire This Time Festival, and the Young Playwrights Festival at the Eugene O'Neill Theater Center. Gordon-Solmon received her M.F.A. in Dramatic Writing at New York University, attended the National Theater Institute, and is a proud 52nd Street Project volunteer.

ACKNOWLEDGMENTS

Coffee Break premiered at the Humana Festival of New American Plays in April 2016. It was directed by Meredith McDonough with the following cast:

WOMAN 1	Brenda Withers
WOMAN 2	Deonna Bouye
1	Barney O'Hanlon
2	Nate Miller

and the following production staff:

Scenic Designer	Justin Hagovsky
Costume Designer	Kristopher Castle
Lighting Designer	Dani Clifford
Sound Designer	Sam Kusnetz
Production Stage Manager	Paul Mills Holmes
Assistant Stage Manager	Jessica Kay Potter
Dramaturg	Jessica Reese
Properties Master	Mark Walston

CHARACTERS

WOMAN 1.

WOMAN 2.

1.

2.

SETTING

A coffee shop.

Barney O'Hanlon, Deonna Bouye, Brenda Withers, and Nate Miller
in *Coffee Break*

40th Humana Festival of New American Plays
Actors Theatre of Louisville, 2016
Photo by Bill Brymer

COFFEE BREAK

A coffee shop. Two women sit down at a table, each a carrying a coffee cup.

WOMAN 2. Apparently they could restructure the entire department.

WOMAN 1. Really?

WOMAN 2. That's what Karen said. But you know Karen

WOMAN 1 & WOMAN 2. She'd say anything

WOMAN 2. The way I see it, they would have to
What?

WOMAN 1. Do you have anything…in your cup?

WOMAN 2. Decaf

WOMAN 1. In the foam

WOMAN 2. It's a regular coffee

WOMAN 1. I have something
In my foam

WOMAN 2. Oh

WOMAN 1. It's a heart

WOMAN 2. I see that

WOMAN 1. He made me a heart
Do you think it's like
A move?

WOMAN 2. A…

WOMAN 1. He's cute right?
Do you think he's cute?

WOMAN 2. I think that's just what they do

WOMAN 1. Boys that like you but don't know how to say it?

WOMAN 2. Baristas

WOMAN 1. You didn't get one

WOMAN 2. It's a regular coffee

WOMAN 1. You said decaf

WOMAN 2. That's the same thing

WOMAN 1. You don't think he likes me?

WOMAN 2. I don't know if he does

WOMAN 1. Why wouldn't he like me?
What about me is there to not like?

WOMAN 2. I'm saying it might be standard coffee art
And not a confession of love

WOMAN 1. We come here every day
I've never had a heart before
And suddenly I do

WOMAN 2. From the new guy who's proba—

WOMAN 1. Should I go talk to him?
I'll wait for him to come to me
Will he come to the table?
I'll stay in my chair

1 & 2. The table and the chair

1. The chair thinks:
Isn't it amazing we were paired up
Like we fit
Like we match
Like somehow we came from the same place and were made for each other

2. The table thinks:
These chairs are fine
We were in the factory together
So now we're here together
Makes sense

1. The chair thinks:
Look at those legs
All four of them

2. The table thinks:
I wonder if someone will fix my wobble today
I don't like it when they start stuffing napkins underneath
You need firm elevation with an injury
Cardboard
Or a wood chip

1. The chair thinks:
Sometimes
When table and I touch
I catch it wobble a little
I think I make it nervous

2. The table thinks:
This wobble is a pain in my oak
And it gets worse every time a damn chair bangs against me

1. The chair thinks:
I think this is love

The next day. WOMEN 1 & 2 *go to sit at their table, as before, with their coffees.*

WOMAN 2. So I asked Dan if he thought there would be layoffs and he said no. But you know Dan, he's…
Are you okay?

WOMAN 1. Sure
You were saying
About

WOMAN 2. Potential layoffs

WOMAN 1. Uh huh

WOMAN 2. Well when I spoke to Dan, unreliable source that he is
You seem a little on edge

WOMAN 1. I'm fine

> *Beat.*

I'm afraid of love
Not afraid excited
Afraid of being excited
Afraid if I'm excited, I'll be disappointed
But why would he disappoint me now, if he hasn't yet, right?

WOMAN 2. What are you…

WOMAN 1. Andrew

WOMAN 2. Who?

WOMAN 1. It says his name on his nametag

WOMAN 2. The foam guy?

WOMAN 1. I need to know but
You do it
What do you see?

WOMAN 2. A cappuccino

WOMAN 1. In the foam

WOMAN 2. A squiggle of chocolate syrup maybe

WOMAN 1. What kind of squiggle

WOMAN 2. It could be…a messy cloud?

WOMAN 1. Let me

> *She looks, gasps.*

WOMAN 2. What
What

WOMAN 1. It's a
(vagina)

WOMAN 2. Pardon?

WOMAN 1. See how there's the loop on that side and…

WOMAN 2. I can see how it kind of looks like petals, maybe a flower

WOMAN 1. My flower

Oh Jesus

> *She picks up a scone from her saucer that was hidden on the other side of her cup.*

He gave me a scone

On my saucer

He gave me a free scone

And drew a you-know-what in my foam

And gave me a scone

This is getting so intense

1 & 2. The saucer and the scone

1. The scone thinks:

I can't wait for my dip in the coffee

To get warm

And wet

To sink into the murky deep

2. The saucer thinks:

Oh scone

I feel the vibrations as you languidly move in the coffee

Then lie back on me

Softened, spent, dripping, crumbling

To pieces on my surface

1. The scone thinks:

If only there was someone to hold all my pieces

2. The saucer thinks:

I could hold the pieces

1. The scone thinks:

Oh that saucer below me

2. The saucer thinks:

Oh that scone above

That unbleached, gluten free, cranberries and traces of nuts

1. The scone thinks:

That porcelain, dishwasher safe, made in China, do not microwave

I'd microwave

If I could

The scone thinks:

If only

2. If only

Same as last time, the WOMEN *sit, coffees, table.*

WOMAN 1. He was being weird

WOMAN 2. He seemed normal

WOMAN 1. It's because I wasn't here yesterday

WOMAN 2. I don't think he's disappointed after two days of serving you coffee

WOMAN 1. That's not all he—

WOMAN 2. Maybe he'd be disappointed after coffees with his friend every single day
And then being ditched out of the blue

WOMAN 1. I'm sorry were you waiting for me yesterday?

WOMAN 2. Where were you?

WOMAN 1. I took a sick day

WOMAN 2. Are you alright?

WOMAN 1. I needed some space
Things were starting to move so fast
I couldn't see him
And I couldn't go into the office because that would make me think of getting coffee, which would inevitably lead back to him
So I called in sick

WOMAN 2. That's um

WOMAN 1. But when four o'clock came along, I realized
I need him
And I miss him
And now it's too late
He was so cold when I ordered

WOMAN 2. I don't think he was cold

WOMAN 1. He asked if I wanted my latte iced

WOMAN 2. It's hot out

WOMAN 1. There's no foam in an iced latte
It was his passive aggressive way of questioning whether I'm in this for real
Which is a valid question because I didn't know yesterday
But I do today and it's too late

She looks into her cup, decomposes a little.

Yup

WOMAN 2. What is it

WOMAN 1. Nothing

WOMAN 2. I'm sure it's not that bad

WOMAN 1. (*Fighting tears.*) It's nothing
There's nothing in the foam
Excuse me I need a napkin

1 & 2. The napkins
They think:

1. We were altogether

2. One package
One set

1 & 2. Layer
upon Layer
upon and upon and upon
endless infinite togetherness

1. And then one day

2. One goes away

1. And another

2. And other

1. Upon layer Upon layer

1 & 2. upon and upon and upon

2. endless

1. infinite

2. aloneness

>   *A week later. The* WOMEN *sit at the table, with their coffees.*

WOMAN 2. It's good to see you

WOMAN 1. I missed our coffee breaks

WOMAN 2. Me too

WOMAN 1. It was too hard to be around…
I've been using the instant in the employee kitchen

WOMAN 2. The one on the sixth floor?

WOMAN 1. Seventh

WOMAN 2. Aren't you going to look?

WOMAN 1. It didn't even cross my mind

WOMAN 2. You're going to be thinking about it the whole time
Well

WOMAN 1. A smiley

WOMAN 2. That is definitely two eyes and a happy mouth

WOMAN 1. That's nice
Even though it's over
It feels good knowing you meant something you know?

That it wasn't all me
That he wishes me the best
I wish him the best I do even though it's hard
I think this is the closure I needed.

WOMAN 2. That's good

WOMAN 1. We should find a new place
Maybe with tea

WOMAN 2. I got laid off

WOMAN 1. When?

WOMAN 2. Last week

WOMAN 1. You met me in the lobby

WOMAN 2. I wanted to say goodbye

WOMAN 1. I'm so sorry was it the

WOMAN 2. Restructuring

WOMAN 1. What are you gonna do?

WOMAN 2. I have some interviews

WOMAN 1. We should still keep in touch

WOMAN 2. Definitely

WOMAN 1. You live downtown, right?

WOMAN 2. Uptown

WOMAN 1. We can meet in the middle
For coffee
Or tea

WOMAN 2. That sounds nice

WOMAN 1. (*Lightly.*) Yeah, we're more than coworkers

      WOMAN 1 *sips her coffee.*

2. The coworker
The coworker thinks:
Of Her
Drinking her coffee
The way she holds the cup
The way she takes a sip
With an ease that is disarming
A grace that is alarming
Never noticing
Who buys her coffee every day
Who pulls out her seat
Slips a scone onto her plate
The coworker thinks:

I wonder what She thinks
This colleague this acquaintance this friend
I wonder if she'll ever think of me
The way I think
The way so many things think
But are rarely thought of

WOMAN 1. Hey
It's gonna get cold

WOMAN 2. Thanks.

She takes a sip from her cup.

End of Play

THIS QUINTESSENCE OF DUST
by Cory Hinkle

BIOGRAPHY

Cory Hinkle was the winner of the 2015 Heideman Award for his play, *This Quintessence of Dust*. He has received the McKnight Advancement Grant, two Jerome Fellowships, and a Jerome Travel and Study Grant. He was a co-writer of *That High Lonesome Sound,* which premiered at the 2015 Humana Festival. His plays *Little Eyes* and *SadGrrl13* premiered at the Workhaus Collective, a company he co-ran with eight other playwrights from 2007–2012. His other plays have been produced or developed at the Guthrie Theater, Jackalope Theatre, Chalk Repertory Theatre, The Theatre @ Boston Court, Mixed Blood Theatre, the Southern Theater, HERE Arts Center, the Bay Area Playwrights Festival, Cape Cod Theatre Project, the Humanitas Play LA Workshop, the Sundance Theatre Lab, and New York Theatre Workshop, among others. His work is published by Playscripts, Dramatic Publishing, Smith & Kraus, Vintage, and Heinemann. More information can be found at www.coryhinkle.com.

ACKNOWLEDGMENTS

This Quintessence of Dust was produced at the Humana Festival of New American Plays in April 2016. It was directed by Les Waters with the following cast:

JANE	Kelly McAndrew
CHIP	Todd Lawson
HENRY	Pun Bandhu

and the following production staff:

Scenic Designer	Justin Hagovsky
Costume Designer	Kristopher Castle
Lighting Designer	Dani Clifford
Sound Designer	Sam Kusnetz
Production Stage Manager	Paul Mills Holmes
Assistant Stage Manager	Jessica Kay Potter
Dramaturg	Jessica Reese
Properties Master	Mark Walston

This Quintessence of Dust was commissioned by Pavement Group (Chicago, IL) and performed at the Den Theatre from April 14–16, 2014 with the following cast: Yunuen Pardo as Jane, John Zinn as Chip, and Brian Stojak as Henry. It was directed by Tyrone Phillips.

CHARACTERS

JANE: She's caustic and funny, a survivor.

CHIP: He's vain, but lovable.

HENRY: He's like a little boy—sensitive, naïve, wide-eyed.

All characters are in their late 20s to early 30s.

SETTING

The future. Los Angeles, California.

Pun Bandhu, Kelly McAndrew, and Todd Lawson
in *This Quintessence of Dust*

40th Humana Festival of New American Plays
Actors Theatre of Louisville, 2016
Photo by Bill Brymer

THIS QUINTESSENCE OF DUST

A light rises on JANE.

JANE. I don't really miss how everything used to be.

Like

Not at *all*

Yes, in many ways things totally *suck* now

Like I can only eat *canned goods*

And not having the possibility of any sort of medical attention if you like cut off a finger is kinda *scary* and my hair is all ratted up like dreads cause I haven't washed it in ten months

BUT

What did I give up?

I was always stressed and depressed and moody and bitchy

Due to *social networking*

And *you tube-ing*

And *upworthy-ing*

And *netflix-ing*

I don't miss it!

(Admittedly, I really liked (and *miss*) *Orange Is the New Black,* not the main character, but the secondary characters? Like a LOT)

But I was always seeking adoration and LOVE and now I realize

OH MY GOD

I don't need it!

All of that love I thought I wanted?

I DON'T NEED LOVE

(Though I've lost my family and most of my friends, but the thing is when I *really think* about it, you know, I was never that close to any of them anyway, *not really*)

I like the quiet... The quiet is soooooo nice...

I watched the sunset last night.

(It was kind of hard to see, due to a weird dust storm?)

But I have an appreciation now for the *light* here in California

(How did I *never* look at a sunset before?)

And, yes, I feel sorry for all of the "island peoples" that no longer have homes and the cultures that have been LOST and the languages that are now DEAD and you can't swim in the ocean anymore due to all the JELLYFISH

But on the other hand

I won't ever have to LIKE one of your STATUSES ever again

And I won't have to watch videos of your kids.

Because…
You're dead.
And your kids are dead.

> (*Small pause.*)

Aaaanyway, everything would be fine
I would totally really be digging the apocalypse right now
Except that
Here I am trapped inside this tiny little super hot dank dirty apartment cum shelter that isn't even MINE, hiding from bands of cannibals
(Cormac McCarthy was totally right on that)
And I just happened to get trapped with
My ex, Chip.

It's like I'm stuck inside a sitcom from the nineties
Except, you know,
This sitcom is set—at the end of the world?

> (CHIP *suddenly enters.*)

CHIP. It's funny actually
Because we *did* date in the 90s
And then I broke up with her //

JANE. //No, not true

CHIP. And we both went our separate ways
And I was "doing my thang" in Hollywood
And she was out here visiting a friend
Even though there was this whole water shortage thing
And like people were dying, like, totally all over
It was super ugly

JANE. I should've stayed in New York.

CHIP. And then we had one of those "catch up" coffees

JANE. How are you?

CHIP. I'm great.

JANE. Yeah? What's new?

CHIP. Oh, national commercial for Ray-Ban you know what about you?

JANE. The usual. KILLING IT.

CHIP. And that's when—

JANE. The shit—

CHIP. Hit—

JANE. The fan. Los Angeles went DARK.

CHIP. Dark as Mumbai had been for months.

JANE. And Cape Town.

CHIP. And *so* many other places.

JANE. But America was different.

CHIP. Or so we thought…

JANE. And then…

CHIP. In order to survive, I killed someone, which I *still* feel really kinda bad about? And for like *weeks* my right hand smelled like Intelligentsia coffee (from our catch up date)—

JANE. It wasn't a date.

CHIP. And my left smelled like, well, human blood?

JANE. The strange thing is— Everything got *so quiet in this world* that I actually started to see things clearly for *the first time in forever* and I was just, like, living in the present, in the *now*, in my *body*, not needing love or adoration from anyone, *one* with the world, the animals and the *plants* (well the plants and the animals are mostly all dead, except for the jellyfish)

CHIP. So you were one with the jellyfish.

JANE. I was one with *myself*.

CHIP. I think you might have like PTSD from everyone, you know, *dying?*

JANE. NO! I'm happy.

CHIP. Anyway, now we're living in my neighbor's apartment?

(*He shows us physically in space*—)

There's a wall here

And it's completely covered floor to ceiling with canned goods.

My neighbor was like a Boy Scout when it came to the end times.

JANE. He's the guy Chip had to kill?

CHIP. (*Through clenched teeth.*) *I still feel bad so please don't bring it up.*

JANE. There's a bottle of whiskey.

And we get *SO* drunk and it's *SO* dark

CHIP. It turns out, the end of the world is dark and QUIET

JANE. Which is good for me because I can finally hear myself THINK

CHIP. But not for me because, actually, I kind of hear VOICES?

JANE. We get drunk and Chip likes to talk about his ex-girlfriends—

CHIP. It's just so WEIRD (you know) to think

that all of these girls I broke up with

they're all DEAD

and here I am ALIVE

and they won't ever see me again

well, except for YOU.

JANE. (*Through clenched teeth.*) *You didn't break up with me.*

CHIP. And then…

(From off, a loud knocking.
They stand completely still.
Another knock… And another…)

CHIP. What do we do?

JANE. Shh!

(More knocking.)

CHIP. It's the cannibals, isn't it?

JANE. Shut, up.

(HENRY *enters.*)

HENRY. I come in
Through an open window
My leg's broken
A bunch of cannibals like nearly killed me and—

JANE. Henry!?

HENRY. Jane!?
YAAASSSS
Jane!
HERE IS HOPE
Here's a ray of LIGHT—

CHIP. Who's this guy?

HENRY. I dated Jane in Brooklyn
We were SOOOOO into each other

JANE. No, YOU were into ME.

HENRY. JANE!
She was like
The most unattainable girl I ever dated.

JANE. What are you doing here!?!

HENRY. All of this end-of-the-world-stuff went down during pilot season,
I was gonna do a thing with Shia LaBeouf?

CHIP. *(Suddenly angry.)* Whatever, man!

HENRY. I'm sorry?

CHIP. She was waaaaaaaaaaaay into me too.

HENRY. She was?

CHIP. She like TOTALLY dug me
We dated in college?
She had to go to the hospital once for
Like um
HER WRIST?
Cause she like

BROKE IT from giving me HANDJOBS.

(JANE *and* HENRY *both stare at him.*)

Yeah I made that up I don't know why I'm sorry but she loved me, she did.

JANE. I don't love people.

HENRY. How can you not love people? They're awesome.

JANE. Because when I finally *truly did love someone*, this guy in New York named Rich, less than a month after we got together he turned REALLY COLD FOR NO REASON and said he NEEDED SPACE and so I came out here to hang out with my friend, Stacey, so she could *console me* because my heart was broken! And in a moment of desperation I got a cup of coffee with Chip and THEN THE *WORLD ENDED!?!*

(JANE *and* CHIP *bicker as* HENRY *confides in us.*)

HENRY. They're *screaming* at each other
And I think I'm going to *die* from loss of blood
(which actually I *do* die later, but for a different reason)
But anyway, because of their screaming
I never get to tell them what happened.
See, I went out looking for food
Something
Anything!
A squirrel
Or I would have eaten a rat I was so hungry
And I see this group of cannibals
Heads shaved
Long black fingernails
Their clothes *black* from dried blood
And I run!
But I'm so fatigued
Delirious
Malnourished
That I can't get away!
I beg for mercy
And I can't believe it!
They actually give it to me!
They take me in, as their slave, for a time
I work for them
Boiling human scalps and turning them into candle wax
(Very interesting process, actually)
But, still, I'm—I am *hungry*… I have to *eat… Something…*

(*Pause.*)

What else was I supposed to do?

I know! I know!

But honestly…?

It was delicious.

I've always loved people, people are awesome, but never this much.

CHIP. He *cannot* be here.

JANE. He's my ex.

CHIP. He may also be a cannibal.

JANE. Your breath does smell like human flesh.

HENRY. I can't leave.

Now that I've found you Jane!

I've been with *a lot* of women

And I never wanted to stay the whole weekend with any of them except *you*

I never wanted to shower with them

I never wanted to rub their feet with oil

Or watch movies in the afternoons

Or read yesterday's *New York Times* even though it's old, but we're too lazy to go out of bed and get today's paper? Or do crafts remember THAT?

JANE. Not REALLY

HENRY. My mom LOVED you

I NEVER introduced women to my family, like, ever

But you were different

You were my friend

You know how they say you, like, fall in love with your best friend?

> (*Pause.*)

I always loved you.

> (*Long Pause.*)

JANE. Later, that night…

HENRY. I lie down to sleep in the quiet darkness of the apocalypse

And it's the last time I do.

I don't know if it's because I told her I loved her, or because she intuited I now have an insatiable taste for human flesh?

JANE. Little bit of both.

HENRY. But she killed me, in my sleep…

> (*Pause.*)

JANE. I won't tell you how I did it because it was quite gruesome

And sometimes I feel, like, a little pang of guilt?

Because actually I think I took a lot of my anger toward Rich out on Henry?

But…

It's almost like I can feel Henry from beyond

Sending me these little, like, pings

Little messages?
I'll be sitting eating some canned beans
Trying to make out the sunset behind the orange dust
And I feel almost, like, like I want to respond to him in some way.
Like if I was still on Facebook?
I mean I AM ON IT
There's just no power right now to boot all the systems up
But if I *could* post something
I would post a really cool and poetic quote on Henry's wall.
Like, um, I don't know something from Shakespeare?
Do you know any Shakespeare, Chip?

CHIP. To be or not to—

JANE. Not that!
Something moving!
Like a picture of the earth with a quote from Shakespeare superimposed
Something about
How we had something we could really love, but we didn't care about it, you know?
No, you know what?
Like Hamlet! (I read that in college)
What's that quote?
Oh shit, *what is it?*
He's talking about how beautiful the world is and he talks about the sky, how it's a golden roof—yeah! "fretted with fire," though actually, maybe that's a different part (whatever) and he says something about the "paragon of animals," just how *incredible* it all is!
Everything, you know?
But when Hamlet looks at all that beauty?
He's just all like, "What is this quintessence of dust?"
Like he looks at everything and all he sees is *dust*
Which is
Just kind of... How I feel about people?
You know?
How Hamlet feels about the earth is how I feel about people.

Aaaaanyway
Enjoy it while you can, I say.
I mean there's still the sunset right?
Look at that sunset!
Wow!
You can barely see it, but you can *just* make it out...

       (*Small Pause.*)

I wouldn't trade the sunset for anything.

> (*The lights begin to change*
> *And they all watch the sun set*
> *Then lights fade.*)

End of Play

RESIDENCE
by Laura Jacqmin

ABOUT *RESIDENCE*

This article first ran in the Limelight Guide to the 40th Humana Festival of New American Plays, *published by Actors Theatre of Louisville, and is based on conversations with the playwright before rehearsals for the Humana Festival production began.*

A new mom returning to work, desperate to make the sale that will pull her out of debt. A 30-something stoner who seems content to let his life stall. A perky college student determined to achieve her ambitions. On the surface these three may not have much in common, but over the course of a month at an extended-stay hotel in Tempe, Arizona, struggling saleswoman Maggie, front desk clerk Bobby, and Theresa, the management trainee, form an unexpected bond. By turns funny and quietly devastating, Laura Jacqmin's play *Residence* takes an intimate look at people trying to establish distance from their messy lives, and somehow coming together in the process. For this story's searching characters, the Residence, with its promise of a "five-star experience," becomes a strange refuge, a home away from home—but they can't escape the intrusions of the outside world, which isn't nearly so hospitable.

For Maggie, visiting Tempe to market portable ultrasound equipment to area doctors, this isn't an ordinary sales trip. She's back at work for the first time since a recent hospitalization, which left her family overwhelmed with medical and credit card debt. As the sole breadwinner, it's up to Maggie to earn the commission that will allow her and her husband to pay their bills, and support their six-month-old son. And as if those stakes aren't high enough, Maggie's also grappling with ongoing mental health issues within her family. "This is very much a play about people coping, and Maggie epitomizes that," comments Jacqmin. "We meet her at a moment of crisis; she's trying to get back on the horse and regain some semblance of normalcy, fighting against the idea that this state of chaos may actually be the new normal."

Though her fellow denizens of the Residence might seem more cheerful and settled, Maggie isn't the only one whose life is on shaky ground. Upon checking in, she befriends Bobby, the chill, good-natured front desk clerk who smokes pot in the parking garage and takes her on grocery runs. As the two get to know each other, Maggie discovers that she and Bobby are in some ways more alike than they could have anticipated. Meanwhile Theresa, Bobby's work crush, seems to have everything figured out. She aspires to become the hotel's manager and is pursuing the degree she needs to turn that dream into reality—but her comically over-eager attempts to appear professional betray an ill-concealed anxiety about the future.

As these characters grow closer, a sense of danger creeps into their interactions. Jacqmin explains: "This play is a containment study, in a way. If you're trapped in one place with a group of people for a certain chunk of time, you reveal things that you wouldn't have otherwise and things can go off the rails. We watch these characters bounce off one another and there's some positive impact, but there's a fair amount of bad behavior, too." Jacqmin's speaking partly from experience: she drew inspiration for *Residence* from her own stay at a Residence Inn in Tempe while working on a project. "When you're living somewhere that's supposed to feel like home—but isn't your home—for a long period of time, you start to get weird," she recalls. "You make friends in unlikely places, or engage in activities you don't usually engage in, because it's an opportunity to get away from your regular life. There's a restlessness that develops."

In addition to following the twists and turns in these temporary friendships, *Residence* also digs into difficult truths about the economics of the healthcare industry. For example, Maggie's sales pitches nod candidly to the costs and limitations of primary care services. In particular, Maggie's own financial predicament speaks to how hard it can be to receive affordable care and insurance coverage for mental health conditions. It's an issue that's very personal for Jacqmin: "For years I've wanted to write a play about my experiences with my dad, who has Parkinson's disease. One of the terrible side effects of Parkinson's is that it can induce psychosis. With a degenerative brain disease, it's a wildcard situation where you never know what you're going to get; people's personalities can change in ways that are very frightening. And the resources to deal with these mental health cases just aren't there."

But for all its provocative investigation of such issues, the unlikely and sometimes hilarious connections between Maggie, Bobby, and Theresa lie at the heart of the story. "*Residence* is very much a character piece," says Jacqmin. "We diverge for a scene here and there, but we always return to this stew of people. It's almost like a family drama, except the family members aren't related. They just happen to be in the same place for a month." Sometimes stepping briefly into a new life—"taking up residence with a new personality, without fully inhabiting it," as Jacqmin puts it—is what helps you feel at home again in your old one.

—Hannah Rae Montgomery

BIOGRAPHY

Laura Jacqmin is a playwright, television writer and video game writer, originally from Cleveland, now splitting her time between Chicago and Los Angeles. Her plays include *Residence* (40th Humana Festival of New American Plays at Actors Theatre of Louisville), *January Joiner* (Long Wharf Theatre), *Ski Dubai* (Steppenwolf Theatre Company), *A Third* (Finborough Theatre London), *Look, we are breathing* (Rivendell Theatre Ensemble; Sundance Theatre Lab), *Dental Society Midwinter Meeting* (Williamstown Theatre Festival; Chicago Dramatists / At Play, 16th Street Theater), and *Ghost Bike* (Buzz22 Chicago). Other works have been produced and developed by Atlantic Theater Company, Roundabout Underground, Vineyard Theatre, LCT3, Cape Cod Theatre Project, Ars Nova, Second Stage, The Lark, the National New Play Network, and more. Awards: Wasserstein Prize, two NEA Art Works Grants, the ATHE / Kennedy Center David Mark Cohen National Playwriting Award, two MacDowell Fellowships, and an Illinois Arts Council Individual Artist Grant. Television: *Get Shorty* (forthcoming, EPIX), *Grace and Frankie* (Netflix), and *Lucky 7* (ABC). Video Games: *The Walking Dead* Season 3 and *Minecraft: Story Mode* (Telltale Games). She received her B.A. from Yale University, and earned an M.F.A. in Playwriting from Ohio University.

ACKNOWLEDGMENTS

Residence premiered at the Humana Festival of New American Plays in March 2016. It was directed by Hal Brooks with the following cast:

MAGGIE	Danielle Slavick
BOBBY	Alejandro Rodriguez
THERESA	Leah Karpel
BEN	Avery Glymph
NITA	Amelia Workman
THE DOCTORS	Avery Glymph

and the following production staff:

Scenic Designer	Daniel Zimmerman
Costume Designer	Kathleen Geldard
Lighting Designer	Paul Toben
Sound Designer	Christian Frederickson
Media Designer	Philip Allgeier
Stage Manager	Katie Shade
Dramaturg	Hannah Rae Montgomery
Casting	Kelly Gillespie
Properties Master	Joe Cunningham
Production Assistant	Leah V. Pye
Directing Assistant	Jonathan Harper Schlieman
Assistant Dramaturg	Kate Cuellar

Residence was developed by the Cape Cod Theatre Project.

CHARACTERS

MAGGIE: 38, white, from Wisconsin, medical supply saleswoman. Not entirely stable right now. Guest at the Residence.

BOBBY: 30ish, Cuban-American, but his Spanish sucks. A bit of a stoner, but with swagger. Front desk clerk at the Residence.

THERESA: 22, white, perky, current State University student. Used to be a front desk clerk but has recently been promoted to management trainee at the Residence.

DOCTOR: 40s. Preferably a person of color. Plays a family medicine doctor, then a mobile-house call doctor, then an OB/GYN. (Also plays BEN.)

BEN (voice only): 40s. Maggie's husband. (Also plays DOCTOR.)

NITA: 34, gorgeous, half Mexican, half black. College professor. Rich girl. Bobby's ex.

SET/TIME

The play takes place over four weeks at the Residence, a moderately upscale extended-stay hotel in Tempe, Arizona. It just opened a few months ago and everything is pristine, even if the colors are a bit garish. Full kitchens, new linens, and lots of different light fixtures everywhere. We spend time in: MAGGIE's hotel room, the rooftop outdoor pool/lounge area, an employee break area near a parking garage, and a back employee office. We also make several visits to various DOCTOR's offices.

A NOTE ABOUT TRANSITIONS

Whenever possible, we should roll right into the next scene, particularly if there are two MAGGIE scenes back to back.

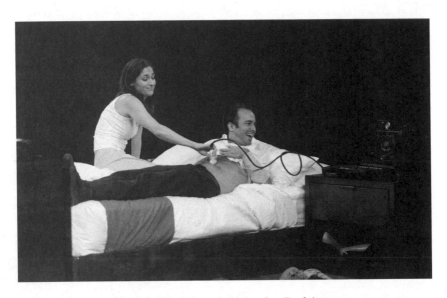

Danielle Slavick and Alejandro Rodriguez
in *Residence*

40th Humana Festival of New American Plays
Actors Theatre of Louisville, 2016
Photo by Bill Brymer

RESIDENCE

One.

MAGGIE's hotel room at the Residence. MAGGIE is here with BOBBY. Her big rolling suitcase is still near the door, like she abandoned it there upon arrival.

MAGGIE. (*Not an apology:*) Just that I thought there'd be a balcony.

BOBBY. Yeah, most rooms, you got a desk *or* a balcony. Your reservation's for like —

MAGGIE. Four weeks.

BOBBY. So I guess they thought you needed a desk. You know: Business Traveler?

MAGGIE. So there are no rooms with a desk *and* a balcony?

BOBBY. (*Trying to recall where those specific rooms might be:*) Uhhhh there are some? There are *some.*

MAGGIE. So maybe I could switch to one of *those* rooms.

BOBBY. It's just that we're really full this weekend.

MAGGIE. Yeah, I saw all those guys with golf clubs in the lobby. Like sixty guys with golf clubs.

BOBBY. (*Flirty:*) They're gettin' away from their wives, *you* know.

MAGGIE. (*Not reading it whatsoever:*) And at the airport, all these fifty-something men, waiting for their clubs to come through the oversized luggage sorter.
I thought Arizona was like —
Baseball. Right?

BOBBY. Spring training doesn't start for another two months. January: it's golf.

MAGGIE. So those golf guys, they reserved *all* the rooms with a desk *and* a balcony?

BOBBY. I mean — I don't know what the situation is for every *room?* —
If you wanna wait until after the weekend, we could maybe get you switched then. I don't wanna make any promises, though, because I'm not a hundred percent familiar with the *system?*

MAGGIE. (*Not exactly a question:*) Could you maybe just ask?

(BOBBY gestures: you got it. Then, turns away from MAGGIE, unholsters his radio, holds down the button.)

BOBBY. (*Low-pitched, into the radio. He loves this:*) Theresa, come in Theresa.
(*Long pause. Nothing.* BOBBY *gestures to* MAGGIE: *I got this. Holds down the button again.*)

Yo Theresa, Are You There?

THERESA. (*V.O., over radio.*) What's up, Bobby?

BOBBY. I'm in 803 with a Guest and she's interested in an upgraded room.
(*A moment of panicked silence, then:*)

THERESA. (*V.O., over radio. Concerned:*) Is there a problem with her current room?

BOBBY. No nonono, she just wants a balcony.
She *needs* a desk, but she *wants* a balcony.

THERESA. (*V.O., over radio.*) Did you tell her we can check after the weekend?

MAGGIE. (*Bright:*) Hi, Theresa.
(*Beat.*)

THERESA. (*V.O., over radio.*) Um. I'll come up!

BOBBY. (*Can't resist:*) Bobby out.
(BOBBY *re-holsters his radio.*)

If anybody can help you out, it's Theresa.

MAGGIE. It's just I'm going to be here for a month –

BOBBY. Yo, I get it. I'd want a balcony, too.

MAGGIE. Are you the person who takes us grocery shopping?

BOBBY. (*A little braggy:*) Sometimes I'm behind the desk, but yeah – I'll take you wherever. We got a Whole Foods fifteen minutes away.

MAGGIE. Isn't there anywhere else?
I just – don't want to spend that much money.

BOBBY. There's like a Ralph's.

MAGGIE. Great.

BOBBY. It's not very good, though.

MAGGIE. I don't care.

BOBBY. Like they shut the bakery down every other month because of mice.

MAGGIE. I just won't go to the bakery, then.

BOBBY. Okay. I'll take you to the Ralph's. The Customer Is Always Right.
(*A beat of semi-awkward waiting.*)

What's your company?
Like, what are you in Tempe for?

MAGGIE. Oh.

Medical equipment.

Compact volume ultrasound system.

BOBBY. Sounds like some NASA shit.

Stuff. NASA stuff.

MAGGIE. It's the best thing to come on the market in the past five years.

BOBBY. (*Joking:*) I'll take it.

MAGGIE. (*Not getting it:*) Ha. You got thirty grand?

BOBBY. I was kidding. What do I need an ultrasound for?

Unless I'm worried I got a bunch of women pregnant.

MAGGIE. Are you? Worried?

BOBBY. (*Thrown – but … :*) Uh –

I mean, you never know. Right?

> (*A knock from the door. BOBBY opens it, revealing THERESA, 22: perpetually perky and hyper-professional – which can seem ridiculous, given the context. THERESA, armed with a clipboard, marches straight over to MAGGIE.*)

THERESA. You must be Mrs. Elliott! Welcome to the Residence, and *welcome* to Tempe! We are *so* privileged to have you as our Guest.

MAGGIE. Are you the manager?

THERESA. I'm actually a management trainee? But I'm going to do *everything* I can to get this sorted out.

MAGGIE. I don't know how much there is to sort out – I just wanted to see if I could get a room with –

THERESA. Both a desk and a balcony. I know.

I am so sorry to have to disappoint you today, but I have *triple*-checked our system and there's just *zero* wiggle room.

Now, if you were interested in switching rooms *next* week, *that's* something we could talk about.

MAGGIE. You know what –

Forget it.

THERESA. Oh, no, I don't want to forget it!

MAGGIE. It's fine.

THERESA. (*Desperate to please her:*) Our staff can transfer rooms for you. You wouldn't even have to be here!

MAGGIE. I don't want strangers going through my bags.

THERESA. Well – if you change your mind, my name's Theresa, and I'm the management trainee.

You let me know if there's anything I can do to improve your stay.

MAGGIE. There is something, actually.

THERESA. What.

MAGGIE. You could find me a room with a desk and a balcony.

(THERESA *tries to laugh, uncomfortably.*)

Kidding.

(THERESA *exits.* BOBBY *is beaming a little.*)

BOBBY. She's pretty great, isn't she?

Lemme know when you wanna go to Ralph's. Just ask for "Bobby."

(*Points to his shirt, realizes there's nothing on it.*)

Whoops. I'm supposed to have a badge there. Where's my badge? Anyway. "Bobby."

MAGGIE. See you later, Bobby.

BOBBY. Enjoy Your Stay At The Residence.

(BOBBY *exits.* MAGGIE *looks around the room for a second: her home for the next four weeks. Remembers: shit. There's something she has to do. She places an iPad on its stand, then runs her fingers through her hair, pinches her cheeks to give them some color. This is a performance, and she's determined to be convincing.*

MAGGIE *makes a call on FaceTime. It rings just once — maybe one and a half times — before being picked up. After a moment, we hear* BEN's *voice through the speakers of the iPad.*)

BEN. (*V.O.*) Hold on a second.

MAGGIE. (*Confused, caught off guard:*) Oh, uh –

Am I not –

BEN. (*V.O.*) Just – hang on – *there* we go.

(MAGGIE *waits for* BEN *to pick up the baby.*)

MAGGIE. (*Warm enough:*) Is that who I think it is?

BEN. (*V.O.*) Somebody's supposed to be napping, but he wanted to stay up and say hi to you…

(*A baby's gurgle.*)

MAGGIE. (*Faux-stern, but shaky – she's not natural at this:*) Somebody's going to keep his dad up all night…

BEN. (*V.O. He really doesn't:*) I don't mind.

How was your flight?

MAGGIE. You know, we went up, we came down. That's pretty much the best you can hope for!

BEN. (*V.O.*) How's the hotel? You wanna give us the grand tour?

(MAGGIE *holds up the iPad, reverses the camera to show him.*)

MAGGIE. There's a bed. Like a desk. That's the view through the window.

BEN. (*V.O.*) Huh. No balcony?

MAGGIE. Wouldn't you know, they ran out.

> (*Trying to make conversation:*)

Is it, um. Still snowing there?

BEN. (*V.O.*) Three inches, with another two overnight.

MAGGIE. Oh, that's not *that* bad!

BEN. (*Oh, really?:*) Yeah? What's the temperature *there?*

MAGGIE. I think the little screen thing in the elevator said 79 degrees.

BEN. (*V.O.*) Oh, come *on!*
Good thing I had you pack sunblock. That little sticker on the side of your meds – you know the sun with an X through it? – that's no joke.

MAGGIE. (*She can't help but clock that "had you":*) All my sales meetings are inside.

BEN. (*V.O.*) Yeah, but even that walk to and from the car – that adds up.

MAGGIE. (*Perky:*) I will wear my sunblock. I'll wear *extra.*

> (*Beat.*)

BEN. (*V.O.*) You okay?

MAGGIE. Yeah!
Four weeks is nothing. I mean, it's gonna go by like –

> (MAGGIE *snaps her fingers. She sort of misses her snap.*)

I missed my snap. God. How does that even happen?
I meant it'll go by in a snap.

BEN. (*V.O.*) I just want to make sure you're ready.

> (*Long beat.*)

MAGGIE. I mean who can say whether anybody is actually ever ready for *anything.*
You know?
I just wanna be back at work.
I just wanna –
You know?
Normal.

BEN. (*V.O.*) Listen …
Visa called again.

MAGGIE. Why? I talked to them like every day last week.

BEN. (*V.O.*) They said they still haven't gotten anything from the clinic. I left three messages with them, but –

MAGGIE. They said they'd fax my records; Visa has to give them *time* to fax the records.

BEN. They said – while we're waiting – we could have your primary care physician write a letter.

MAGGIE. My *primary care physician* wasn't the doctor that treated me. My *primary care physician* would have pitched a fit if she knew how much the *clinic doctor* was going to charge.

What's it up to?

BEN. (*V.O.*) Fourteen thousand.

　　　　(*Beat.*)

Not that I want that in your *head*, but.

They called.

　　　　(*Beat.*)

Look – before you go.

I know I don't even have to say this, but –

I know these sales meetings can get a little – frustrating – and I know sometimes they wanna go out for lunch – or a drink – but it's just really, really important that you don't. Drink. I mean: at all.

MAGGIE. I know that, Ben.

BEN. (*V.O.*) No, I know, but it's just really important.

Alcohol. And sun. Are just really bad for you right now. So –

MAGGIE. So no alcohol, and no sun.

I've got this, Ben.

Okay?

BEN. (*V.O.*) Okay.

Talk to you again later tonight.

MAGGIE. Yup. Later.

BEN. (*V.O.*) Love you.

　　　　(MAGGIE *smiles an instant, huge smile.*)

MAGGIE. Love you, too.

　　　　(MAGGIE *disconnects the call. Her smile instantly drops. She might even have*
　　　　to close her eyes: exhausted from the effort of the call.
　　　　She sits staring at the iPad screen for a moment, then closes it inside of its case.
　　　　Then, one by one, she removes from her purse and sets in a row on the desk:
　　　　one, two, three different orange prescription bottles – an antidepressant, an
　　　　antipsychotic, and an anti-anxiety drug – and a 20cl bottle of Jack Daniels.)

Two.

An employee break area, basically inside the parking garage. You can see some sky, but it smells like concrete in here. Cigarette ash is ground into the cement despite there being a modern cigarette-butt disposal stand here.
BOBBY is surreptitiously trying to pack a one-hitter. He is precise, surgical — until the bud drops out and onto the concrete.

BOBBY. Oh, fuck.

(*He tries to pick it up, but just sort of mashes it further into the ground. He gets down on hands and knees to try to scoop it back into the bowl. It's semi-successful.*
He stands again, carefully packs it in a bit more, prepares to light it —
When he's interrupted by THERESA, *carrying a clipboard. She's wearing a girly little suit with a shortish skirt and fitted jacket.* BOBBY *immediately slips the one-hitter into a pocket and tosses the lighter over his shoulder, is instantly annoyed with himself — the lighter isn't the problem — then tries to smooth his hair for* THERESA.)

THERESA. Hi, Bobby!

BOBBY. (*He has a crush on her, but tries to hide it:*) Heeey, Theresa.

THERESA. I'm so happy you're on shift with me today! The breakfast room staff is mad at me again.

BOBBY. Who, Marisela or Su-Jin?

THERESA. Both of them.

BOBBY. (*You're in troublllle:*) Ooooh what'd you do?

THERESA. (*A guilty admission:*) I didn't finish my pancakes the other morning and they saw me throwing my plate in the trash.

BOBBY. You threw out some mini pancakes? I love those things!

THERESA. They put chocolate chips in them. It's just too much! Anyway, they have such bad attitudes. It's like, go work at the Courtyard if you want to act like that, but don't even begin to think it's going to fly at the Residence.

BOBBY. Yeah! *Fuck* the Courtyard.

THERESA. Didn't you work there for a while?

BOBBY. For like a week.

THERESA. Didn't they fire you?

BOBBY. It was a mutual parting of ways.

THERESA. What happened?

BOBBY. Racism.

THERESA. (*Genuinely concerned:*) Oh, no!

BOBBY. I was doing short-order breakfasts and this golf dude didn't like how I made his eggs –

THERESA. The golf guys are such a problem.

BOBBY. And I was like, "I made it exactly how you ordered it, sir," and he was like, "I said Florentine not frittata," and I was like, "Those two are pretty hard to mix up," and he *shoved* it in my face, all like, "DO YOU SPEAK ENGLISH, ASSHOLO" like that was supposed to be the Spanish word for asshole!

I spiked that plate all over his feet and walked out.

THERESA. Ohmigod the Courtyard is the *worst.*

BOBBY. (*An aside:*) I do think the lobby is nice, though.

THERESA. (*An aside right back:*) I mean the lobby is *okay* but ours is newer so just by definition it's nicer.

Those golf guys, though!

BOBBY. Fuck the golf guys!

THERESA. One of them, like, asked me to show him up to his room the other day? And I'm trying to make every Guest experience a five-star experience because we're the newest hotel in Tempe and need to make a good impression, but on the elevator ride up he would *not* take his eyes off my, you know.

(*She gestures to her breasts. BOBBY nods, sagely.*)

Like he could barely even concentrate when I was telling him about all the amenities: the rooftop pool, the 24-hour gym. And then when we got to his room, he was all: "Is there turndown service?" and I was like – "um, not so far, that's not something we offer," and he was like, "I think the Vista Playa offers turndown service," and I was like, "Okay, first of all, the name 'Vista Playa' literally translates to 'beach view,' and this is Tempe, Arizona, so right off the bat you know that's a hotel full of liars," and then he tried to *kiss* me.

BOBBY. No. Nonono, that's *bull*shit.

THERESA. So now I'm like watching all the travel sites like a hawk, waiting for this guy to write something mean about our service or hospitality because I wouldn't make *out* with him.

BOBBY. (*Still distracted and angry:*) Yo, what'd *Jordan* say about that shit?

THERESA. That I was a cute girl and it probably wasn't the last time it was gonna happen and it sucks but what are you gonna do?

BOBBY. That's *it?* Some manager…

THERESA. He *did* say I could have a free ice cream bar from the sundry store.

But – we were out of the Milky Way Ones.

(*A mournful beat, then:*)

Honestly, I wish there was a whole class in my program about this kind of stuff. There's only one paragraph about it in our whole textbook!

BOBBY. Seriously?

THERESA. It's this little infographic called, "The One Time The Customer Is *Never* Right," but it *also* says, "make sure you're not doing anything to *ask* for it."

I tried to talk to my advisor about it, but he said he's adjunct and "doesn't have time for that stuff outside of office hours."

BOBBY. You like that program?

THERESA. Oh, I love it. I love it.

BOBBY. But, like – a degree in hotel whatever-it-is?

THERESA. It's a fully accredited Bachelor's in Tourism Development Management, colon, Resort and Accommodations Leadership track.

BOBBY. What do you do there?

THERESA. We study how to be good leaders.

Different motivational techniques, and how to deal with people who are very different from you. Customer service. How to build a business. It's – really great stuff. It's going to set me up for the rest of my life.

BOBBY. But doing a whole degree – isn't it expensive?

THERESA. I mean – I'm taking out some loans, for living expenses and stuff. But my dad is paying my tuition, and that's the expensive part.

BOBBY. How much in loans?

And we make, what, like, ten-eighty-five an hour?

THERESA. Well, I'm making a little more than that now, because I'm a management trainee?

BOBBY. Still. How is *this* gonna pay for *that?*

THERESA. (*Getting a little flustered:*) When I make manager, I can pay my loans back. And like I said: my dad is taking care of the rest, so – it's fine. I'm investing in my future.

BOBBY. Yeah, but like –

THERESA. *Anyway.*

> (*A weird little silence between them.* BOBBY *shuffles his feet a little;* THERESA *pretends to be examining a weird-feeling cuticle.*)

BOBBY. I like your suit.

THERESA. Thank you! I just thought now that I'm a management trainee.

BOBBY. Yeah. Totally. You got your suit, you got your heels 'n' stuff. You got your clipboard.

> (BOBBY *teasingly grabs for the clipboard.*)

THERESA. Uh –

(THERESA *grabs for the clipboard.*)

Can I have that back, actually?

BOBBY. "To-do list." Ooh.

"Call supplier about third floor vending machine issue." Yeah, you better –
that thing's been shooting Snickers at 20 miles an hour.

"Schedule with pool chemical guy."

(BOBBY *hesitates when he sees something.*)

"Discipline Bobby."

THERESA. No, that's not really – it was just like, a note, to remind me – it
wasn't, like –

BOBBY. Discipline me about what?

THERESA. The other morning, I noticed a Guest checking in, and she was
speaking to you in Spanish…but you were speaking to her in English.

BOBBY. So?

THERESA. Just – next time, if a Guest wants to use Spanish, please use
Spanish, too.

BOBBY. I don't speak Spanish.

THERESA. … What?

BOBBY. Yeah, no hablo. Like, I understand some? Like I understood
everything that lady was saying, I just – I don't speak it myself. I never really
learned it.

(THERESA *is shocked.*)

THERESA. Well – that's a problem.

BOBBY. How come?

THERESA. Part of the reason Jordan hired you is because he thought you
spoke Spanish.

BOBBY. (*Getting a little pissed:*) Nah –
Jordan looked at my name, and he looked at me, and he *assumed.* And you
know what they say about assuming.

THERESA. (*Straightfaced:*) What do they say?

(BOBBY *stares at her a split second – is she for real? Uh, she is.*)

BOBBY. It's *bad* for people to speak Spanish around here, man. In Arizona?
It's like the *last* thing you wanna do. Like, when I get pulled over? You better
believe I don't even use my real voice. I do a Jordan.

(*A really white voice:*)

"I'm so sorry, officer, what's the problem?" If I was like, "Hey, you're DWM-
ing me," I'd get arrested like *that.*

THERESA. What's DWM-ing?

BOBBY. Driving While Mexican.

THERESA. (*Confused:*) I thought you said you were Cuban.

BOBBY. Cops don't know the difference between Cuban and Mexican, that's what I'm trying to tell you. We're all the same. That's what Jordan thinks.

THERESA. And why are you getting pulled over?

BOBBY. Look –

I don't speak Spanish, okay?

THERESA. You really should. I'm learning it – it's a mandatory part of my program.

Like –

(*Her accent is <u>not</u> good. Seeing stuff parked in the garage:*)

Motocicleta.

El auto.

(*Pointing at* BOBBY:)

Compañero de trabajo.

BOBBY. (*It's sort of cute how bad her accent is:*) Yeah … *compañero.*

THERESA. See, you'd be really good at it – your *énye* is so much better than mine.

BOBBY. You gotta sorta: *ñ. Ñ.*

THERESA. (*To herself:*) *Ñ. Ñ.*

BOBBY. (*Expert:*) Keep trying. *Compañero.*

THERESA. (*She's embarrassed to say it in front of him – his accent is so much better:*) …It's hard.

I need to practice. It's really important that I learn it.

BOBBY. I know. "Spanish is the language of the future." I *know.*

THERESA. (*Small:*) Actually – my professor said – it's so we can talk to the housekeeping staff.

(BOBBY *just stares at her for a moment.*)

BOBBY. I can't even get into this shit right now.

So are you done "disciplining" me now, or what?

THERESA. Actually –

BOBBY. *What.*

THERESA. Can you please ask your girlfriend to stop calling the front desk when she wants to speak to you? That's the whole reason we have the staff number in the back office.

And it's just really – she can't keep doing that, or it's going to turn into a problem.

(*Beat.*)

BOBBY. Ex.

THERESA. What?

BOBBY. My ex-girlfriend. We're not together anymore, so. I don't even know why she's calling.

THERESA. Maybe you should ask her.

BOBBY. I'll take care of it.

THERESA. Thank you, Bobby.

I really think the Residence is lucky to have you. I just want to see you going above and beyond because I know you're capable of that.

BOBBY. (*A little flattered, despite himself:*) Okay. Thanks.

THERESA. I have to get back inside.

(THERESA *turns to go. Just before she goes back inside, she tosses back:*)

Um-and-can-you-stop-smoking-pot-on-shift-please-because-everyone-can-smell-it-and-I-don't-want-you-to-get-in-trouble.

(*She's gone.* BOBBY *is nervous, then realizes she doesn't want him to get in trouble, which might mean … he smiles.*
He takes the one-hitter back out. The bud spilled everywhere in his pocket. Unsalvageable.)

BOBBY. (*Quiet:*) Fuck.

(BOBBY *takes out his cell phone and dials. It rings just once then goes to voicemail.* BOBBY, *annoyed that he's been screened, leaves a message.*)

Oh, okay, Nita, so you're allowed to call me at work like every day but when *I* call, all of a sudden you're not available?
Whatever.

(*Beat, then:*)

If you want money, I wanna see a paternity test. Till then, I'm not giving you shit.
Peace.

(*He hangs up. Twitches there a moment, annoyed, then goes inside.*)

Three.

A small office. DOCTOR *has takeout containers at his desk.* MAGGIE *hurries in, lugging the portable ultrasound case behind her. She has trouble getting it through the door.*

MAGGIE. Thanks for taking the time to meet with me –

DOCTOR. No, thank *you.*

(*Then, all business:*)

You have until I finish my lunch.

(*Is he serious? Oh, yeah. He's serious:*)

I'm taking my first bite.

MAGGIE. Oh. Okay!

I'll just get started then.

What I want to talk about is the pre-hospital ultrasound experience.

Sometimes, people have complicated stuff going on. And if the level of patient trauma is too great, they're probably going to skip right over scheduling an appointment with you in favor of an emergency medicine department. And as a small practice, how are you supposed to compete with a Level 1 Trauma Center, right?

But what if they could *keep* that appointment with you? And be confident that no matter what was going on internally, they could avoid the ER, and quickly and safely find out what was going on – without requiring the services of a radiologist!

As a family medicine physician who deals with every kind of patient complaint under the sun, this point-of-care unit could mean the difference between sending someone away, or welcoming them with open arms.

Jesus you eat fast.

As we say back at the office:

"Astounding accuracy leads to astounding outcomes."

DOCTOR. "Astounding."

MAGGIE. Yes: astounding!

DOCTOR. *"Astounding!"*

MAGGIE. … Uh-huh!

DOCTOR. So answer me this:

Does it take pictures?

MAGGIE. So our Tissue Differentiation setting offers the highest resolution soft tissue imaging available – plus, it comes with our touch-of-a-button Auto Clarity Suite, standard.

DOCTOR. I'm gonna ask you again, and this time, cut the gobbledy-gook: does it take pictures?

MAGGIE. Yes, it does.

DOCTOR. I already have an ultrasound that takes pictures.

MAGGIE. But the pictures the Precision E takes have a 20% improvement in contrast ratio from the previous models.

DOCTOR. Does it go on a cart?

MAGGIE. Uh – yes –

DOCTOR. I already have an ultrasound that goes on a cart.

MAGGIE. … This cart would be smaller.

DOCTOR. So how much is it?

MAGGIE. So the ultrasound itself retails for twenty-eight thousand a unit, but of course we'd offer flexibility in that pricing if your practice decided to buy multiples.

DOCTOR. *Multiples?*

MAGGIE. Uh-huh!

(DOCTOR *sweeps the detritus of his lunch into the trash.*)

DOCTOR. So lemme get this straight.

You're visiting a small, independent practice today, financed entirely by the doctors who run this place, not a one of them suckling on the government teat, to see if we want to spend something like a hundred thousand dollars of our own money to buy *multiple* portable ultrasounds to replace the perfectly good – if somewhat older – unit, and for what? So you get a big fat commission from the fascists behind the ACA?

MAGGIE. That's not how it works, actually –

DOCTOR. I'm gonna save you the trouble, and you can save your breath: You Will Not Make A Sale Here.

You people should be ashamed of yourselves.

MAGGIE. (*With a tiny bit of an edge:*) I'm just a working person, doctor. Same as you. Same as all the doctors at this private practice.

DOCTOR. (*Hearing that edge:*) Usually you salespeople like private practice – at least you know our checks won't bounce.

MAGGIE. I wasn't trying to imply there's anything *wrong* with the way you do business –

DOCTOR. Really? Because it sounds to me like you think I've got something to be *embarrassed* about.

This is America, young lady. I get to choose which patients I want to see and which ones I don't. I have the *freedom* to do that.

MAGGIE. Okay – wait – just – wait a second.

Maybe – if you let me start over – it's just, I've recently come back to work from – a leave of absence, and so there's a pretty good chance that I forgot some – important little piece of information that might change your mind –

DOCTOR. Sorry, I'm not gonna give you a do-over because you just got back from *vacation.*

MAGGIE. Okay –

DOCTOR. What, you spent a week getting wasted in Vegas?

Still jetlagged from *Meh-hee-ko?*

Just got off a *Disney cruise* or something?

MAGGIE. Actually I was in an inpatient psychiatric clinic for six weeks. That place *also* happened to be a private practice.

(*Beat.*)

DOCTOR. (*Chastened but unsure of how to recover:*) Well –
I hope you found it – effective.

MAGGIE. You get what you pay for, right?

(DOCTOR *is silent.*)

I remember where the exit is.

Four.

The roof of the Residence. We don't see them, but there's a small pool here, and a hot tub, and a fire pit and seating area on the other side.
What we do see is MAGGIE, *sans sunblock, stretched out on a lounger in the sun, against* BEN's *orders. It's* <u>bright</u>. *Nobody else is stupid enough to be out during these peak sun hours except for* MAGGIE. *She doesn't have a hat or sunglasses, but she does have a towel rolled up and placed over her eyes.*
BOBBY *enters, carrying some strands of Christmas lights. He wears sunglasses because he's not an idiot.*
He gets set up, trying to untangle the lights. It's pretty hopeless. He sneaks a couple glances at MAGGIE, *trying to figure out who she is – the towel makes it a little hard. He tries clearing his throat, but there's no response from* MAGGIE. *He clears his throat again, louder, and* MAGGIE *lifts the towel to look at him.*

BOBBY. Ha. Thought that was you.

MAGGIE. Yeah? How?

BOBBY. Recognized your – just recognized you.

MAGGIE. Whatcha got there?

BOBBY. Just some lights that somebody tied in like thirty billion knots, no big deal.

MAGGIE. Christmas is over.

BOBBY. Yeah, but the celebration never stops at the Residence.

(*Taking note of her lack of sun protection:*)

You're gonna fry out here like that.

MAGGIE. It's just a little sun. Why does everyone keep telling me to stay away from it, like I'm going to *die* if I spend a single second outdoors?

BOBBY. 'Cause you are. Like no question. You're from the Midwest, right?

MAGGIE. Wisconsin's not the Midwest, it's Dairy Country.

BOBBY. Yeah, Dairy Country people get burned *up* in sun like this.

(MAGGIE *responds by draping the towel over her head like a hat.*)

MAGGIE. How's this?

BOBBY. Yeah, that, plus a little SPF fifty thousand.

MAGGIE. I'll be fine.

    (MAGGIE *lies back down.* BOBBY *suddenly starts to unravel a really complicated knot and gets instantly excited.*)

BOBBY. Oh, shit – oh oh oh oh oh oh!

    (*Until he realizes it just leads to an even bigger knot.*
    THERESA *enters, carrying a bag of decorations.*)

THERESA. You haven't started?

BOBBY. Whoever packed up these lights didn't coil 'em or nothing.

    (*Sucks his teeth a second when he reaches another clump.*)

Who was on cleanup after the holiday party?

THERESA. (*Casually:*) Jordan.

BOBBY. (*Half under his breath:*) Figures.

THERESA. Be nice.

BOBBY. Bet he tied these knots himself, just to mess with me.

    (*Noticing* MAGGIE, THERESA *switches to her voice-for-Guests.*)

THERESA. Well, hello! How are you today?

MAGGIE. … Me?

THERESA. Of course, you! I hope you're enjoying our pool and lounge area. Let me know if there's anything I can do to improve your experience.

MAGGIE. Will do.

    (THERESA *moves to unfurl a massive sun umbrella near* MAGGIE.)

What are you doing?

THERESA. Just opening up this umbrella for you!

MAGGIE. You don't have to.

THERESA. It's my pleasure.

MAGGIE. No, you really don't have to. I don't want you to.

THERESA. You're going to burn up if you don't have a *little* shade!

MAGGIE. I'm fine.
I have this towel. See? This towel – is all I need.

THERESA. This umbrella is a lot bigger than that towel!

BOBBY. (*"Stop trying":*) Yo, Theresa – I tried already, believe me. If Maggie says all she needs is that towel – that's all she needs!

THERESA. (*Pointed:*) I hope you've been helping provide a five-star experience for our Guest: Mrs. Elliott.

MAGGIE. Oh, he has. He took me to Ralph's.

THERESA. (*Concerned:*) We have a Whole Foods.

MAGGIE. I wanted to go to Ralph's.

(BOBBY *snickers;* THERESA *clocks it.*)

THERESA. What? What's funny?

BOBBY. She *wanted* to go to Ralph's, yeah. She don't wanna go any*more.*

THERESA. Why not? What happened?

BOBBY. I told her, Ralph's has mice.

MAGGIE. You said the *bakery* had mice.

BOBBY. Yeah, but the bakery's right in the middle of the store!

MAGGIE. (*To* THERESA:) So I'm rolling my cart down the cereal aisle. I put a box of cereal in my cart, keep on rolling. I check out. Load the groceries into the van. Start heading back.

BOBBY. Couple minutes later, we pull up to Alameda and Broadway, and we hear this *rustling.*
She looks in the back, like maybe a bag had fallen over.

MAGGIE. Nothing.

BOBBY. We thought we imagined it.

MAGGIE. Minute later, we hear another noise. This time, I look back, the box of cereal is tipped over on its side. It fell out of the bag. No big deal, right? Until –

BOBBY. She starts screaming her head off, like *screaming.*
I pull over, run around to the back, open the hatch –

MAGGIE. A dozen pink, hairless baby mice are *spilling* out of the cereal box, along with fur, and little bits of cardboard, and *so* much mouse shit – like more shit than mice –

THERESA. Oh, my gosh!

MAGGIE. He scoops everything up, drops it by the side of the road –

BOBBY. Squirt a whole bottle of Purell on my hands, and got the hell *out* of there.

        (*Beat.*)

THERESA. You just left the mice there, by the side of the road?
That's awful. They were babies.

MAGGIE. Yeah, but.
They didn't belong there.

BOBBY. Not in my van. Hell, no.

        (BOBBY *and* MAGGIE *are smiling at each other, reliving the moment.* THERESA *watches this.*)

THERESA. They're probably going to die there.
When did this happen?

MAGGIE. Tuesday.

THERESA. They're probably dead already.

(*Awkward little silence.*)

MAGGIE. What are you guys doing up here?

THERESA. We're setting up for the 6 p.m. Manager's Reception.

MAGGIE. It wasn't on the schedule on my fridge.

THERESA. The more, the merrier, right?

(THERESA *turns away from* MAGGIE. BOBBY *approaches* THERESA, *speaks a little softer.*)

BOBBY. Hey – she's right. It wasn't on the schedule.

THERESA. So?

BOBBY. So – are we actually allowed to be doing this?

THERESA. Managers take initiative.

BOBBY. Yeah, but do management trainees?

THERESA. If you don't want to help me, I'll hang up the lights myself.

BOBBY. I didn't say I wasn't going to help you –

THERESA. Did you even see *Jordan's* Manager's Receptions for this month? He claimed he was doing Hawaiian Luau every other Tuesday, and then what does he serve? Pigs in a blanket from Costco and pineapple chunks. From a *can.* And he has awful taste in wine, everything was *Riesling* and the golf guys just want beer, he should *know* that.

And then the whole thing you said about the *lights?!*

BOBBY. Whoa whoa whoa.

THERESA. My theme is Paris in Springtime and I'm serving macaroons. By the time we're done up here, it's gonna look like a garden at Versailles.

(*They squint into the ungodly bright, non-Parisian, non-springtime, nothing-close-to-Versailles-esque sun.*)

BOBBY. I think it's "macarons."

THERESA. What?

BOBBY. The little sandwich things – right?

THERESA. Meringue sandwiches, yeah, that's what they are.

BOBBY. It's "macarons." Not "macaroons."

THERESA. … It's French, not Spanish.

(*Beat.*)

I just wanted to host an event to show how good I would be at actual, genuine managerial duties. Not – regular front desk stuff, which is *all* Jordan has me *doing.*

I mean, what's the point of even being in this trainee program if that's all it's gonna be? You know?

BOBBY. So you *are* breaking the rules.

THERESA. Yeah. But. It's not a big deal.

I bought the food, *I* got a discount on the liquor, I'm taking care of the whole thing.

> *(Beat.)*

You won't tell on me?

BOBBY. You know I got you.

> *(THERESA smiles at him.)*

THERESA. I'm gonna go get the macaroons.

> *(She heads towards the exit.)*

BOBBY. It's "maca – "

Forget it.

> *(Beat as BOBBY makes another attempt at the lights. Then, a buzzing from BOBBY's pocket – or maybe an odd ringtone. BOBBY takes out his phone, glances at it – WTF.*
> *To himself:)*

You serious?

> *(Despite his better judgment, he braces himself and answers the call.)*

I can't talk right now.

> *(Beat.)*

Why can't I talk right now? 'Cause I'm at my *job*, that's why.

You know: my job? Where I *work*?

Yeah, that's what I thought. That's *what I thought*.

> *(Beat.)*

And don't call the front desk anymore, are you *trying* to get me fired?

> *(Beat.)*

Call the office then. 322-4148.

Nope. Nope. Call the office.

> *(Beat.)*

Four one four eight.

Bye.

> *(BOBBY hangs up, depuffs his chest, repuffs, shrugs it off.*
> *He's still annoyed though. Goes back to the lights, but it's a losing game. No way he can focus now.*
> *After a moment, to MAGGIE:)*

Hey, Sun Goddess. C'I ask you something?

> *(MAGGIE doesn't say no.)*

So, you're an attractive woman, right?

MAGGIE. Are you asking me or telling me?

BOBBY. You see yourself in the mirror every day; don't play.

MAGGIE. Okay. Yeah.

BOBBY. So you must've dealt with somebody just, like, *not leaving* you *alone*, no matter how much you try to tell 'em you're done, right?

MAGGIE. (*Referring to the phone call, joking:*) Oh, is that what that was? Sounds like she really wants to talk to you.

BOBBY. Yeah, but she wants it on her terms, you know? 'Cause if I try to call her from my phone, like at *my* convenience, she screens the call. Like she blocked the number or something.

MAGGIE. Why would she block the number?

BOBBY. I mean, I'm not saying it's not *complicated*. Like I might have been calling *her* a little too much? At one point?

MAGGIE. You harassed her; so she's harassing you back?

BOBBY. No, but this chick is *crazy*, though.

MAGGIE. (*Sharp:*) Hey.

> (MAGGIE *slaps the chaise.*)

Don't say shit like that.
Don't call a woman crazy unless she's actually crazy.
Don't call her crazy if she *seems* crazy.
Don't call her crazy if she *sounds* crazy.
Only if she's *actually* crazy. Are you allowed to say that word.
Okay?

BOBBY. Okay.

MAGGIE. *Okay?*

BOBBY. Damn, okay.

> (*They're both taken aback for a moment. Silence. MAGGIE surveys her limbs.*)

MAGGIE. I'm gonna be pink tomorrow, man.

BOBBY. You're gonna be bright red.

MAGGIE. I'm gonna look just like those baby mice.

> (*Beat. She's trying to work through it:*)

"Awful."
I mean – they were just mice.
Who cares?
You know?

Five.

MAGGIE's hotel room. The portable ultrasound is out, on the desk.
MAGGIE is pacing a little, nervously waiting for something.
Then, we hear something from the bathroom.

MAGGIE. Anything?

THERESA. *(O.S.)* Not yet!

(Some noises. Pause.)

MAGGIE. You gotta get a really good seal.

THERESA. *(O.S.)* I have a pretty good seal.

MAGGIE. No, but you need like an airtight seal.

THERESA. *(O.S.)* I know!

(Some noises.)

Jeez Louise ...

MAGGIE. *(Embarrassed.)* I'm so sorry. I thought they'd send some burly guy
with a special machine.

THERESA. *(O.S.)* Nope! Just me!

MAGGIE. I had lunch at the hospital.
And you know what they say about eating lunch at the hospital.

THERESA. *(O.S.)* What do they say?

MAGGIE. ... Don't.

(Beat, then a successful flush.)

THERESA. *(O.S.)* Yes!!!

MAGGIE. You got it?

(After a moment, THERESA emerges from the bathroom with a plunger in a
mop bucket, ripping off a surgical mask.)

Oh, thank god.

THERESA. *(Still a little in shock.)* You're telling me. I thought I was gonna
have to switch your room!

MAGGIE. Wow.

THERESA. *(Trying to make the best of it.)* It's not a five-star experience if you
don't have a usable toilet.

(Beat. THERESA looks like she wants to say something, then doesn't, then
decides to.)

Um – I found these in there.

(THERESA holds out the three orange prescription bottles. They're full.)

In the trashcan?

(Caught, MAGGIE's face morphs into an aggressive blank.)

MAGGIE. Oh.

Oh.

Whoops.

THERESA. Good thing I found them before housekeeping did. If they'd –
accidentally thrown them out – I mean, you'd be in some real trouble.

Just 'cause they're all still full.

Not that I was *looking* at the labels or anything – just that – the trashcan's
right next to the toilet, and when I looked down, boom, there they were.

MAGGIE. (*Not an excuse. More like a dare:*) I must've –

Like by accident or something.

THERESA. Here.

MAGGIE. Thanks.

> (*Awkward beat.* MAGGIE *holding the bottles.*
> *Both of their gazes come to rest on the bottle of Jack on the desk.* MAGGIE
> *feels compelled to say – something about it.*)

A client just *gave* me that.

THERESA. (*Awkward; impressed:*) The life of a business traveler!

> (*Then:*)

MAGGIE. Lemme get you some cash.

THERESA. Oh, no, I can't accept a tip for this. This is just regular service.

MAGGIE. They can't possibly be paying you enough for *this* to be regular
service.

THERESA. They pay us okay. I got a raise when I became a management
trainee – and I'll get another when I make manager, but you have to have
your degree for that. I'm still in school.

> (*Beat.*)

Did you go to school for – um – that stuff?

> (THERESA *gestures to the ultrasound.*)

MAGGIE. I went to school. Not really for that stuff specifically.

THERESA. I mean, but you're like this successful independent businesswoman now, so, even if you didn't go to school for that specifically, you still
think school is worth it, right?

MAGGIE. Well.

Sometimes you have to weigh how great something is against how much it
costs, and decide if it's – worth it.

> (*Sensing that* THERESA *still wants to talk:*)

How much does *your* school cost?

THERESA. I mean, it's a fully accredited degree.

They raised the tuition a little bit second semester, which is – annoying.

Some loss of state funding thing – some education – tax – credit – whatever. And it's not a huge amount? Only like – sixteen hundred dollars more? But. I don't think it's right they told us after classes started back up.

MAGGIE. Don't take out a loan.

THERESA. I already have a loan.

MAGGIE. Don't take out another loan.

THERESA. No, it's fine, I just have to – my dad's paying for it.
He lives in Sugar Land, Texas. I don't see him a lot. He lives in Sugar Land, so.
But, when I was a kid, when he and my mom were in court figuring out alimony and child support and the future and stuff, he agreed to pay my college tuition, so he's contractually obligated, I just –
He was a little like, a Bachelor's in Tourism Development Management? Is that even a real *degree*?

MAGGIE. Sounds real enough.

THERESA. (*Relieved:*) Right? That's what *I* said. That's what I told him, too.

MAGGIE. (*Intense:*) How many hours a week do you go to school?

THERESA. Like fifteen.

MAGGIE. And you work – what – 40 hours on top of that?

THERESA. It's usually closer to 60… depending… but I mean, that's just part of what being a manager *is*. I *like* pressure!

MAGGIE. But that's too much. You're just one person. And this can't be what you want to do for the rest of your life, right? Work and school and school and work and all that *debt*?

THERESA. (*Starting to blanch:*) I'll be okay.
I should… I should go, I think.

(MAGGIE *goes to a drawer, takes out a checkbook and a pen.*)

MAGGIE. I want you to take this.
For your tuition.

THERESA. What are you doing?

MAGGIE. What's your last name?

THERESA. What is that?

MAGGIE. A check for $1600. What's your last name so I can make it out to you?

THERESA. Mrs. Elliott, I can't take that.

MAGGIE. If you don't tell me, I'll just ask whoever's at the desk and then you won't be able to stop me.
Tell me your last name.
I want you to have this.

THERESA. I can't, though.

MAGGIE. (*Getting much sharper:*) You need it. Take it.

THERESA. I *can't.*

MAGGIE. What, do you think it's going to bounce or something?
It's not going to bounce.
You said: I'm a successful independent businesswoman. I know what I'm doing.

> (MAGGIE *rips the check out of the checkbook and holds it out.*)

Take it – write in your last name yourself.

THERESA. No, Mrs. Elliott, I'm not *allowed* to, I'd lose my *job.* Can you please put that away?

> (*Beat.* MAGGIE *tears the check in two. A flustered* THERESA *gathers her equipment and heads towards the exit.*)

Sorry.
Goodnight.

MAGGIE. (*In retaliation for the slight, and the discovery of the pills:*) You know, I don't need, uh.
I don't need housekeeping to come so often.

THERESA. No?

MAGGIE. No.

THERESA. How often do you –

MAGGIE. I'll call the front desk when I do.
If I don't call – then I don't need anyone in my room.
Okay?

> (THERESA *nods, then exits. A beat of quiet.*
> *Still flushed/amped,* MAGGIE *drops the pieces of torn-up check into the trashcan. Then, drops the prescription bottles into the drawer in the bedside table.*
> *The warble of a FaceTime call from* MAGGIE's *iPad. She lets it ring for a bit, then answers the call.*)

MAGGIE. (*Jangled:*) Hey. Hi. Hey.

BEN. (*V.O.*) Oh –
He did the craziest thing today – I gave him a cup of his puffs and I guess he wasn't in the mood, so he actually grabbed the cup they were in and like really slowly, really deliberately, turned it face-down on his highchair tray, like, nope, not any more of these.
With such a serious little face.
And I was like: buddy. You love those puffs. And he just looked at me, like: nuh-uh. So I guess we don't have to spend so much fucking money on those things anymore.

MAGGIE. Where is he?

BEN. (*V.O.*) Put him down already. He had a *long* day.

    (*Microbeat.*)

MAGGIE. What does *that* mean?

BEN. (*V.O. Caught:*) Oh. Well:

He sort of – like he cut himself a little.

MAGGIE. How'd he cut himself "a little"?

BEN. (*V.O.*) He wouldn't stop fussing, so – I let him play with my keys.

MAGGIE. You *know* we're not supposed to do that.

BEN. (*V.O.*) Yeah, because of *lead*, not because of –

Anyway, I think it was the mountain bike key – it's got that sharp edge. God, I haven't even taken that thing out of the *ga*rage since Jamie was born…

MAGGIE. (*Short:*) It's been a lot longer than that.

BEN. (*V.O. Trying to turn it into a nice joke:*) Guess I am just a weekend warrior after all.

Anyway, Jamie's fine – I used Neosporin, and the pediatrician said to just let it air out –

MAGGIE. You took him to the doctor for a cut?

BEN. (*V.O. Defensive:*) Well, he was bleeding.

    (*Beat.*)

MAGGIE. (*Trying to end the conversation:*) I should probably go to bed, too. Actually.

BEN. (*V.O.*) Already?

MAGGIE. Long day. And I've got an early appointment.

BEN. (*V.O.*) Oh – good! That's great.

MAGGIE. It's only "great" if they buy something.

BEN. (*V.O.*) I know it's been a slow start –

MAGGIE. It's not a "slow start."

It's a non-starter.

BEN. (*V.O. Making an excuse for her:*) Well, you're only twelve days in.

    (*Just a little bit of desperation creeping in:*)

You're still using that fold-out brochure, right? The laminated one? That's always impressive.

And – you told me that one hospital in Minnesota, the one that bought 12? *They* really liked it when you let them hold the transducer.

Just remember: go in with confidence. And remember not to get too aggressive during the ask.

MAGGIE. I don't need you to tell me how to do my job.

BEN. (*V.O. Plowing ahead:*) No, I know, just if you wanna talk strategy, I'll talk strategy any time!

MAGGIE. Back off, okay?

BEN. I'm just trying to *help.*

MAGGIE. Why are you being so pushy about this?

(*Beat, sensing something:*)

What's going on?

(*Beat, then:*)

BEN. (*V.O.*) Blue Cross is denying our appeal.

(MAGGIE *collapses into herself briefly.*)

They're sticking with the partial payment. They said, since there was no prior authorization –

They're saying, because I checked you in for observation before we saw your primary care physician –

But… we can appeal again.

(*Long beat.*)

I know you're feeling a lot of pressure.

But I *know* you can do this. *All* of this.

I am Here to support you.

MAGGIE. You are. You're right there. In that little screen.

(*An admission:*)

It feels – different now.

BEN. (*V.O. He can't hear this from her:*) You just have to get used to the meds.

MAGGIE. It doesn't feel easy. It used to feel – easy. Like as soon as I got in the room, bam.

BEN. Just – be patient, and it'll come back.

(*Reminding her, but with an edge:*)

Everything they prescribed… it's for a reason. And the benefits outweigh the costs.

MAGGIE. Right.

BEN. (*V.O. Continuing to push:*) And – overall, I mean – wouldn't you agree you're *feeling* better?

MAGGIE. Better… how?

BEN. (*V.O.*) Just – generally. Better.

MAGGIE. Are you asking me if I actually feel any happier?

Or do you just wanna know if you're going to have to drive me somewhere in the middle of the night locked in the trunk of our car?

Again.

(Beat.)

BEN. *(V.O.)* Honey –

What do you want me to *say*.

MAGGIE. *(A real question:)* Were you hoping that having Jamie would fix me? Like completely? Like whatever the hormones do would just fill in all the gaps and connect the things that don't connect and make my brain just – relax?

BEN. *(V.O.)* I don't want to talk about this over FaceTime.

MAGGIE. *(Another real question:)* Or just having him, like holding him, that first second in the hospital, that something new would just click, and boom: normal?

BEN. *(V.O.)* I don't want to talk about this.

MAGGIE. *(The final real question:)* Are you honestly still hoping that six months in, something might change?

(Silence.)

BEN. *(V.O.)* G'night.

(BEN *hangs up. Silence. Then,* MAGGIE *goes to the bottle of Jack and cracks it open. Drinks. Doesn't stop drinking. Still doesn't stop drinking. Until – she forces herself to. Caps the bottle. Shoves it inside the desk drawer like she's not sure what she might do if she doesn't hide it.)*

Six.

MAGGIE *is seated, with another* DOCTOR. *She looks a little rough, like she hasn't slept, and more disheveled than usual. Her hair isn't perfect, her clothes are a little wrinkled and untucked. Even her demeanor isn't quite right – she's more casual, less focused than she usually is. Hungover? Or – still drunk?* DOCTOR *is excitedly flipping through pictures on his cell phone, showing them to* MAGGIE.

DOCTOR. That's our first van. Everything's new, right down to the paint job.

We hired a graphic designer and everything: this graffiti specialist guy. That's called a "fill-in" right there.

MAGGIE. *(Flat:)* Awesome.

DOCTOR. I thought it was a bit bold, but the other physicians on my team are a little younger, and they're plugged in. We signed up for a Twitter account and everything. "At FastDocs."

You should follow us! We already have 182 followers!

(Another photo.)

That's the interior lab set-up. It's not equipped for everything, but we have pretty much what a basic urgent care would have, plus we're on-the-move.
Technology is so amazing. Like – the more advanced our civilization becomes, the more we can find purpose in going backwards.
I mean: doctors who make house calls? What could be more backwards than that, right? But what we've found is that people really appreciate how upfront we are about cost-benefit. We have all of our pricing, right there, on our website! And *we* come to *you!*

(*Continuing to swipe.*)

Granted, we've gotten a *little* backtalk about not accepting insurance… but *insurance* is the reason I was getting so burned out in traditional practice! Now I can actually *tell* my patients how much services cost – because I *know!*

MAGGIE. Really great stuff. So, doctor –

(*Another photo.*)

DOCTOR. That's just Jack, goofin' off.
Jack. Whatta nut.

MAGGIE. If I could just –

(*Another photo.*)

DOCTOR. That's a fridge full of urine samples. I just thought it looked funny.

MAGGIE. (*Harder:*) Lotta photos.

DOCTOR. I just got this phone.

MAGGIE. But if we could just talk about the ultrasound now?

DOCTOR. Yeah, so they're – how much did you say they were?
Like, could you say the number out loud?

MAGGIE. It's twenty-eight thousand per, but if you're buying multiples, which it looks like you would be, there's some, um, flexibility.

DOCTOR. How much flexibility?

(*Beat.*)

MAGGIE. I mean. Name a number you're looking to buy, and I'll name a number you could buy for.

DOCTOR. So if we wanted ten.

MAGGIE. If you wanted to buy ten …
This is what I'd be thinking per unit.

(MAGGIE *writes a number.* DOCTOR *looks, winces.*)

DOCTOR. It's a lot of money.

MAGGIE. It's a higher standard of care.

DOCTOR. Yeah. But. I mean.
Money's money. You know?

(*Pause. Another tactic:*)

MAGGIE. You're not the only mobile house call practice in town, are you?

(DOCTOR's *face darkens.*)

DOCTOR. No. There's ImmediateMedico in Phoenix.
They're bilingual.
They do say Spanish is the language of the future.

MAGGIE. ImmediateMedico has portable ultrasound units in their vans.
So, if somebody finds out ImmediateMedico has a better lab than you do –

DOCTOR. I wouldn't say that.

MAGGIE. I would. They have ultrasounds. And you don't.

(DOCTOR *is staring at* MAGGIE *pretty hard.*)

DOCTOR. Here's the thing. I already talked to a GE rep last week. They want our business. They don't *have* our business – yet. But they promised me a price ten percent under this.

MAGGIE. Can I see that promise in writing?

DOCTOR. Our negotiations haven't gotten that far yet.

MAGGIE. What model were they offering you, the Logiq, the Voluson, what?

DOCTOR. The Voluson. I think.

MAGGIE. Yeah, you know why they were offering you a price ten percent under the one I'm offering you? Because that model is two years out of date, that's why. They're trying to pull a fast one on you. A fast one on FastDocs. Don't be *stupid* and fall for it.

DOCTOR. (*Defensive:*) Look. I don't want to spend that much money.

MAGGIE. I can take off an additional two percent. That would make *this* number –

(*She writes.*)

That.
How does that sound?

DOCTOR. I already have a relationship with GE. And, no offense, but GE's rep was a little bit – friendlier.

MAGGIE. I can take off *three* percent.

DOCTOR. It's just –

MAGGIE. (*Beginning to lose it:*) If you ask me to go below that, you're asking me to scratch my commission.
You're asking me to sign off on making zero money on this sale, when you're clearly opening this practice to avoid dealing with insurance just so you can make a few extra bucks.
This is the absolute lowest I'll go. This is the number I'm willing to accept.

Now do we have a fucking deal or not?

> (DOCTOR *draws up tight, offended.*)

DOCTOR. Not.

Seven.

> *A few days later.* MAGGIE's *room. It's messier than earlier — housekeeping hasn't been by in a while.* MAGGIE *is lying motionless on the bed.*
>
> *After a moment, a knock on the door.* MAGGIE *sits up, looks towards the noise, but doesn't move to answer it.*
>
> *Another moment, another knock. Then:* BOBBY, *carrying a bag of groceries, uses his keycard to let himself in. He stops short when he sees* MAGGIE.

BOBBY. Oh. Didn't think anyone was home.

> (*No response from* MAGGIE.)

Uh, you never called me back.

I left a message on your room phone, asking when you wanted me to deliver your groceries. Didn't you see the light blinking?

MAGGIE. No.

BOBBY. I just got off shift at 6 and I didn't wanna go home and leave you without dinner.

> (BOBBY *looks around the room, takes in the mess.*)

Housekeeping's kinda been slacking off, huh?

MAGGIE. Oh. Uh –

> (BOBBY *peeks inside the dishwasher.*)

BOBBY. They ain't even run the dishwasher? That's not cool.

MAGGIE. (*Re: the groceries, distracting him:*) Just – here, lemme take those from you.

BOBBY. You want me to unpack 'em for you?

MAGGIE. Um –

BOBBY. I'll unpack 'em for you.

It's part of the five-star experience.

> (BOBBY *begins putting away her groceries.*)

Hey, I couldn't actually find the eggs you wanted – I mean, they had "cage-free" but not "*cruelty-free*" cage-free," and I didn't wanna get you, like, *cruel eggs*, so I didn't get you any eggs. Sorry about that.

> (MAGGIE *sits, watches him put away her groceries.*)

Got your V8.

And – instant oatmeal.

"One medium-sized lemon."

Easy Mac, three boxes. You got carbs for days …

>   (*He starts to stack the dishes.*)

These are nasty, too…

MAGGIE. (*Suddenly:*) What if there's something else I realized I want?

BOBBY. If you fill out another list, I'll drop it at the desk on my way out –

MAGGIE. No.

What's if it's something – like the eggs?

Like what if it's something you won't be able to find at the store?

BOBBY. Uh –

MAGGIE. Can you get me pot?

BOBBY. Can I get you pot.

MAGGIE. Yeah.

And not shitty pot – like, good stuff.

>   (*Pause.*)

BOBBY. I mean – I don't know where I'd even get something like that…

MAGGIE. Oh, c'mon.

I see you when I walk to my car. You guys think you're invisible in that little overhang in the garage, but you're not.

BOBBY. (*Ever so slightly flirtatious:*) You watching me?

MAGGIE. It's Tempe, Arizona. What the fuck else is there to do?

>   (BOBBY *laughs. He takes an Altoids box and the one-hitter out of his pocket. Inside the box is a joint he's already rolled, plus a prescription bottle with more weed inside.*)

BOBBY. (*Proud:*) I drive up to L.A. to get this. It tastes like a smoothie, sweartogod.

How do you want it?

MAGGIE. (*Pointing to the one-hitter:*) I just want a little.

>   (*As BOBBY starts to pack it:*)

How much do I owe you?

BOBBY. (*Waving her off:*) Nah, nah, nah.

MAGGIE. No, seriously, how much?

BOBBY. No charge. *Seriously.*

MAGGIE. Is this another, unadvertised part of the five-star experience?

BOBBY. This is the *six*-star experience.

>   (BOBBY *hands her the one-hitter. She's done this before, but not for a while: BOBBY lights it for her. She holds in the smoke for a long time, leaning her head back, eyes open, concentrating. Then, she releases it slowly, through her mouth, like a sigh, still gazing up.*)

MAGGIE. Strawberries.

BOBBY. I told you. Smoothie.

> (MAGGIE *looks back down, at him now.*)

MAGGIE. Keep me company?

> (*Beat.* BOBBY *nods: he'll stay. Then, he takes the one-hitter back and starts packing it for himself.*)

I'm not interrupting any plans you had tonight?

BOBBY. Cartoons on Netflix.

MAGGIE. My iPad has Netflix.

BOBBY. Hell, yeah.

> (BOBBY *smokes. He's efficient. Still holding it in:*)

You want another?

> (MAGGIE *nods,* BOBBY *exhales, taps out the bowl and packs it again.* MAGGIE *watches him.*)

MAGGIE. I don't know why boys doing drugs are so handsome.
It's not the same with girls: when girls do drugs they're just trying to look like boys doing drugs.

BOBBY. I'm not a boy – I'm a man.

> (MAGGIE *smokes. She moves to recline on the bed, still holding the smoke, exhaling when she lands.*
>
> BOBBY *sits in the chair, grabbing her iPad. He looks at the cover photo for a moment. He's surprised –* MAGGIE *didn't mention she was married, or that she had a baby.*)

Uh. Nice photo.

> (*Beat.*)

This your husband?

MAGGIE. Yeah.

BOBBY. Cool, cool.

Your baby?

MAGGIE. Uh-huh.

BOBBY. What's his name?

MAGGIE. Which, the husband or the baby?

BOBBY. Baby.

MAGGIE. Jamie.

> (*Judgmental beat.*)

BOBBY. Huh.

MAGGIE. What?

BOBBY. Like short for James?

MAGGIE. Just Jamie.

BOBBY. Huh.

MAGGIE. Jamie's a nice name.

BOBBY. Who said it wasn't?

MAGGIE. Does everything have to be short for something else? I'm Maggie; not Margaret. Just: Maggie.
Is Bobby short for – Robert?

BOBBY. Roberto. But – that's my dad's name, so.

> (*Beat.*)

How're your sales going?

MAGGIE. They're not.

BOBBY. Shit.
Why aren't people buying it?

MAGGIE. You don't need a good reason *not* to buy something.

BOBBY. So you're out here, for four weeks, and you're just *hoping* somebody'll bite?

MAGGIE. I work on commission. Hope is all I have.

> (*Beat.*)

BOBBY. Can I see it? The ultrasound, I mean.

MAGGIE. This is turning into a really awesome party.

> (MAGGIE *moves to get off the bed. Takes a second to make sure she's okay to stand.*)

BOBBY. You good?

MAGGIE. I'm great.

> (*She successfully stands, crosses to the nightstand and opens the case, revealing the ultrasound.*)

Here it is.

BOBBY. No, like. I wanna see it take a picture.

MAGGIE. You want me to ultrasound you?

BOBBY. I mean, there's no radiation or whatever, right? It won't mess up my testosterone or anything?

MAGGIE. Nope.

BOBBY. Let's go, then.

> (BOBBY *lies back on the bed.*)

MAGGIE. Here we go, apparently.

> (MAGGIE *connects the wand to the ultrasound, turns it on.*)

I'm gonna pull up your shirt.

> (BOBBY *pulls up his own shirt.*)

This is gonna be cold.

>   (MAGGIE *squirts a small amount of gel on* BOBBY'*s stomach. He squirms.*)

BOBBY. Ow.

MAGGIE. It shouldn't *hurt.*

BOBBY. No, it's just cold.

MAGGIE. I told you it was gonna be cold.

BOBBY. Well – I didn't think it was gonna be *that* cold.

>   (MAGGIE *uses the wand to scan him. She turns the screen so he can see.*)

MAGGIE. That's your stomach wall.

BOBBY. Whoa.

There're all these lines.

MAGGIE. That's the tissue.

>   (*Beat as they look.*)

BOBBY. Why's it moving around like that?

MAGGIE. Just regular old digestion.

BOBBY. Whoa.

>   (*Beat.*)

It's just – so empty in there.

I thought it'd look really full.

MAGGIE. (*Something happened inside of her when he said that:*) Yeah.

>   (*Beat.*)

Here, wanna try it yourself? It's "easy to use."

BOBBY. Sweet.

>   (MAGGIE *hands him the wand and lies down on the bed again, next to* BOBBY. BOBBY *moves the wand around his own abdomen, looking at his insides.*)

Lookit me. I could be a – a male nurse.

MAGGIE. They're just called nurses.

BOBBY. (*In his radio voice:*) "Nurse Bobby to the ER."

>   (*After a few moments, he stops, puts the wand down. Switches off the ultrasound. Fans his stomach for a second to try to dry the gel.*
>   BOBBY *reaches over* MAGGIE, *towards the nightstand, to retrieve the one-hitter. It's oddly intimate.* BOBBY *taps it out, packs it again, smokes. Holds the smoke in for a long time, breathes out.*
>   MAGGIE *and* BOBBY *lay next to each other on the bed for a quiet moment, looking at the ceiling.*
>   *Then,* MAGGIE *rolls slightly, her body turning towards* BOBBY'*s. She leans into him a little, inhaling his scent. She puts a hand on his thigh, near his knee.*)

She moves to kiss his neck.
Gently, BOBBY *shakes his head and nudges her off.* MAGGIE *closes her eyes, instantly ashamed.)*

MAGGIE. Sorry. Sorry.

BOBBY. (*Kind:*) It's cool.

MAGGIE. Sorry.

(MAGGIE *rolls back onto her back.*)

Fuck. I don't even –

BOBBY. Nah, it's cool, Maggie. Don't even worry about it.

(*Quiet again. They don't look at each other.*)

I'm gonna find us a cartoon to watch. Yeah?

(MAGGIE *nods.* BOBBY *grabs the iPad, scrolls through Netflix, looking for something for them to watch. He doesn't look up when he says this.*)

You like being a mom?

(*Off of her expression:*)

Sorry. Is that private?

MAGGIE. Why do you want to know?

(*Pause.*)

BOBBY. I kinda lied to you when you checked in.
You asked me – if I had gotten a bunch of girls pregnant, and I said no, but. I did. One girl, at least. My ex, Nita.
She got pregnant and she told me she didn't wanna keep it, and then she changed her mind and she said she *did* wanna keep it after all and I dumped her and she was like, fine, get lost, I don't give a fuck, and she had it, the baby, and I haven't seen her in months. Nita, I mean. I've never seen the baby at all.

(*Beat.*)

Like I don't think everybody's supposed to be a dad.

MAGGIE. I don't think everybody's supposed to be a mom.

BOBBY. Yeah! Like, I don't think just having a kid qualifies you to have a kid. You know?

MAGGIE. When I got pregnant … it just felt like, this is something I have to get through.
Like a medical condition. Temporary. Nine months, and then it's done.
I didn't really think … I didn't really think about the fact that the temporary condition is something you go through to get to a much much much more permanent condition.
I thought I'd feel –
Relieved.

BOBBY. And you didn't?

(*Beat.*)

MAGGIE. You hear that when people hold their kids for the first time, they feel – *so much.*

All I could think when I held Jamie was:

It's so empty.

I thought it would be full.

And it's – *so* empty.

> (*Quiet.*
> BOBBY *starts a cartoon:* Home Movies, Bob's Burgers, *something like that. They watch the screen of the iPad.*)

Eight.

Employee back office. A few days later, in the evening. Raucous music from the lobby drifts in. THERESA is here, at the computer, an open bottle of tequila near her. She's tipsy: and off, *somehow. Not her usual perky self, and it's not just that she's a bad drunk. BOBBY enters, carrying a net.*

BOBBY. Damn, you're still here?

THERESA. What does it look like?

BOBBY. You're still working that reception?

THERESA. They *will not* LEAVE.

Like I know their sign thingy said "8 until question mark" but *come on!*

Jordan told me they were *physicists,* here for some conference or something.

He told me I'd be out by *nine thirty.* Because they're *physicists.*

But those *physicists* are drinking *everything!*

Look – they *gave* this to me! They have like a million more bottles. *And* a ton of pizzas, *and* buffalo wings, *and* like really way too many vegetable trays with *four dipping sauces per tray!* And that is *Too Much Sauce.*

BOBBY. You drunk, T?

THERESA. A little.

> (*Beat.*)

You want a drink?

BOBBY. (*Holy shit. Is she really asking?*) Hell yeah, I want a drink.

> (THERESA *hands him the bottle.* BOBBY *takes a swig.*)

Tequila tastes like ass.

THERESA. I *love* tequila.

BOBBY. That's crazy.

THERESA. (*Taking a swig:*) I *love* it.

I thought your shift ended at 9.

BOBBY. I was up on the roof, fishing turds out of the hot tub.

THERESA. *No.*

BOBBY. Oh, yes.

Don't worry about it, though. It's already drained, bleached, and ready to go.

THERESA. Who *pooped?*

BOBBY. I haven't looked at the security footage yet, but – my money's on the golf guys.

THERESA. (*Hissing:*) *The golf guys!*

BOBBY. What are you doing?

THERESA. Replying to TripAdvisor reviews.

BOBBY. How we doing so far?

THERESA. I mean, we have a 93% overall positive rating –

BOBBY. Wait, what? 93? What's going on with that other 7 percent?

THERESA. That's what I said!

BOBBY. (*Reading over her shoulder:*) "New and Clean." Well, that's very true. "Very upscale.

Nice lobby and rooms are very spacious and clean. Lots of places to plug. In your electronics which is a must these days. The desk is spacious and easy to work at. Good for business!!!" Three exclamation points. Damn. What'd you write back?

THERESA. (*Showing off a little:*) "Thank you for taking the time to review the Residence! We're so glad your suite accommodated all of your needs, especially your comment regarding the plugs. We know they are a must for today's busy lifestyles. We hope to see you again in the very near future. Sincerely, Manager."

(*Beat.*)

BOBBY. Um. That's really good –

THERESA. Thanks!

BOBBY. But – I mean – so you wrote that?

THERESA. I mean – yeah.

BOBBY. But you're not the Manager, Theresa. Jordan is.

THERESA. Jordan said I could do some online engagement activities. Like, start a Twitter account or whatever. You'd think *he* could do that, especially because he makes $19 an hour, but apparently he's "too busy."

BOBBY. But this isn't Twitter.

THERESA. It's not a big deal, Bobby.

BOBBY. Okay.

THERESA. It's *not.*

(*Small silence.* BOBBY *tries to break the tension.*)

BOBBY. Where'd you learn to do this stuff? School?

THERESA. Actually, my mom made me write thank-you notes growing up. I used to hate them, but now I kind of love them. I love putting a whole story into five sentences.

(*Begins a lazy series of spins in her rolling chair.*)

"Dear Person."

"Thank you for whatever I'm writing this thank-you note for."

"This is why I'm thankful, or this is how I'm using the thing I'm thanking you for."

"Here's something that's going on with me."

"Hope everything is going well with you."

"Sincerely/Best/All My Love, Theresa."

So when I'm writing my responses on TripAdvisor, I just think of it sort of like a thank-you note!

BOBBY. (*In awe of her.*) Wow.

(THERESA *stops spinning.*)

THERESA. (*Thoughtful.*) I'm gonna throw up.

BOBBY. Whoa.

THERESA. No, I'm not.

(*Beat.*)

I'm gonna have another drink.

BOBBY. Yeah, me too.

(THERESA *takes a swig.* BOBBY *takes a swig.*)

Do another one, do another one.

THERESA. Okay – I haven't actually read this one all the way through yet because the title is kinda mean. "Worst Phoenix-area Experience Ever."

BOBBY. Oh, shit.

THERESA. "First of all, the AC vents blow directly onto the bed: thanks for the no-sleep, guys!

It's right in the middle of a total party neighborhood! I'm listening to a drunken tuba player outside on the corner as I type this.

Worse, the service was NOT up to my standards. When I asked the front-desk girl to show me how something in my room worked, she turned into an ice queen" – OH MY GOD IT'S THE GOLF GUY.

BOBBY. The guy who tried to make out with you?! Oh, *hell* no!

THERESA. Maybe TripAdvisor will delete it if I email them…

BOBBY. *Delete* it? No, you gotta fight back!

THERESA. I don't know.

BOBBY. If you're not gonna do it for you, do it for the Residence. He gave us one star!

THERESA. Where would I even *start?*

BOBBY. Here: type this.

(THERESA *gets ready to type. As he speaks, she types.*)

"Thank you for your comments. I'm sorry that you were disappointed by our HVAC system and by that tuba player."

That is weird.

"As we are not officially affiliated with the university, we have no control over its students."

THERESA. *Nice.*

BOBBY. Thank you.

"However!"

THERESA. *(Typing:)* "*However.*"

BOBBY. "Your comment about a member of our front desk staff is uncalled for. Maybe you should work on improving your golf game instead of hitting on our management trainee. We'd appreciate it; and so would your *wife.*"

THERESA. Good burn.

BOBBY. "*In*sincerely, Manager."

Post that shit.

THERESA. Are you sure?

(BOBBY *leans over* THERESA *and hits Enter to post the response.*)

BOBBY. That'll show him.

THERESA. What a jerk.

BOBBY. That shit is unbelievable!

When you're manager, you're not gonna stand for that stuff. Not the golf guys, not people like *Jordan* who leave their best employees stranded with weird drunk professors –

(THERESA *stands, crosses away from* BOBBY, *her face a dark cloud.*)

THERESA. Yeah. Well. I don't think I'm gonna be a manager anytime soon.

BOBBY. What are you talking about? You're, like, fast-track.

THERESA. Not anymore.

I had to withdraw.

BOBBY. Withdraw?

THERESA. From classes?

I have an outstanding tuition bill for like twenty-two thousand dollars and they can't reach my dad and he, like, disconnected his *phone* so I couldn't call him to ask what the hell is going on.

(*An upset beat.*)

The bursar's office called me yesterday.

Said my account was "negligent," so.

Unless I take out the world's stupidest loan … I'm not going back. And that means … I'm not going to be a manager.

BOBBY. (*Worried for her:*) Yo, but like – just because corporate has a buncha rules about what you need to be a manager, that doesn't mean they can't pull some strings for you.

I bet if you talked to Jordan –

THERESA. Uh-uh.

BOBBY. Then let *me* talk to him!

THERESA. No! I mean – Jordan doesn't even know! If he finds out I'm not in school anymore, he's going to kick me out of the trainee track, he might fire me –

BOBBY. Never in a million years would *that* guy fire *you.*

THERESA. *Please* don't say anything to Jordan, okay? Promise me.

(*Beat.*)

BOBBY. I mean – yeah, okay, T. It's gonna be okay.

THERESA. (*Exposed:*) God, you are so nice to me.

BOBBY. (*Exposed:*) Course I'm nice to you. Everyone's nice to you. 'Cause you're so –

Whatever, you can't help – like, how you are.

THERESA. How am I?

BOBBY. I mean –

You know exactly how you are.

THERESA. But I want you to tell me.

(*They're very close together. Suddenly,* THERESA *is kissing* BOBBY. *He's kissing her back. Somehow, her jacket's coming off, somehow, his tie is getting pulled off.* THERESA *unzips his pants and pushes up her skirt. Oh my god. It's about to happen. It's about to happen. It's actually happening.*

A few frantic moments of sex until – BOBBY *finishes. Way earlier than either of them planned.*)

BOBBY. Shit shit shit shit shit shit.

THERESA. No, it's okay, it's okay –

(*The phone rings.* THERESA *freaks out.*)

Shit shit shit shit shit shit!!!

(THERESA *pushes* BOBBY *off of her, adjusts her skirt as* BOBBY *turns away and zips up. She composes herself, then answers the phone.*)

Hello?

(Beat. THERESA's face changes. She speaks more formally, trying to suppress her drunkenness.)

I'm afraid I can't.

No, I CAN'T.

(Beat. More heated:)

Because you're not his girlfriend anymore, you're his *ex*-girlfriend.

(BOBBY freezes. He gesticulates: that's her? Is that her? THERESA waves him off.)

Because –

(Silence as THERESA listens. Then, slowly, hangs up.)

BOBBY. What?

Theresa, what?

THERESA. She says – you need to call her.

Because.

She wants to talk about your *baby*.

So …

(Silence. Quietly furious, THERESA puts her jacket back on, smoothes her hair.)

BOBBY. Listen … Theresa –

THERESA. I think the party's over.

(THERESA exits.)

Nine.

BOBBY *is seated at a coffee shop table, waiting. He's playing with a paper sleeve – he hasn't ordered anything. He makes the paper sleeve into a bracelet, then immediately stands and hurries to take it off when* NITA *– 34, half Mexican half black, the kind of self-possessed and kickass professor everyone dreams of having – enters. This is no mere baby mama. This is someone way out of* BOBBY's *league – and boy, does he know it.*

Tentatively, from across the coffee shop, she waves: a cute little wave. BOBBY *just raises one hand, then puts it down.*

Awkwardly, they come together for – what's this going to be? A hug? Whatever it is, it sucks.

When they separate:

NITA. That was awful.

BOBBY. Yeah.

NITA. *Que carajo…*

BOBBY. Really weird.

NITA. I mean, I know we haven't seen each other in a while, but –

BOBBY. Take two, take two.

> (*They try again. It's less weird this time.*
> *They sit. Maybe this won't be so bad.*)

You look good. Like – I mean, like you always look good, but.

NITA. Thanks.

BOBBY. I thought you'd be all…

I don't know.

NITA. Fat?

BOBBY. (*He can't even hide his attraction to her, not even after all this:*) But like not even a little? *Damn*, you know?

NITA. (*Looking at a menu:*) Did you order something? Their pastry chef makes these *polvorones de canele* that are just like the ones Martita used to make.

BOBBY. I'm not really hungry.

NITA. They have great coffee.

BOBBY. Ha. For five dollars, it better be.

> (NITA *half-laughs at his attitude. She can't help it. It's not the friendliest.*)

Are *you* gonna get something?

NITA. (*"Uh, no":*) I'm breastfeeding. No caffeine, no wheat, no hydrogenated fats.

BOBBY. Well –

I didn't even bring any cash, so.

> (NITA *just looks at him for a moment. It has a disarming effect on* BOBBY
> – *always has.*)

NITA. I teach at 2, anyway.

BOBBY. You're working already?

NITA. I already took off most of first semester; two in a row won't look good for tenure.

I hired a nanny.

BOBBY. (*A little judgmental:*) Really?

I thought maybe you'd ask your sister to come up from Polanco for a bit – or your mom –

NITA. If I can afford to hire a nanny, why shouldn't I?

BOBBY. Just that she's so young. I thought you weren't supposed to, while they were still so young.

NITA. I pump in my office. I store it in my mini-fridge. My assistant drives my milk home at lunch.

It's easy.

BOBBY. Right.

"Easy."

NITA. Bobby –

BOBBY. No, sounds *real* easy, for *you*. Go ahead. Hire your "Martita."

NITA. I don't wanna get into this with you again –

BOBBY. Don't get into it then.

> (*Beat. BOBBY's still upset about the expense of it all. The ghosts of old arguments.*)

Jesus, why'd you even date me? I mean, look at you.

Why would you even – like, why'd you even mess with me?

> (NITA *shrugs.*)

NITA. I liked you.

BOBBY. Enough to have a *kid* with me?

> (NITA *doesn't respond.*)

Admit it.

You were slumming.

NITA. I knew you would do this…

BOBBY. We never went *out* anywhere, you just like *kept* me. Like *paid* for everything. How do you think that made me *feel*?

NITA. You know, a lot of guys would *like* having a rich girlfriend.

BOBBY. Please, you think I thought you were paying for everything on an assistant professor's salary?

I know the deal with that money: that's your *dad's* money. Am I supposed to feel good about fancy restaurants and weekends in Sedona on Señor Emilio Gonzalez Barrera's Platinum card? The only thing you ever let me buy was, like, *condoms*. I mean what the *fuck*. And apparently, I didn't spend enough on 'em 'cause look what happened!

> (*Silence.*)

I work 40 hours a week.

I make 10.85 an hour.

That's $434 a week, before taxes.

My rent's 680. Bills a hundred twenty.

My car's a '98 Honda.

That's the breakdown, that's the situation, that's all I got. So:

How much do you want from me?

> (*Beat.*)

NITA. Nothing.

BOBBY. Nita, don't play.

NITA. I don't want your money!

BOBBY. Then why the fuck have you been calling me? Why the fuck are you calling me, at work, every day, if you don't want child support? What the fuck do you *want*?

> (NITA t*akes her phone out of her purse. She scrolls to something and shows it to him.* BOBBY *looks away very quickly, then looks back.*)

NITA. This is from like ten minutes after she was born. After they'd cleaned all the blood off of her.

And me. I didn't know a human being could bleed that much and still be alive.

That's your nose. Those are your ears. Her hair is the same as your hair.

So.

What do *you* want here, Bobby?

> (BOBBY *can't look away from the photo now as he matches every body part in the picture to one of his own in his mind. He looks at it until he's overwhelmed and has to look away, emotional. A long silence, then:*)

BOBBY. I. Um.

> (BOBBY *says nothing else.* NITA *exhales, nods a bit. Then, she removes a folded contract from her purse. Places it on the table in front of* BOBBY.)

What is this?

NITA. A petition to the court for the voluntary termination of your parental rights.

I'm getting married and he wants to adopt the baby.

BOBBY. What – like, what does that mean?

NITA. You won't have to pay child support.

You'll have no legal ties to her.

You can just – not be in her life.

> (*Shocked silence.*)

BOBBY. Married?

> (NITA *holds up her hand. The ring is massive.*)

Who?

NITA. The chair of the history department. Philip.

BOBBY. That *gringo*?

NITA. *A* white dude, yes.

BOBBY. Wow.

Wow, okay.

You want me out of your life that bad? Out of *her* life?

> (NITA *doesn't respond.*)

This Philip. He doesn't care that this baby looks *exactly* like me? He doesn't care that this baby is *mine*?

NITA. You don't care.

And don't insult me by pretending you do.

Step up, Roberto. Be a man.

> (*Pause as* BOBBY *considers the paperwork. Then, looks back up at* NITA. *Softer now. Lost.*)

BOBBY. What's her name?

> (*Long beat.* NITA *just looks at him.*)

I could call the number on those Father's Rights billboards. I could get partial custody. Shared custody, fifty-fifty.

NITA. You could.

> (*Beat.* BOBBY *and* NITA *look at each other.*)

You let me know what you decide. Okay?

> (NITA *stands, pushes back her chair. Moves to exit, then:*)

I liked you because you asked me to dance that first time like we were a couple of middle school kids and you blushed the whole time the song played, I could tell, even in the dark, and it made me blush, too.

Por eso me gustabas.

> (NITA *exits, leaving* BOBBY *at the table, still staring down at the papers.*)

Ten.

> *Same day, a few hours later.* MAGGIE's *hotel room. Even messier than before. She's in her pajamas and talking to* BEN *over FaceTime on the iPad, trying to figure out the bills from a distance.*

MAGGIE. (*A bit manic:*) So if you put the electric bill on the American Express, the water bill on the Discover, and write a check for the mortgage – Actually, wait. No.

BEN. (*V.O.*) *Don't* pay the mortgage?

MAGGIE. Obviously pay the mortgage; just don't *mail* the check – it'll get there too late.

Bring it over to the bank before they close this afternoon. Okay?

BEN. (*V.O.*) (*As he's writing this down:*) Mortgage… check… in… person. And – which account should I write that from?

MAGGIE. The one that's not overdrawn?

What's next?

BEN. (*V.O.*) Theeeee gas bill. That's a big one.

MAGGIE. How big?

BEN. (*V.O.*) Three hundred sixty dollars and seventy six cents.

And that's with the thermostat at 64.

MAGGIE. Okay. Here's what you're gonna do. You're gonna call the gas company, explain the situation, and ask for another 30 days. There's a program – there's a program we can apply for, because it's winter.

BEN. (*V.O.*) What kind of program?

MAGGIE. The We-Don't-Let-People-Freeze-to-Death-Even-If-They're-Broke program.

BEN. (*V.O.*) Okay.

All that's left is… the phone bill.

MAGGIE. That's not due until Thursday.

BEN. (*V.O.*) Today *is* Thursday.

MAGGIE. No, it's not.

BEN. (*V.O.*) It's definitely Thursday.

MAGGIE. Oh my god it is.

      (*Beat.*)

Fuck.

Fuck.

I was supposed to be in Tucson at 3:15 on Thursday. Today. Thursday?

BEN. (*V.O.*) Okay – Maggie, calm down.

MAGGIE. *Fuck.*

      (MAGGIE *stands in place, paralyzed.*)

BEN. (*V.O.*) If you leave right now, you'll be late, but you'll make it.

MAGGIE. I'm not even dressed! I can't get to Tucson today! Not like this!

BEN. (*V.O.*) Then call and ask to reschedule. They're human beings – they'll understand.

MAGGIE. (*Spinning out:*) No, they won't!

They're never gonna buy anything from me now, not from a rep who misses an appointment.

And *Tucson*. I mean, I know these people, I've heard about these people, they're mean. Everyone in Ari*z*ona is just so *mean.*

Usually I've sold at least two with a trip this length.

I don't know.

I don't know.

I don't know! You know?

Maybe I wasn't ready.

Maybe – I can't *do* this anymore.

BEN. (*V.O.*) You forgot one appointment.

It's not the end of the world.

Just work a little bit harder tomorrow to make up for it.

      (*Pause.*)

MAGGIE. 'Cause that's the problem? I'm not working hard enough?

BEN. (*V.O.*) That's not what I said.
You're twisting my words.

MAGGIE. Maybe *you* should think about finding a job.

    (*Hard quiet.*)

BEN. (*V.O.*) Maybe we should pat ourselves on the back for figuring out these bills, and just – say we'll talk later.

MAGGIE. Nope. No. I wanna talk about this first.

BEN. (*V.O.*) We've already talked about this.

MAGGIE. Let's talk about it again.

BEN. (*V.O.*) I looked for jobs.

MAGGIE. You looked a *year* ago.

BEN. (*V.O.*) Right: and we both agreed that *your* job pays more than anything I could find in the area, and then we *both agreed* I'd stop looking.

MAGGIE. There might be more jobs out there than there were a year ago. Different jobs.

BEN. (*V.O.*) And then – what would we do? You would keep working, we would put Jamie in daycare?

MAGGIE. Daycare is nice.

BEN. (*V.O.*) Daycare would zero out your salary, bringing us right back down to one again. *Huge* disruption with no net gain.

MAGGIE. Then I'll stay home with Jamie, and *you* can commute somewhere. A 9 to 5. Steady. Reliable. You could buy all the twenty-eight-hundred-dollar mountain bikes you want.

    (*Silence.*)

Ben? What do you think?

BEN. (*V.O. A change in tone here: flatter:*) You know what I think, Maggie, why even ask if you already know?

MAGGIE. No, I don't know – tell me.

BEN. (*V.O.*) You know.

MAGGIE. Tell me –

BEN. (*V.O.*) Stop it.

    (*Beat.*)

MAGGIE. You'll let me pay the bills.
You'll let me do – *EVERYTHING* – for us.
But you won't leave me alone with my own baby? *Still?*

    (*A thrumming silence. Then:*)

BEN. (*V.O. Flat:*) Show me your meds.

MAGGIE. Don't change the subject.

BEN. (*V.O.*) You've been gone 22 days. Show me your lithium and *show me* that it's two-thirds empty, or else I'm gonna –

MAGGIE. (*Flinging the challenge in his face:*) You're gonna what? Fly out here and *make me?*

BEN. (*V.O.*) I am trying *so hard* not to blame you. But you are making it *very* hard for me.

MAGGIE. Oh, yeah, you have it really hard.
Fucking asshole.
You're still so mad at me, and you have no right to be, because this bullshit right here, this *situation?*
It's all your fault.

BEN. (*V.O.*) Do you remember what you were *doing* when I found you, do you remember where *Jamie* was –

MAGGIE. (*Doubling down:*) You took me to the clinic, against my will. You had me admitted, against my will. You *kidnapped* me.

BEN. (*V.O.*) I'm not gonna do this.

MAGGIE. Stop saying all the things you're not going to do!

BEN. (*V.O.*) You were out of your *mind* that night, you were fucking *crazy.* I didn't know *what* the fuck you were going to do! And you could have done *anything!* So I'm not apologizing!

MAGGIE. You're not going to apologize for locking me up –

BEN. (*V.O.*) *I am never going to apologize! I am never going to apologize to you! I have been very clear about my priorities here and what order they go in and that is the way things are going to be!*

> (MAGGIE *stares at the screen, breathing hard, adrenaline racing.*
> *Quiet.*)

Our son is 24 weeks old.
You were in the hospital for 6 of those weeks.
Now you're away for another 4, and that's fine, I know you have to, I understand that.
But.
I have been his primary caregiver for almost half his life.
You have been gone – for almost half his life.

MAGGIE. I swear to fucking god, Ben, I swear to god, if you leave me –

BEN. (*V.O.*) I'm not *saying* that, Maggie, I'm not threatening you!

MAGGIE. No.
Ben.
Listen.

> (*Beat.*)

If you leave me.

I'll let you have him.

I won't fight you.

I'll let you – just …

BEN. (*V.O.*) No. No!

I'm not asking for that!

If we can find the right combination of drugs –

If we can get back to something *normal* –

If you just keep *trying.*

MAGGIE. And if it doesn't work?

Then what? Back to the clinic? Another seventy-thousand dollar bill? Is that really what you want?

Maybe this is how I'm a good mother, Ben.

Maybe walking away is the only way I can *be* good.

> (BEN *is silent. Over the speakers, the baby stirs, begins to fuss.*
> *Sincere:*)

Hi, Jamie. Mommy says hi.

Eleven.

> *Later that same night.* MAGGIE *is seated on a lounger in front of the rooftop fire pit. The low and semi-constant rumble of planes on their final descent into PHX underscores the scene. She stares into the fire. A bottle of wine and a glass are on the ground next to her. The remains of a joint are in a makeshift ashtray,* BOBBY'*s lighter from earlier near it.*
> *A moment, then* BOBBY *enters, squinting in the dark.*

MAGGIE. Hey!

BOBBY. (*He's harder with her, here. Not having it. Not tonight:*) Yo yo yo.

How's your evening going?

MAGGIE. So good.

BOBBY. Cool, cool.

Um, so I came up because the desk got a call, actually, that someone had glass in the pool area? So.

> (MAGGIE *stares at him for a long moment.*)

That is your wine and everything, right?

MAGGIE. You know it's my wine and everything, I bought it from your fucking "sundry store" downstairs for $16.95 plus tax.

You mean somebody *told* on me? Like a guest?

BOBBY. I wasn't the one who took the call.

MAGGIE. There's not even a fucking sign, you know that, don't you? How am I supposed to know I'm not allowed to have glass up here if there's no sign?

BOBBY. We keep meaning to put up a sign. The hotel's just new, so like.

MAGGIE. This isn't even the pool area. It's the fire pit. The pool is all the way over there.

BOBBY. Sometimes people like to warm up around the fire pit after swimming in the pool.

MAGGIE. At 11 o'clock at night?

>   (BOBBY *shrugs once again.*)

Was it that woman with the mullet and her two slutty teenage daughters?

BOBBY. Like I said –

MAGGIE. I can't believe they told on me. Assholes.

>   (BOBBY *notices the joint.*)

BOBBY. You, uh –

>   (*He makes a weed-smokin' gesture.*)

MAGGIE. (*Defiant:*) Yup. Am I in trouble for that, too?

BOBBY. I mean, not with me. I just gotta confiscate the wine bottle. But I brought you some plastic cups, so you can like, save the wine.

MAGGIE. Stupid.

BOBBY. I know.

MAGGIE. Here, help me with this.

>   (BOBBY *holds one cup steady, then a second, as* MAGGIE *pours the wine into them.*)

So stupid.

BOBBY. Tastes the same in plastic.

>   (*The fire pit clicks off.* MAGGIE *looks at it, startled.*)

MAGGIE. What happened? Did I break it?

BOBBY. Nah, it's just on a timer, for safety.

I got you –

>   (BOBBY *crosses to the switch, turns it; the fire pit pops back to life.* BOBBY *crosses back to it and stands there, looking into the fire for a long moment. Some caveman hypnosis shit.*)

I fuckin' love fire.

MAGGIE. Yeah?

BOBBY. When I was a kid, I was such a little pyro. I stole a lighter from the gas station and I'd just burn stuff for fun.

MAGGIE. What'd you burn?

BOBBY. Teenage Mutant Ninja Turtles action figure.

The issue of Spiderman where he dies 'cause it made me sad.

Ants.

My mom's checkbook.

Like eight report cards.

This photo of me going down a rollercoaster 'cause I looked dumb.

Part of my hair once, by accident. (Sort of by accident, sort of not.)

Underwear.

Aspirin.

Girls loved me. Girls like guys who set shit on fire, did you know that?

> (MAGGIE *laughs*. BOBBY *laughs*.)

MAGGIE. Set something on fire for me.

BOBBY. What, like here?

I don't really have anything to burn.

MAGGIE. Too bad there's not a sign saying no glass in the pool area, or you could burn that.

BOBBY. I told you, that sign's still coming.

MAGGIE. (*A dare:*) Burn something for me.

> (BOBBY *wants to, senses the danger, hesitates while he thinks about it, decides against it.*)

BOBBY. It's not really fun, like this. It's like – putting something on a barbeque. Like – what's the point, you know?

> (MAGGIE *just stares at him.*)

Another time.

MAGGIE. Whatever.

Finish your wine.

BOBBY. It's a lot.

MAGGIE. Just drink it.

> (BOBBY *drinks his wine, tries to burp, can't.*)

BOBBY. S'good.

Tastes like –

Like really wine-y.

> (*Some silence.*)

Maybe time for you to head inside, huh?

MAGGIE. (*Ignoring him:*) What are the good neighborhoods here?

BOBBY. In Tempe? Most of it's pretty good.

MAGGIE. Where do you live?

BOBBY. Like fifteen minutes west of here. It's near a fire station, but – I smoke enough of *that*, I'm dead to the world.

MAGGIE. How much are apartments?

BOBBY. Well, *my* place is like six eighty a month.

MAGGIE. That's cheap.

BOBBY. I mean – it's not *cheap*, but it's all right.

MAGGIE. I could afford that, no problem.

BOBBY. Yeah, but you can't fit a husband and a baby into the kinda place I've got.

MAGGIE. If it was just me – I'd fit.

BOBBY. Yeah, but. It's not. So …

MAGGIE. Maybe not.
Maybe.

>   (*Beat.*)

BOBBY. What are you saying?

MAGGIE. I'm thinking about staying.

BOBBY. Like, staying at the Residence longer?

MAGGIE. No, like, staying here, in Tempe. Permanently.

>   (*Beat.*)

BOBBY. Um.
But you have a house and everything, back in Ohio or wherever –

MAGGIE. Wisconsin. Dairy Country.

BOBBY. Your life is in Wisconsin.

MAGGIE. Yeah. But. What if it wasn't?

>   (*Beat.*)

BOBBY. I don't know what you want me to say.

MAGGIE. You don't have to *say* anything. I'm not asking your *permission*. I like it out here.
It's sunny.
There are fire pits.
What's not to like?

>   (*Beat.*)

BOBBY. (*His final "no" to her:*) Maggie.
You have a kid.

>   (MAGGIE*'s eyes narrow. No he fucking didn't.*)

MAGGIE. You left your kid.
Why can't I leave mine?

>   (BOBBY *rears back, stung.*)

BOBBY. Hey. Come on.

MAGGIE. Oh, now you're getting all sensitive? Lean into it! You *ran*.

BOBBY. I'm telling you. Back off.

MAGGIE. Hey, I'm not saying you made a bad call. Like you said: just *having a kid* – doesn't qualify you to *have a kid*.

You're not qualified. Look at you.

BOBBY. You don't know anything about me! I told you about my situation, but I didn't tell you the *whole* situation, I told you a *part* of it. And you can't use what I did to try to fuck up your own life!

> (MAGGIE *looks at him.*)

MAGGIE. My husband had me involuntarily committed because he caught me trying to drown Jamie in the sink.

He had to punch me twice in the side of the head and lock me in the trunk of our Corolla to get me to stop fighting.

I was in the hospital for six weeks.

Every single one of the twenty-three days I've spent at home since then, Ben has slept with Jamie in a locked room that I'm not allowed into.

> (*Beat.*)

He won't leave me alone with him.

> (*Beat.*)

And why would he? Right?

'Cause I've gotta say...

When I had the sink full, and I had Jamie on that Afternoon Tea Time dish towel, and he was looking up at me, that open little face, that tiny little blank, and I scooped him up, one hand under his back, the other supporting his head, and I started to sliiiide him down underneath –

It felt like the rightest thing in the world to do.

Like the *only* thing.

Like if I just did that...

Everything else would come into focus.

> (*Beat.*)

I *miss* that feeling. Even though I *know* that feeling is...

> (*She can't finish – it's too enormous. Then:*)

So, I'm moving to Tempe.

What else am I supposed to *do*. Right?

> (*Beat.*)

Unless I just kill myself.

It doesn't – *feel* like something I would do?

But.

I don't really know *what* I do anymore.

> (BOBBY *is shocked into silence. He looks at the ground, then at* MAGGIE, *then angrily at the ground again.*

Then, his eyes locked on MAGGIE*'s,* BOBBY *unholsters his radio, pushes the button.*)

BOBBY. Yo Theresa it's Bobby respond ay-sap.

(*Radio silence for a long moment.* BOBBY *pushes the button again.*)

Yo The*resa* get the fuck on the *radio, thanks.*

MAGGIE. (*Furious; betrayed:*) Really? You're calling *management?*

BOBBY. Fuck you.

MAGGIE. Fuck you, too.

BOBBY. If I lived with you, I'd sleep in a locked room, too.

MAGGIE. Yeah?

Well.

Good.

I'm a dangerous person.

THERESA. (*V.O., over the radio.*) Bobby? What do you want?

BOBBY. Theresa! I need you up on the roof, *right fucking now.*

THERESA. (*V.O.*) You can't just *order* me around, Bobby –

BOBBY. (*Urgent:*) 10-56, Theresa, 10-56.

(*Long beat.*)

THERESA. (*V.O. Having realized the gravity of the situation now:*) Oh my god.

Wait – wait –

(*Beat as the radio clicks off.*)

MAGGIE. What's 10-56?

Bobby. What's 10-56?

(BOBBY *doesn't respond.* MAGGIE *gestures to the bottle.*)

This isn't 10-56, right?

(*She points to the weed, repeats* BOBBY*'s weed-smokin' gesture from before.*)

Or this?

(MAGGIE *stands. She leans down, dangerously close to the fire pit.*)

This isn't 10-56, either. Is it?

(MAGGIE *takes a few steps forward. Towards the edge of the roof.* BOBBY *inhales, watching her. Her eyes on his, she takes another step.*)

Am I getting warmer?

BOBBY. Stop it.

MAGGIE. (*Taking another step:*) Stop what?

BOBBY. Just *stop it.*

MAGGIE. You reported a 10-56; I don't want to make you a *liar.*

BOBBY. This is my *job*, you know, this is where I *work*, you think it's *okay* to just like check into a hotel and come up here to get drunk and make a bunch of bullshit threats about – about fuckin' *killing yourself*?

MAGGIE. (*Hard, taking a step over the railing:*) Hey, I wouldn't have *had* to come up here if you'd gotten me a room with a balcony.

(THERESA *suddenly bursts in, flushed and simultaneously upset/excited.*)

THERESA. *MRS. ELLIOTT WHAT IN THE NAME OF CHRIST ARE YOU DOING?!*

(*Even* MAGGIE *is startled by this.*)

BOBBY. (*To* THERESA:) Where the fuck were you?

THERESA. Mrs. Elliott *please* step back from the edge, *please* don't 10-56 while I'm on shift, I have done so much to make this a five-star experience for you, I unclogged your toilet and I didn't even complain once or even tell anyone how gross it was, *please* don't ruin it all now.

BOBBY. Yes! *Listen* to Theresa!

THERESA. (*Should she, though?:*) A fucking *SUICIDE?* Do you know what a *suicide* would *do* to the Residence?

BOBBY. Um.

THERESA. Do you have any idea what it would do to *me?*

BOBBY. Uhhhhh –

THERESA. (*Working herself into a tizzy:*) I thought Midwesterners were nice. This isn't nice, this is *terrible*.
Should I call the police? I need to call the police. The poolside phone doesn't work. I've told maintenance so many times about the poolside phone not working. We could get sued for that! That's a big problem! My cell phone doesn't get reception up here. I don't have any bars. Bobby, do you have bars?

(BOBBY *shakes his head, no.*)

MAGGIE. (*Pointing to the table:*) Mine does –

THERESA. Mrs. Elliott! Don't talk to me right now! Don't get distracted! Don't do anything that could make you fall!

MAGGIE. (*Realizing something funny:*) Ha.

THERESA. Don't *laugh* at me! This isn't *funny!*

MAGGIE. No, but wouldn't that be hilarious? If I climbed up here to jump, but I just – fell?

(*Freaking,* THERESA *grabs the fire extinguisher, strides to* MAGGIE's *other side, and points it at her.*)

THERESA. Mrs. Elliott, please back away from the roof or I will be forced to shoot you!

MAGGIE. What the fuck?!

THERESA. I'll be forced to shoot you with the *fire extinguisher*, not – oh my *god!*

MAGGIE. Put it *down*, Theresa!

THERESA. (*Struggling with the extinguisher:*) You get back from there – or I *will* pull the clip!

Or – the lever.

I'll figure it out!

> (MAGGIE *puts her hands up. Retreats from the edge of the roof.*)

That's right! Back! Back! Get back!

> (MAGGIE *sits back down by the fire pit.* THERESA *turns the extinguisher on* BOBBY.)

You too! You asshole!

BOBBY. Me?!

Put that fucking thing down already!

THERESA. I will not! I will fire this!

BOBBY. We get charged $300 to refill those!

THERESA. *Oh, fuck!*

> (*She puts down the fire extinguisher, tries to breathe.*)

Oh, my god. Oh, my god.

> (MAGGIE *moves to lay a hand on* THERESA*'s back, but* BOBBY *nudges her out of the way: stay away from her. Surprised,* MAGGIE *steps back, letting* BOBBY *comfort – or at least hover over –* THERESA. THERESA *breathes. She's calming down. After a moment, she absorbs her surroundings:* MAGGIE*'s shoes kicked off. The bottle. The cups. Sniffs the air. Sees the joint in its makeshift ashtray. And:*)

THERESA. (*To* BOBBY:) Isn't that your lighter?

> (*Beat.*)

MAGGIE. He loaned it to me.

> (*Beat.*)

THERESA. What's going on out here?

BOBBY. Nothing's going on –

THERESA. How did you know there was a 10-56 going on, Bobby? Why were you up on the roof in the first place?

MAGGIE. It was my fault. I was breaking the rules. Someone reported me. Glass in the pool.

He brought me plastic.

THERESA. (*Noticing:*) Two cups.

MAGGIE. To pour the bottle into. You can't fit a whole bottle of wine into one cup.

THERESA. (*To* BOBBY:) Why are you *up* here, Bobby?

BOBBY. I came up to take the glass container away from Maggie. I was actually doing my *job*.

(*Beat.*)

THERESA. If I watch the footage from the roof camera, will it show you getting fucked up with a Guest?

(BOBBY *doesn't respond.*)

I'm asking you a question.

BOBBY. Are you seriously going to look at the *roof camera footage?*

THERESA. Were you or were you not drinking and smoking marijuana on shift?

Because I'm sorry if you're *still* unclear about this, but that's not actually part of your job description.

BOBBY. And drinking tequila and messing around with your subordinates isn't part of yours.

But.

You still did that. Didn't you?

(*Beat as* THERESA *stares at* MAGGIE *and* BOBBY.)

THERESA. Whatever *this* is, between you two? With the mice, and the lighters, and the –

It's not appropriate. And it hasn't been since the moment she checked in. Oh yeah, I'm talking to you, "Maggie."

BOBBY. Hey, Mrs. Elliott is a Guest.

THERESA. Oh, *now* she's "Mrs. Elliott"?

You do realize I could call the police and tell them about the marijuana and the *pills* I found in her trashcan and *this* and have you locked the fuck up, *tonight.* You crazy bitch.

(*It's as though someone has thrown cold water in* MAGGIE*'s face.* BOBBY *gets to his feet, angry now.*)

BOBBY. Watch it.

THERESA. Or what?

BOBBY. Mrs. Elliott just needed somebody to talk to, and that's what I was doing up here, and now she's *fine.*

THERESA. Mrs. Elliott needed someone to talk to, Mrs. Elliott needed *weed* – what *else* did Mrs. Elliott need? What else did you *give* her?

(*Silence.*)

BOBBY. You know me better than that, Theresa.

THERESA. I don't fucking know you. You have a *baby*. You have a *child* with someone, a child you apparently don't want anything to do with, which is *so shitty* I can't even –

I didn't know that. You never told me that. That's a pretty big thing to leave out.

BOBBY. I don't have to tell you my business.

THERESA. Oh, you don't?

BOBBY. No! You're not my *girlfriend*, Theresa. I don't have to tell you shit.

(*Beat.*)

THERESA. You're right.

I'm not your girlfriend.

I'm your manager.

BOBBY. Management trainee.

You can't even throw a reception on your own.

A reception that nobody came to.

A reception that nobody *wanted* to come to.

(*Hard pause.*)

THERESA. I can *fire* employees on my own.

BOBBY. You can fire an employee for providing a five-star Guest experience?

THERESA. I can fire him for impersonating a manager on the official Residence TripAdvisor page.

(*Beat.*)

BOBBY. No.

THERESA. Yup.

BOBBY. *You* typed that shit!

THERESA. Yeah, well, you posted it. At least, that's how Jordan saw it when we talked about it just now.

(*Quiet for a moment. Then:*)

BOBBY. Yo, why's your skirt on backwards, Theresa?

(*Beat.*)

THERESA. What?

BOBBY. Your skirt. It's on – backwards.

THERESA. It's *not*.

(*It is. In one motion, she turns it around to face the right direction.*)

I – I mean –

Coffee. I spilled coffee *all over*, so I *had* to change.

BOBBY. (*Realizing:*) Jordan? *Jordan?*

In the fuckin' *office?*

(THERESA *blushes furiously, angrily.*)

THERESA. It's not my fault!

I had to drop out of school! Okay? And *she* told me not to take out another loan! A *business*woman told me that! So –

How else was I gonna be a manager?

> (*Long beat.* BOBBY *holds his hand out, for a shake.*)

BOBBY. Congratulations.

THERESA. Stop it.

BOBBY. No, congrats.

You earned it, right?

THERESA. (*Coldly furious now:*) You're done. You are done.

Leave your badge on my desk.

I want you out of the building in ten minutes or I'm calling security.

> (THERESA *exits. A long moment.* MAGGIE *looks at* BOBBY, *guilty and wretched.*)

MAGGIE. Bobby –

BOBBY. *Don't.*

> (*Beat.*)

Just go back to your room, okay?

> (MAGGIE *slowly stands and exits.* BOBBY *is left alone, swaying from the dismissal.*
> *He stares resolutely into the fire. He stares. He stares. Then: it clicks off.*)

Twelve.

> *We land in a third and final* DOCTOR's *office.* MAGGIE, *quiet and drawn, has just finished her pitch. The ultrasound is out and ready to go.*

DOCTOR. I've read all your literature, and I've done a fair amount of research on my own. So, really, what I'd like to do now is just test the thing out, see how I like it.

Problem is, my nurse is out to lunch, and I don't want to impose –

MAGGIE. (*With a tired smile:*) Part of the job.

DOCTOR. Just lie back for me?

> (MAGGIE *hops up on the examination table. She knows the drill: she unzips her pants and folds them back slightly while the* DOCTOR *preps the ultrasound.*)

MAGGIE. I couldn't find much about your practice online. How many locations do you have?

DOCTOR. Three so far in this state. We're pushing further east, into the Plains, and north.

MAGGIE. Private practice?

DOCTOR. Foundation-funded. Women's clinics in underserved regions. OB/GYN, preventative care: the works.

MAGGIE. (*Wow:*) That's … pretty incredible.

DOCTOR. We're chipping away.

I'm going to move your shirt aside and apply some gel. Just a warning: it's gonna be a little cold.

(*He squeezes out some gel. MAGGIE gasps a little involuntarily.*)

MAGGIE. God.

DOCTOR. I told you.

(*DOCTOR uses the wand, gazes at the picture. MAGGIE does, too.*)

Hm. Your uterus is slightly enlarged.

(*Beat.*)

MAGGIE. I had a baby.

DOCTOR. How long ago?

MAGGIE. Six months.

DOCTOR. Congratulations.

(*MAGGIE is quiet.*)

Image resolution is the best I've seen so far. I could take this on the road with me?

MAGGIE. Just pack it in the case and go.

DOCTOR. (*Handing her a towel to clean off the gel:*) What are the power requirements?

MAGGIE. If you can plug your hairdryer into it, you can plug this into it, too.

DOCTOR. (*As he hands her a towel to clean off the gel:*) And the price?

MAGGIE. Slightly flexible.

DOCTOR. You know I have to bargain you down a *little*, but. I like to keep it fair.

(*DOCTOR considers.*)

If we bought twenty.

(*MAGGIE's heart skips a beat. She tries to stay calm.*)

MAGGIE. Twenty.

DOCTOR. Like I said: we're pushing east. No point in opening up a clinic if we don't have any equipment. And I'm tired of buying castoffs from county hospitals.

Twenty'll get us a fair multiples discount?

(*MAGGIE just nods. It will.*)

Then twenty it is.

(MAGGIE *cries a little. She can't help it.* DOCTOR *hands her a tissue. After a moment:*)

Six months old, huh?

Good age.

MAGGIE. Is it?

(DOCTOR *laughs.*)

He's still just sort of – a little alien.

DOCTOR. They're always just sort of little aliens.

(*Beat. This is difficult to say:*)

MAGGIE. I don't –

I don't feel much.

Or.

I mean.

I feel the wrong things.

And that's all I feel.

(DOCTOR *looks at her for a moment.*)

DOCTOR. My son is ten. A whole year after he was born, my ex-wife and I turned to each other, and said: "I mean – he's *okay*, I guess."

It takes time.

MAGGIE. How much time?

I mean: what if it takes a really long time?

DOCTOR. It takes what it takes.

(*A moment between them. Then:*
In the transition between scenes, MAGGIE *crosses back to the hotel room. Goes to the bedside table and retrieves the three prescription bottles. Takes a pill out of each and downs them.*)

Thirteen.

MAGGIE *waits in the parking garage. She fans herself with a piece of paper we can't read: it's hot out here.*

After a moment, BOBBY *enters from the hotel, in street clothes, carrying a plastic grocery bag. He stops when he sees* MAGGIE. *Neither of them knows how to behave around the other.*

BOBBY. Hey.

MAGGIE. Hey.

I'm just, uh – waiting on a shuttle. He's on his way back from the Whole Foods.

BOBBY. (*Holding up the plastic bag:*) Cleaned out my locker.

MAGGIE. What was in it?

> (BOBBY *opens the bag. They both peer inside.*)

Garbage, basically.

BOBBY. Pretty much.

MAGGIE. You came back for garbage?

BOBBY. I just wanted to –

You know. See the place one more time.

MAGGIE. And – Theresa?

BOBBY. (*A little harder – he didn't come here for her:*) She's not on the schedule today.

MAGGIE. She had a new badge on Monday. A manager's badge.

BOBBY. I mean, good for her, you know? It's what she wanted. I'll be all right.

MAGGIE. Where are you gonna go?

BOBBY. Somewhere. You know.

> (*Long beat.*)

MAGGIE. I'm sorry.

About that night.

What I did, and – you getting fired, that was my fault –

> (*Beat.*)

And I'm sorry about what I said to you about you leaving your kid. I didn't know what I was talking about and it was mean and I shouldn't have said it.

> (*The awkwardness is now broken between them.*)

BOBBY. Nah.

I mean.

I left. Didn't I?

MAGGIE. (*Hopeful: about him? About herself?:*) But just because you leave for a little doesn't mean you can't ever come back. Right?

BOBBY. Actually.

It does. Legally.

I signed a buncha stuff, and – that's that.

It's cool, though! My daughter is gonna get a real dad. It's just not gonna be me.

MAGGIE. Bobby –

BOBBY. (*Sincere, selling it:*) Nah, it's good!

I'm fine with it.

I mean, you're doing the same thing. It's *fine*.

> (MAGGIE *just looks at him. Sad.*)

What?

(MAGGIE *holds out her fan. It's a boarding pass.* BOBBY *glances at it, then looks down, fast, like he's just been slapped.*)

That's a boarding pass. That's a boarding pass – for today?

(MAGGIE *confirms.*)

Wow. Okay.

So: airport shuttle. Not grocery shuttle.

They got your bags inside at the desk?

(MAGGIE *nods.*)

Good. Good. They'll get 'em loaded up for you once the shuttle gets here. They know how to stack 'em just right.

MAGGIE. That's what they said.

BOBBY. (*Still in disbelief:*) So you're, uh. Heading back? To Dairy Country?

MAGGIE. I am.

BOBBY. Good. Good for you.

D'you ever end up looking at any apartments?

(MAGGIE *shakes her head, no.*)

Yeah, I mean, you don't wanna live in Tempe. You mighta thought, for a second, but: trust me. Nah.

(*Long devastated beat.* BOBBY *should go, but he doesn't want to leave yet.* MAGGIE *senses this.*)

MAGGIE. I don't even know if I'm gonna make it!

BOBBY. (*Hopeful:*) For real?

MAGGIE. Yeah, there's snow in Milwaukee. Some huge storm. I don't know if my flight's gonna go.

BOBBY. (*Even more hopeful – maybe she won't leave, after all:*) I guess you could always come back here, stay another night.

MAGGIE. I think I'm just gonna camp out. Sleep in the airport. If it gets too bad, I might just stay in one of the airport hotels.

BOBBY. I don't know about that – those airport hotels are expensive as hell. Like a hundred-fifty, two hundred a night more than we are.

I mean –

(*Recovering from the slip:*)

I'm just saying: they take advantage of shit like – *snow.*

MAGGIE. It's okay.

I sold some Precision E's.

(BOBBY *brightens, proud of her despite his sadness.*)

BOBBY. You sold some?

MAGGIE. I did.

BOBBY. Yeah?

(MAGGIE *laughs.*)

MAGGIE. Yeah. Yeah.

(*Quiet. Then:*)

BOBBY. You gonna be okay?

(MAGGIE *has no idea if she will or not.*)

'Cause if you – I mean, who the fuck am I, but – and I know you're going back home and everything, back to your husband, back to being a mom and all, but if you need *anything – anything –*

(BOBBY *exhales, upset. What can he really offer? What can he really say? She's going.*

Sort of spontaneously, they hug. It's a long hug, broken only by the sound of a shuttle rounding its final corner. A loud engine thrum. They separate, reluctantly.)

Whoops. Time to go.

MAGGIE. Looks like, yeah.

(*Beat.*)

BOBBY. I hope you have a really nice life, Maggie.

MAGGIE. I hope you have a really nice life, too.

(*They smile at each other. Neither going anywhere just yet. Lights fade.*)

End of Play

CARDBOARD PIANO
by Hansol Jung

ABOUT *CARDBOARD PIANO*

This article first ran in the Limelight Guide to the 40th Humana Festival of New American Plays, *published by Actors Theatre of Louisville, and is based on conversations with the playwright before rehearsals for the Humana Festival production began.*

It's the eve of the millennium, a night that should be spent celebrating the promise of new beginnings. But for 16-year-old Chris, tonight's the night that an ongoing civil war ravaging Northern Uganda will invade her village, changing her life forever. And for Pika, a heartsick child soldier, it's a night filled with dangerous confrontations and decisions that he'll never forget. In Hansol Jung's stirring drama, *Cardboard Piano*, two fractured souls fight to escape a past filled with brutality and hate, and rebuild their shattered lives—but what if there are some things that, once broken, can never be fixed? Are there some wrongs for which the cost of forgiveness is too high?

When we meet Chris, she's just snuck into the village church in the middle of the night. Unbeknownst to her father, the church's American missionary pastor, she's planned a secret wedding to a local girl, Adiel, with only a tape recorder to hear their vows. Since their families would frown upon the relationship and homosexuality is cause for persecution in Uganda, Chris and Adiel decide to run away together. This plan is derailed when they collide with Pika, an injured child soldier seeking refuge from his captors. Haunted by the horrors he's seen and been forced to perpetrate, Pika's convinced that God has forgotten him. Chris becomes an ally in his search for absolution— but neither the church, nor the fragile bond that forms between the children inside it, is safe from the bloody surrounding conflict.

While the emotional and spiritual struggles of its characters lie at *Cardboard Piano*'s heart, its focus on people confronting the boundaries of religious belief and the devastating impact of intolerance is also highly timely. "The first seed of inspiration for this play was a PBS documentary I saw about child soldiers who returned to their home villages, and how their families didn't accept them back because they'd done these horrible things," Jung says. She then began researching the insurgent group responsible for forcibly conscripting these child soldiers into its ranks, the Lord's Resistance Army. According to its leader, Joseph Kony, the LRA's driving purpose was to overthrow the existing Ugandan government and replace it with a new regime based on Kony's interpretation of the Bible's Ten Commandments. "Since the conflict with the Lord's Resistance Army could be described as a faith-based war, it made me think about how religion can do two opposite things," Jung reflects. "It can destroy, hurt, and be an instigator of violence, but it can also be the only thing capable of controlling that violence." While writing *Cardboard Piano*, Jung was also very aware of the controversy around Uganda's recent Anti-Homosexuality Act, as well as the debate over marriage equality in this country. The playwright recalls: "The U.S. was having a lot of conversations about gay marriage and whether to make it legal, and that was a loud voice inside my head."

The story is based in Jung's lived experience as well. Jung herself is the daughter of a pastor and, like Chris and Pika, her relationship to her faith is complicated. "I am Christian, but I've always interrogated what that means," she says. "That really influenced the writing of this play. Chris and Pika's story isn't my own story, but the essence of the play—especially the questions it asks about faith—is very personal. In a way, it's a love letter to my dad." For Jung, this personal resonance adds emotional depth to the storytelling, just as a trip to Uganda helped her make *Cardboard Piano*'s portrayal of daily life there feel authentic. "I thought, I'm writing a play about this place and I don't know what it smells like, what it feels like," she explains. Jung stayed with several Korean missionaries in Kampala, working with children as a youth program counselor during a national missionaries' retreat. She also traveled to villages, which she found incredibly valuable "because of all the things I got to see and make a part of my body," Jung elaborates. "And what the people there sound like, how they talk, was so helpful to have in my ear while creating these characters."

With *Cardboard Piano*, Jung has crafted a lyrical parable about faith, loss, and the power of forgiveness that captures the emotional complexity of its inspirations. It's a story that asks tough questions: Can the beliefs that were our saving grace also become our downfall? How do we go on loving in the face of hatred? And, even when we attempt to put painful memories behind us, is breaking free from the repercussions of past mistakes always possible? As Jung wonders: "What happens when you're confronted with a truth you'd tried to bury, and everything you've built breaks?" Jung's hope is that the play doesn't offer ready answers; that as its characters struggle to figure out what and who is right, so will we. "I'm interested in the audience's empathy actively shifting around," she declares. "I want people to interrogate their own perspectives."

—Hannah Rae Montgomery

BIOGRAPHY

Hansol Jung is a playwright and director from South Korea. Plays include *Among the Dead* (Ma-Yi Theater Company), *Cardboard Piano* (Humana Festival at Actors Theatre of Louisville), *No More Sad Things* (co-world premiere at Sideshow Theatre Company in Chicago and Boise Contemporary Theater), *Wolf Play*, and *Wild Goose Dreams*. Commissions include Playwrights Horizons and Seattle Repertory Theatre, as well as the Virginia B. Toulmin Foundation grant with Ma-Yi Theater and a translation of *Romeo and Juliet* for Play On! at Oregon Shakespeare Festival. Her work has been developed at the Royal Court Theatre (London), New York Theatre Workshop, The Ground Floor at Berkeley Rep, the O'Neill National Playwrights Conference, Sundance Theatre Lab, The Lark Play Development Center, Salt Lake Acting Company, The Theatre @ Boston Court, The Bushwick Starr, Asia Society New York, and Seven Devils Playwright Conference. She is the recipient of the P73 Playwriting Fellowship at Page 73 Productions, the Rita Goldberg Playwrights' Workshop Fellowship at The Lark, a 2050 Fellowship at New York Theatre Workshop, a MacDowell Colony Artist Residency, SPACE at Ryder Farm Residency and International Playwrights Residency at the Royal Court Theatre (London). She has translated over thirty English musicals into Korean, including *Evita, Dracula, Spamalot,* and *The 25th Annual Putnam County Spelling Bee*, while working on several award-winning musical theatre productions as a director, lyricist and translator in Seoul, South Korea. Jung holds a M.F.A. in Playwriting from Yale School of Drama, and is a proud member of the Ma-Yi Writers Lab.

ACKNOWLEDGMENTS

Cardboard Piano premiered at the Humana Festival of New American Plays in March 2016. It was directed by Leigh Silverman with the following cast:

CHRIS .... Briana Pozner
ADIEL/RUTH ....Nike Kadri
PIKA/FRANCIS .... Jamar Williams
SOLDIER/PAUL..Michael Luwoye

and the following production staff:

Scenic Designer ....William Boles
Costume Designer ....Kaye Voyce
Lighting Designer ....Keith Parham
Sound Designer ....M.L. Dogg
Original Music & Composition ....Jason Webb
Fight Director ....Drew Fracher
Dialect Coach .... Kate Glasheen
Stage Manager ....Jason Pacella
Dramaturg ....Hannah Rae Montgomery
Casting ....Telsey + Company, Karyn Casl, CSA
Properties Master .... Joe Cunningham
Directing Assistant ....James Kennedy
Assistant Dramaturg .... Helena D. Pennington

Cardboard Piano was developed during a residency at the Eugene O'Neill Theater Center's National Playwrights Conference in 2015.

CHARACTERS

PART I

CHRIS (16)	a child in love
ADIEL (16)	a child in love
PIKA (13)	a child soldier
SOLDIER	a soldier

PART II

CHRIS (30)	a visitor
PAUL (27)	a pastor, Soldier from Part I
RUTH (29)	a pastor's wife, Adiel from Part I
FRANCIS (22)	a local kid, Pika from Part I

SETTING

A township in Northern Uganda

Part I is New Year's Eve 1999
Part II is A Wedding Anniversary 2014

PUNCTUATION NOTES

—	a cut off either by self or other
/	a point where another character might cut in
Line break	a switch of thought
[…]	things that aren't spoken in words

LUO TRANSLATIONS

jal – le	I surrender
apwoyo matek	thank you very much
mzungu	(light-skinned) foreigner

Briana Pozner and Nike Kadri
in *Cardboard Piano*

40th Humana Festival of New American Plays
Actors Theatre of Louisville, 2016
Photo by Bill Brymer

CARDBOARD PIANO

PART I

Night.
A church—not one of stone and stained glass,
more a small town hall dressed up to be church.
There's a hole in the roof of the church.
Two men, two women.
In separate spaces, they sing together, simple a capella
that might blow up into something bigger and scarier.

ALL.
Just as I am, without one plea*,
But that Thy blood was shed for me,
And that Thou bidst me come to Thee,
O Lamb of God, I come, I come

Just as I am, though tossed about
With many a conflict, many a doubt,
Fightings and fears within, without,
O Lamb of God, I come, I come

Just as I am, Thy love unknown
Hath broken every barrier down;
Now, to be Thine, yea, Thine alone,
O Lamb of God, I come, I come

Just as I am, of that free love
The breadth, length depth, and height to prove,
Here for a season, then above,
O Lamb of—

> (*Rain. Loud. Pours through the hole in the roof.*
> *Pews, chair, cushions arranged to create a hollow in the middle of church.*
> ADIEL, *age 16, is asleep in the middle of the hollow, strewn with wild flower*
> *petals.*
> CHRIS, *age 16, slips in, big suitcase in tow.*
> *She hides the suitcase somewhere in the shadows*
> *She tiptoes around the chairs, benches to lean into* ADIEL's *sleeping ear.*
> *Whispers.*)

---

* Hymn 313, Words by Charlotte Elliott, Music by William B. Bradbury.

157

CHRIS. The end of the world is near.

    (ADIEL *starts.*)

ADIEL. Hm!?

CHRIS. Hi.

ADIEL. Where am, what,

CHRIS. It's me, just me.

ADIEL. For heaven's sake Chris. You frightened me. What is the time. You are very late.

CHRIS. Had to wait till the folks fell asleep.

ADIEL. Your parents?

    (CHRIS *finds party blower.*)

CHRIS. Blowers!

ADIEL. Why are they still here?

CHRIS. Blue one's mine!

ADIEL. What about the party? What happened?

CHRIS. Nothing. They didn't wanna go, I guess.

ADIEL. So your parents are still in the house?

CHRIS. It's fine. They went to bed. Said they wanna be up in time to see the ball fall in New York.
Miss me?

ADIEL. I saw you just three hours ago.

CHRIS. We didn't know if the world was gonna end, three hours ago.

ADIEL. It did not.

    (CHRIS *blows on blower: yay!*)

ADIEL. Shh!

CHRIS. Happy New Year.

ADIEL. Happy New Year. You'll wake them up.

    (*Blow.*)

Chris it is not funny—

    (*Blow.*)

Come now give it to me.

CHRIS. Make me.

    (*Blow.*)

ADIEL. Haw this is a challenge now?

    (ADIEL *jumps* CHRIS*, misses.*)

CHRIS. Prepare for battle!

    (*Battle trumpets blowblowblow.*)

Upon my honor I shall never surrender!

>   (*Bloooooooooooooooooooooooooo—*
>   *Blowing stops because* ADIEL *kisses her.*)

CHRIS. I surrender.

>   (*Kiss.*)

How do you say I surrender in Luo?

ADIEL. *Jal – le.*

CHRIS. *Jal – le.*

ADIEL. I am very sexy when you speak my language.

CHRIS. I am sexy.

ADIEL. You too?

CHRIS. No, I am sexy, to you. Sexy is a thing I am, that makes You want to get into My pants.

ADIEL. Why are we turning this into English lesson?

CHRIS. I am very sexy when you speak my language wrong.

ADIEL. So both ways we are very sexy.

CHRIS. Okay.

>   (*Hands in pants, hairs undone, shirts flung off, skirts riding up—*
>   *Thunder and lightning.*)

CHRIS. Woah.

>   (CHRIS *bolts upright like a meerkat.*)

ADIEL. What is the matter?

CHRIS. Think he's mad at us?

ADIEL. Who?

CHRIS. I'd be mad if people came to my house at night, mess it up, have sex all over my cushions in front of a picture of me hanging naked on a tree—

>   (ADIEL *kisses* CHRIS.)

ADIEL. I think he is thrilled we included him.

CHRIS. We didn't.

ADIEL. Well I did and I think he is saying congratulations on your big day!

>   (*Thunder.*
>   *Meerkat.*)

He is happy for us! He is giving us extra fireworks. He is saying Happy happy wedding day!

CHRIS. Fuck around in my house of worship and I'll throw a bolt in your head. Is what he's saying.

ADIEL. Ag he did not bring us together to throw a bolt in our heads.

CHRIS. Yeh. Well. We won't know till we know will we?

ADIEL. Chris. What is the matter?

CHRIS. Nothing. Just, thunderstorms. I don't like them.

> (Re: *church:*)

This, is beautiful. When did you have the time to set all this up?

ADIEL. You were late.

CHRIS. Candles…flowers…a, Oreo?

ADIEL. Ah that one is a gift. From Francis.

CHRIS. Francis? The guy who's crushing on you?

ADIEL. No, that is Philip. Francis is my cousin. The one who is crushing on You.

CHRIS. You brought me a cookie from your competition.

ADIEL. The competition is eight years old and he really wanted you to have this one. I am not worried. Very soon you belong only to me.

> (ADIEL *holds out her palms.*)

CHRIS. What?

ADIEL. The rings?

CHRIS. Oh. Um.

ADIEL. What?

CHRIS. —

ADIEL. Ag Chris, that was the one thing you were in charge of.

CHRIS. I'm sorry. My parents, found them and, took them

ADIEL. Your parents? Why?

CHRIS. Because. For safekeeping. They're paranoid, since the news up north. The whole town's so paranoid, it's contagious. Can't wait to get out of this place where we can live like normal people.

ADIEL. This place is my home.

CHRIS. It doesn't always have to be.

ADIEL. Christina I do not want to argue about that right now.

CHRIS. Don't call me Christina.

I wanted everything to be perfect too. I wanted rings. Champagne. Sunlight.

ADIEL. We have candlelight. And here a ring. For now.

> (The *strip of aluminum from a bottle cap*—ADIEL *twists it into a pretty ring.*)

CHRIS. I knew this boy back home. He'd always play with wires, bend them into goats—sometimes other things but mostly goats, he loved goats—goat tribes, goat battle scenes, little goat armies lined up and at attention. He had no friends and was bullied a lot but then one of the teachers found his goats, and helped him apply to this arts school in Colorado, all for free, even the plane ticket. You know what I mean?

ADIEL. No.

CHRIS. I'm saying, you could probably do something like that.

ADIEL. You want that I make armies of wire goats?

CHRIS. No, I want that you apply to a school in America. You can make pretty things. You can go to school for free if you can make pretty things in my country, learn to make more pretty things, sell them, buy a car, buy a boat, a plane, an army of wire goats—

ADIEL. Chris. If you are making stupid jokes because you do not want to do this, tell me right now.

CHRIS. I do. I do want to. I'm sorry. Don't be angry.

ADIEL. I am not angry. Just making sure.

CHRIS. I am sure.

(ADIEL *makes sure.*)

ADIEL. We have everything else, candle, cookie, tape recorder—

CHRIS. Tape recorder?

ADIEL. Because we do not have witnesses, we must record the vows, so when you are mine, you are mine forever.

CHRIS. This isn't legal or anything, I can crush the records and run away whenever I like.

ADIEL. But I will hunt you down to the ends of the earth. I will hunt you down forever. Forever forever I will say, "come back to meeeeeeeeee come back to me my husbaaaaaaaaaand come back to meeeeeeeeeeeeeeeeeeeee I have this tape recordeerrrrrrrrrrrr"

CHRIS. Okay let's do it.

(ADIEL *pulls out a couple of neatly composed handwritten documents.*)

ADIEL. Number one, you must say this, with your name in there, and then I say the same, with My name not yours of course.

CHRIS. Wow. You are not joking around.

ADIEL. I never joke. Number two, You do the ring and say this part. Unless you want to be the bride, then I do the ring to you, and I say this part.

CHRIS. Wait, where'd you get this stuff from?

ADIEL. From our pastor.

(CHRIS *takes a pen to* ADIEL's *vow papers.*)

CHRIS. Okay, strike "lawful," strike "according to God's holy ordinance," / and strike the second part of this whole section,

ADIEL. AH! What are you doing, you are ruining the vow papers!

CHRIS. —we are not endowing anything in the name of the Father the Son or the Holy Ghost. Because they don't care. Amen should go too.

ADIEL. We must do the whole vow.

CHRIS. No we don't. It's our wedding we can do whatever we want.

ADIEL. Well that is not what I want.

(ADIEL *clicks "rec" button on the tape recorder.*)

This is the wedding of Christina Jennifer Englewood and Adiel Nakalinzi. January 1ˢᵗ, Year 2000.

(*She gestures to* CHRIS: *"go ahead, begin the vows."*)

CHRIS. What? Oh okay, me first. I, Chris Blank, take thee,

(ADIEL *hits stop.*)

ADIEL. What are you doing.

CHRIS. I'm gonna find another name. I've disowned my parents.

ADIEL. What does that mean? Shoo, you are making this impossible, You have to have whole name, say I, Christina Jennifer Engelwood. Start again.

(*Rewind. Rec.*)

This is the wedding of Christina Jennifer Englewood and Adiel Nakalinzi. January 1ˢᵗ, Year 2000.

CHRIS. I, Chris Blank, take thee, Adiel Nakalinzi, to be my wife, ugh, that's such dumb word.

(ADIEL *hits stop.*)

ADIEL. Chris!

(CHRIS *takes the recorder. Rec.*)

CHRIS. To be my wife, to have and to hold from this day forward, for better for worse for richer for poorer in sickness and in health to love and to cherish till death do us part, according to, I don't know, according to this dimly lit candle's holy ordinance, and thereto I give thee my troth. What's a troth? Sounds slimy.

ADIEL. I, Adiel Nakalinzi, take thee, Christina Jennifer Engelwood,

CHRIS. Chris Blank

ADIEL. Christina Jennifer Engelwood, to be my lawful wedded husband, to have and—

(CHRIS *hits stop.*)

CHRIS. Stop right there, I refuse to be a husband in this life or the next, do over.

ADIEL. What, we have two wives then? That is a house of widows.

CHRIS. I don't care, make it work, not gonna be a husband. Ew.

ADIEL. A sad grieving house of sad sad widows.

(*Sad face.*)

CHRIS. Ugh.

(ADIEL *hits rec.*)

ADIEL. I, Adiel Nakalinzi, take thee, Christina Jennifer Engelwood, to be my lawful wedded Husband,

(CHRIS *leans into mic on recorder.*)

CHRIS. Ugh.

ADIEL. —to have and to hold from this day, forward, for better for worse, for richer for poorer, in sickness and in health, to love and to cherish, till death us do part, according to God's holy ordinance; and thereto I plight thee my troth.

CHRIS. With this ring I thee wed, with my body I thee worship, and with all my worldly goods I thee endow.

ADIEL. In the name of.

CHRIS. In the name of the Father, and of the Son, and of the Holy Ghost. Amen.

ADIEL. Amen. Now I may kiss the husband.

(*Kiss. With all the nerves and rituals of the Newlyweds' First Kiss.*)

Now we must dance.

CHRIS. No. We must not.

(ADIEL *begins to sing "Unchained Melody" by The Righteous Brothers.* CHRIS *laughs out loud at the song choice, but soon surrenders to* ADIEL's *insistence.*)

CHRIS. Seriously?

ADIEL. Yes.

(ADIEL *continues to sing, pulling* CHRIS *into the performance.*
They dance together, like people in love, soaking in the cheese and tender, all of it.
Just as they're about to reach the end of the second verse, they are interrupted by a noise.
!!
Scuffling of feet on dirt,
random shouts, coming from outside.)

CHRIS. What's the time?

ADIEL. After midnight at the very least.

CHRIS. It must be people getting out from the party. Blow them out, the candles!

(*Silence.*
Then doors opening slamming, feet, shuffling on dirt, whispered sounds.)

ADIEL. Did you lock the door?

CHRIS. I'm getting it now
>   (*BANG gun shots.*
>   CHRIS *and* ADIEL *duck.*)

CHRIS. Jesus!

ADIEL. Chris!

CHRIS. It's alright I'm fine are you? Are you okay?

ADIEL. Get over here, get over here right now!

CHRIS. I know, okay I'm [gonna lock the door first]
>   (*Door opens,* PIKA *leaps in, grabs* CHRIS, *hand over mouth.*)

PIKA. Shh!
>   (*Points bloody gun towards* ADIEL, *then to* CHRIS's *head.*
>   *Motions to* CHRIS *to lock the door. She does.*
>   *More footsteps, pad pad pad past the door, and away.*
>   *Wait wait.*
>   *Wait wait.*
>   *Wait wait.*
>   PIKA *leans against a wall, exhausted, out of breath,*
>   *faints.*
>   CHRIS *leaps back away from him,* ADIEL *leaps forward towards* CHRIS.)

ADIEL. Are you okay.

CHRIS. Mm. [yes]

ADIEL. Did he hurt you? Any—

CHRIS. Mm mm [no]

ADIEL. Okay good okay. Hold on.
>   (*Checks pulse. Breath.*)

CHRIS. Is he [dead]?

ADIEL. He's okay.
>   (CHRIS *looks for a rope type thing.*
>   ADIEL *pries gun from* PIKA, *wipes the blood off the gun.*
>   CHRIS *has found a rope type thing, gives it to* ADIEL.)

ADIEL. What?

CHRIS. For [tying him up]
>   (ADIEL *hands gun to* CHRIS *while she ties up* PIKA.)

ADIEL. Okay.

CHRIS. Okay.

ADIEL. Sit there take a breath / and I will go bring your parents.

CHRIS. Okay
My—

ADIEL. You said they were still here, right? They did not go to New Year Party.

CHRIS. No.

ADIEL. So I will bring them down.

CHRIS. You can't. You can't bring them. You can't wake them up.

ADIEL. Chris we must. That child is hurt.

CHRIS. You can't.

ADIEL. He cannot do anything to us now, I promise.

CHRIS. No it's not that

ADIEL. What is it then

CHRIS. You can't call them.

ADIEL. We need a grown-up, Christina. That child needs help.

CHRIS. That child tried to kill me.

ADIEL. He was only asking for help. He—

CHRIS. He tried to kill me.

ADIEL. He is a rebel soldier, he is hurt. He needs bandage, doctor, do you understand Christina, if we do not wake up your parents that boy might die while we watch.

CHRIS. We can't.

ADIEL. I will not argue about this

CHRIS. No we seriously can't, they won't wake up. They won't wake up, Adiel, I—

I drugged them.

ADIEL. What?

CHRIS. Sleeping pills. In the tea, not very much just, two more than what they usually take,

ADIEL. You did what?!

CHRIS. I needed the car keys. He sleeps with them Velcro-ed in his pockets, I didn't know how else to

ADIEL. Every time? Every time we met, you were poisoning our pastor?

CHRIS. It's not poison! And of course not every time, just tonight, I needed the keys, time to pack and—

Look, I think there's a first aid kit in the office,

ADIEL. Pack?

CHRIS. We have to leave tonight. I have everything we need here, in this bag,

I meant to tell you as soon as—but you were so cute and happy and the vows and song, I didn't want to ruin, I wanted to get through the—

ADIEL. What are you saying?

CHRIS. Escape.

ADIEL. Escape.

CHRIS. We have to escape. This this place, this prison of

ADIEL. We are in a church Chris.

CHRIS. I mean metaphorically.

ADIEL. So, escape metaphorically?

CHRIS. No that part is real. The prison is metaphor, the escape is real.

ADIEL. —you are muddling my brain, there's a boy bleeding over here,

CHRIS. We'll fix it. We can fix it, we'll find the first aid kit, fix the guy who tried to kill me, then we'll get in the car drive to the check point

ADIEL. Get in the car and drive to the— you can hardly find the way to the bus stop, how

CHRIS. We'll figure it out!

ADIEL. Why?!

CHRIS. They know. My parents. They know.

ADIEL. About—

CHRIS. Us.

ADIEL. Ha.

CHRIS. Yep.

ADIEL. How?

CHRIS. The rings. I had our names written on the inside, as a surprise for you,
She asked about—so I told.

ADIEL. And?

CHRIS. They didn't.

ADIEL. Of course not! Why did you / do this, this this—

CHRIS. It's not safe, not safe here anymore, I couldn't just / leave, didn't know if

ADIEL. without even one word / to me, did you,

CHRIS. I thought they might take you too, if I, for us, oh come / on, Adiel,

ADIEL. My auntie is going to have me killed. Killed, Christina, did you even think about what it means to me if the people here find out do you know what that means for me?

CHRIS. It won't mean anything, because we are going to live in Tunisia.

ADIEL. Tunisia?

CHRIS. We'll patch up the kid, pack up the car, and drive past the checkpoint, you can hide in the trunk till we get to the border

ADIEL. You, are the missionary pastor's daughter!

Missionary pastors' daughters do not do this way, poison their parents and then run away to

CHRIS. They're leaving. Moving boxes, plane tickets, Really Leaving Adiel. With me.

I had to tell them, they are these people who are supposed to love me the most in the world

I thought maybe they would, understand, thought they'd—

But it went wrong, okay, it just went wrong and

ADIEL. So we must go to Tunisia?

CHRIS. Adiel if we are gonna do this, each other is all we're gonna have left, we have to put everything on the line. I mean EVERYTHING.

I have to put my God on the altar, you have to put your country on the altar, and say, none of these things matter more to us than each other, each other is our everything, for each other we are willing to burn them destroy them / to to to give them up

ADIEL. Chris you are not making any sense,

CHRIS. Whatever "them" is for either of us. You know that game, that game where they ask you, if you were stranded on an island, and you get to take just the one thing, what would you take? Except it's not a game, we Are stranded on an island, we are all stranded on an island on our own, and we get to choose one thing just the one thing that we will carry with us always. My parents chose God your parents chose country and look what happened to them!

Mine are forced to box up their house and dreams in a weekend, yours are dead.

I can't do that, I can't be stranded on an island on my own,

I Choose You. But it only works if you choose me too.

ADIEL. So you poisoned them?

CHRIS. Adiel!

ADIEL. This is too much Chris.

CHRIS. They were making me leave you.

ADIEL. We had a plan, we were getting married

CHRIS. That's not a real plan! What's the point of getting married when I'm eight thousand miles away

> (PIKA *comes to, finds his bearing, discovers bondage,*
> *Frantic, he tries to grab pocket knife to undo bondage,*
> *Girls lunge away from him.*)

CHRIS. Get in, get in, back of the,

PIKA. Let me go.

ADIEL. We are here to help.

CHRIS. Adiel!

PIKA. You tied me up.

ADIEL. You were being difficult at first. Look. Medicine. For you.

PIKA. Stay there. Let me see inside the box first.

ADIEL. See, just bandages and ice packs.

CHRIS. I say we go inside the office and lock the door.

ADIEL. You do that if you want to.

PIKA. They cut off my ear.

ADIEL. Yes, I know.

CHRIS. Adiel this is not safe.

ADIEL. You are bleeding. We can help you stop the blood. Can I come closer? We can help you.

> (PIKA *lowers the blade.*)

Can you put that down please?

> (PIKA *puts the blade down. [Close, tho.]*)

Thank you. I am Adiel. What is your name?

PIKA. Pika.

ADIEL. Okay Pika, let us sit you up, can you lean your head this way, good. You must not lie down, okay?

> (ADIEL *unties him.*)

CHRIS. Adiel what are you insane?

ADIEL. You poison your parents and I am insane?

CHRIS. This is a bad idea. Worse than my Tunisia idea, in fact, we won't have to go to Tunisia, because we will be dead anyway.

ADIEL. Come here.

CHRIS. Dead!

ADIEL. Chris I need your help, come here.

CHRIS. Dead.

ADIEL. Stop saying dead and keep this rag on his head. You must apply pressure, we cannot do anything until he stops bleeding. We cannot go to Tunisia until he stops bleeding.

> (CHRIS *reluctantly goes to* ADIEL *and the boy.*
> *Takes over the rags.*)

CHRIS. Oh god oh Jesus this is oh wow

ADIEL. You can put more pressure, you must be firm.

CHRIS. How do you know all this.

ADIEL. In my country, you have to learn to do more than just make pretty things.

CHRIS. That's why I'm saying, we should go to Tunisia. Where are you going!

ADIEL. To get water!

CHRIS. Come back here. Come back here! Adiel, get back here right—

> (*She's gone.*
> *Silence.*)

Let's just, get this…

> (CHRIS *pushes the blade away kinda sorta subtly,*
> PIKA *is rigid.*)

No, I'm not gonna, I just wanted to,

> (*The blade is out of easy reach.*)

I'm Chris.

PIKA. Yes.

CHRIS. What happened? Your *[gestures, ear]*, I mean you don't have to say if you don't want to—

PIKA. I tried to run away and then he catch me and then I run away again.

CHRIS. Does it hurt?
Do you want something? Lemonade?
Or, Oreo?

> (PIKA *stares at the Oreo for a bit before taking it.*
> *He eats the Oreo in silence.*)

PIKA. There is a hole in the roof.

CHRIS. Yep.

PIKA. What happened?

CHRIS. Don't know. We woke up one morning and there was this dead bird on the pews, and a hole in the roof above it. I like it, kinda like a skylight. Lets the breeze in, and you can see the stars in the night,

> (ADIEL's *back with a bucket of water.*)

ADIEL. How are we doing?

CHRIS. Great.

> (*She checks beneath the rag.*)

ADIEL. Little bit longer.

> (ADIEL *preps the bandages, alcohol swabs.*)

PIKA. I like it too. The people in this church can pray, see God directly, and pray.

ADIEL. Hm?

CHRIS. The hole. He likes the hole in our roof.

ADIEL. Do you like to pray?

PIKA. The Commander, he makes us pray very very much. In the morning, in the night, the other children, they are not so committed. I am committed. But I want to look at the sky when I am talking to God. Not to close my eyes, or bow my head like the Commander wants.

CHRIS. What do you pray about?

ADIEL. You can let go now.

> (CHRIS *lets go.* ADIEL *wets the rag, cleans the clots of blood around his lobbed off ear.*)

PIKA. My soul.

CHRIS. Your soul?

PIKA. I pray for my soul. I have done many bad things.

ADIEL. Now this will hurt a little, hold on to Chris if you want to.

> (*He does.*
> *Alcohol swabs. Dab dab, while blowing gently,*
> *Wince wince.*)

Good boy, almost finished. Good boy.

PIKA. I am not a good boy.

ADIEL. No? Chris can you help me cut this tape.

CHRIS. Yeah. Of course.

PIKA. In the bush, I dream, my soul is shrinking, like a little raisin, tiny like one rain, and it disappears away into the ocean. God does not hear me in this ocean. I do not hear Him.

ADIEL. Well you are not in the bush, you are not in the ocean, you are here with us, in our church. And He is very happy you are here, Pika.

PIKA. No. I am lost. I am surrounded by bad souls and I cannot breathe cannot remember who I am and now I am also bad soul. I am a very bad soul and cannot remember how to pray I cannot remember His voice I cannot remember how to talk to him. I am a terrible bad soul and so He has forgotten about me. He has forgotten.

> (PIKA *cries, and cries,*
> *Cries like a thirteen-year-old boy cries when he is very scared.*
> *He cries, and cries.*)

CHRIS. Pika how old are you?

PIKA. Thirteen.

CHRIS. Okay, so when I was a kid, even younger than you, I had this thing about a piano. Obsession.

One day, my dad's like, Chris, I got a surprise for you, I'm like, IT'S A PIANO he reaches behind and gives me, well,

he's cut out a cereal box, and built a small piano out of the cardboard.

he plays, singing the notes he's playing, like,

"doon doon doon doon doon doon doon doon"

what do I do? I snatch it, tear it all up.

Soon as I did it I knew I did something bad, because the look on his face was—

And I watch him pick up the pieces, go to his office, close the door.

I'm thinking, he's gone. He hates me. He'll forget me and find another daughter in my place,

Finally I can't take it any more so I go knock on his door, crying Daddy I'm sorry

Door opens, and you know what I see? The piano.

He's been in there this whole time, putting the piano back together.

He goes, "doon doon doon doon doon doon doon," and while I'm crying snot and tears, he lifts me onto his lap, says, "Chris, this is all we have, for now. It's small and fragile, so easy to break.

but look, I fixed it.

Every time we break something, it's okay, long as we fix it. And I did. So it's okay."

>   (*The boy has stopped crying.*)

PIKA. That is the most bad thing that you did?

CHRIS. Ha. No. I wish.

PIKA. I do not know how to fix my soul.

CHRIS. Maybe someone else is fixing it, you just can't see yet.

>   (CHRIS *finds a blanket or throw, wraps around the boy*
>   ADIEL *activates an ice pack and places it on his wound.*)

ADIEL. Here, this is cold, press it to your bandages, yes like that. The blood is not completely stopped, so you must not lie down yet, alright?

PIKA. Thank you.

>   (ADIEL *waits for* PIKA *to settle, and then takes* CHRIS *aside.*)

ADIEL. If we go, you might never see your father again.

CHRIS. I know.

ADIEL. You might never be able to fix it, with either of them.

CHRIS. I know.

ADIEL. Once we leave, we cannot return. We cannot undo what we are about to do. Do you understand this?

CHRIS. Adiel, once I get on that plane with them I cannot come back.

ADIEL. Okay.

CHRIS. !

ADIEL. Not Tunisia. We can go down to the city. It will be easy for us to find something to do in the city. Much easier than me trying to cross the borders without a passport.

CHRIS. Great. Yes. Okay.

ADIEL. First I must go home.

CHRIS. What? No.

ADIEL. I cannot just leave,

CHRIS. I don't think it's safe to be outside right now,

ADIEL. I have to let them know that I am leaving, that I am not, Taken,

CHRIS. We could leave them a note, here?

ADIEL. My auntie will be very heartbroken, she must be allowed to be so, in private.

CHRIS. I'll come with.

ADIEL. No.

CHRIS. I don't think this is a good idea Adiel.

ADIEL. I know this town. The shadows, the paths. I'll be fine.

(CHRIS *takes gun from where it was hidden.*)

CHRIS. Take this.

ADIEL. Chris—

CHRIS. Just, in case. Please be careful.

(ADIEL *leaves. With gun.*)

PIKA. You are leaving?

CHRIS. Yeah. Do you think she'll be okay?

PIKA. Why are you leaving? Is this a bad township?

CHRIS. No. No, it's pretty great, nice township— The men that you were running from, they've gone? You think?

PIKA. Maybe. Are you running away too?

CHRIS. Kind of.

PIKA. You do something bad?

CHRIS. No. Yes, maybe, I don't know, depends on what you decide is bad.

PIKA. I did something bad. I did many things bad. I do not want more bad things, so I run away. They catch me, but then I run away again. If they catch me again, I will be like meerkat

(PIKA *does an unexpected impression of a meerkat.*)

two big black holes at the side of the head.

CHRIS. Oh.

PIKA. You said you are going to the city.

CHRIS. Yes.

PIKA. Can I come with?

CHRIS. With us? Huh, wow, I don't know, Pika

PIKA. If I stay in this township, or alone somewhere else, they will find me. And then I become meerkat. Or maybe they kill me. Mostly they kill second-time finds.

CHRIS. Where's your home? Wouldn't it be better to go home?

PIKA. I do not remember, I was taken when I was ten. Three years ago. Even if I do find my home again, my family will not want me because I am bad.

CHRIS. Look, that's tough, but

PIKA. If I am with other people who are family, they cannot make advance.

CHRIS. We aren't your family.

PIKA. I can help with many things. I am trained for battle I can steal foods or climb over walls and trees I can defend you and your friend Adiel. I can do many many things. If you are worried about my bad soul, I promise you I will fix it.

CHRIS. How do you fix a bad soul?
I mean, it's not about your soul, good or bad, it's just, we don't know each other, we can't just start living together. Maybe if you stay here, talk to my dad in the morning, he might help you out, but maybe not, our pastor won't be in such a soul-fixing mood after his only child runs away.

PIKA. Your dad is the pastor?

CHRIS. Yup.

PIKA. Why are you running away? All your problems can be solved here.

CHRIS. Yeah, no. Look, I don't know how God or pastors do it, but I know how the real world does it.

PIKA. Do what?

CHRIS. Fix your soul.

PIKA. The real world has powers to fix the soul?

CHRIS. Sure.

PIKA. Who is the real world?

CHRIS. You know, countries, governments, people. In South Africa, they had a truth and reconciliation committee, they made it international, everyone could tap in on the hearings. It was super successful and nearly everyone's souls were fixed. The president won the Nobel Peace Prize for it.

PIKA. How is it done? Do you know how to do it?

CHRIS. Sure. It's not that hard. It's just some people listening to other people after a time of, bad things, and then, for the criminals—deciding whether or not to forgive, for the victims—deciding how to rehabilitate, restore, make better. They also decided who were the criminals and who were the victims.

PIKA. Who has the power to decide?

CHRIS. The people.

PIKA. There is just two of us.

CHRIS. So I will be the people. And we can put your hearing on tape, and if we find more people, they can weigh in.

PIKA. I don't understand why you have the power.

CHRIS. Me neither, but it seemed to have worked for them, it's worth a shot? I mean, I am the pastor's kid so maybe I can gather forces from the real world and the God world.

PIKA. I did many bad things.

CHRIS. Here, put your right hand on this Bible.

PIKA. More bad than breaking a piano.

CHRIS. Come on, can't hurt to try?

> (*He does.*
> CHRIS *hits rec.*)

Do you, Pika the ex-soldier, solemnly swear to tell the whole truth and nothing but the truth so help you God.

PIKA. Okay.

CHRIS. It is January 1st, year 2000, we are gathered here today for the public hearing of ex-soldier Pika, who has applied for absolution from the bad things of his past. My name is Christina Jennifer Englewood and I will be representing the people. Pika, tell us what you have done.

PIKA. Everything?

CHRIS. Everything.

PIKA. I cannot remember everything. It is very very long list.

CHRIS. Then pick one of the worst.

PIKA. I do not want to tell. You would not like me. You would not want to take me with you.

CHRIS. Pika we're doing this so we might be able to.

PIKA. Okay.

CHRIS. Go on.

PIKA. There was a man, he was a soldier of the army too. He was high ranks, he ate with the Commander but he was discovered, of helping girls escape the army. The man was tied up to a tree. The Commander called some names, and each soldier whose name was called must come and cut a piece of the man off with the machete while the man was still alive. When My name was called, there was not very much left to cut off so the Commander order me to cut off the head. I did. It was not easy because I was still new and did not have strength with machete. And then after I cut off the head the Commander order me to throw the head in the air and catch it three times, like this, like this, like this. And then kick it like a soccer ball like this. Then we sing the song, *Polo polo yesu larahe, Yesu lara woko ki i bal ayee mi tiyu tic palala oo wa ito.* His head roll on to the road, that is where we left it.

CHRIS. Wow.

PIKA. Do you hate me now?

CHRIS. No.

PIKA. Do you think it worked?

CHRIS. How do you feel?

PIKA. Terrible.

CHRIS. It is the decision of the people to grant absolution to ex-soldier Pika. May your soul find peace in this court's ruling. How about now?

PIKA. A little better. Does that mean I can come with you?

(CHRIS *gets close to the mic on the tape recorder.*)

CHRIS. Yes.

PIKA. Yes?!!

CHRIS. We have to talk to Adiel, but, she's the easy one.

(CHRIS *takes out cassette and presents it to* PIKA.)

PIKA. Thank you. Thank you.

(*Hugs.*)

CHRIS. Yay family!

(CHRIS *blows on her blower: Yes!*
PIKA *grabs the blower and flings it away.*)

PIKA. What is that!

CHRIS. I'm sorry,

PIKA. They will come here. Why did you do that! / They will come here.

CHRIS. Sorry I wasn't— It's been a while, your people have probably left. Adiel went out on her own, there's no way she would've gone outside if she thought they were still

(*Someone rattles the door.*)

That's Adi—

(PIKA *yanks her down.*
Finger to his lips, and creeps along towards the window, takes a peek.
He sees.)

CHRIS. Who—

(PIKA's *frightened eyes shut her up.*
They look for a place to hide,
More sounds, rattle door,
CHRIS *gestures up there!*
They climb up onto the roof.
Door is knocked in.
A SOLDIER *enters.*)

SOLDIER. Pika…

(SOLDIER *looks around.*)

Pika…?

(SOLDIER *notices the bloody rags, water.*)

Pika. You know there is nowhere to go. Nobody else wants you. Come now. Let us go home.

Nobody needs to know about our adventure tonight, it'll be our little secret, eh?

(*Hurried footsteps come closer.*)

CHRIS. Adiel!

(PIKA *shushes her, holds her back, shakes his head.*
ADIEL *runs in through the broken doorway.*
She stops dead in her tracks when she sees the SOLDIER.)

SOLDIER. Hello.

ADIEL. If you were looking for shelter, there was no need to break the door. The house of our Lord is always open.

SOLDIER. This one was closed and locked.

(SOLDIER *holds up the bloody rag.*)

I am looking for a lost soldier. I think he is here?

ADIEL. I don't know. I hope you find what you are looking for.

(SOLDIER *blocks her path.*)

I was simply passing by and I saw the broken door.

SOLDIER. I see.

ADIEL. Good night.

SOLDIER. Where are you going so late in the night?

ADIEL. Just out for a walk.

SOLDIER. With a travel bag?

ADIEL. Yes.

SOLDIER. Running away, like my lost soldier? Or even With my lost soldier?

ADIEL. Just out for a walk.

SOLDIER. I see. We are going to make this a game.

(SOLDIER *takes out a weapon, probably a machete.*)

CHRIS. Fuck, no,

PIKA. Shh!

SOLDIER. I do not like games.

(PIKA *starts to climb down the side of the wall—outside.*)

CHRIS. What are you doing!

(PIKA *shushes her violently.*)

SOLDIER. I ask again. I am looking for a lost soldier.

ADIEL. I think I am looking at one.

SOLDIER. You think you are? How old are you?

ADIEL. Twenty. Five.

SOLDIER. Are you lying?

ADIEL. No.

SOLDIER. That is unfortunate. If you were younger I could take you with me. Now I have to kill you.
It's a joke.

(PIKA *appears in the window or doorway, so that* ADIEL *spots him. He gestures: roof.*)

SOLDIER. I don't like to kill beautiful girls. If I can help it.
So last chance. Where is Pika.

(CHRIS *starts climbing down the way* PIKA *went.*
A slip, CHRIS *makes a sound.*
SOLDIER *hears, turns towards the sound with his machete—*)

ADIEL. He left.

SOLDIER. What?

ADIEL. I saw him outside the window just a few moments ago.

(SOLDIER *starts to leave*
PIKA *leaps into the shadows.*)

ADIEL. Let him go. He is poisoned. Broken. He does not care about this country.
I do. Let me come with you.

SOLDIER. You want to come with me?

ADIEL. I want to help, take care of you.

SOLDIER. You want to take care of me?

ADIEL. Yes.

(PIKA *climbs back up to the roof.*)

SOLDIER. Whoever has taught you how to lie, has done a very good job.

ADIEL. Or maybe I am not lying.

>   (ADIEL *undoes his buckle*
>   PIKA *re-appears to* CHRIS.)

PIKA. Psst. Psst!

>   (*He has a rock. She helps.*)

SOLDIER. You are a strange little girl.

ADIEL. Is it so strange to be attracted to a powerful man

SOLDIER. You are attracted to me?

ADIEL. Yes.

>   (*Her hands in his pants,*
>   SOLDIER'*s hands slide where she has hidden the gun.*)

No. Not yet. Down there.

SOLDIER. Giving orders already

>   (SOLDIER *finds the gun on* ADIEL.)

What is—

Ha.

Good game soldier.

ADIEL. It's not mine. I forgot it was even there / I promise you,

SOLDIER. Were you going to shoot me?

ADIEL. No no of course not

>   (*Sudden movement,*
>   SOLDIER *leaps towards* ADIEL,
>   PIKA *falls on top of the man with the rock aimed for his head.*)

PIKA. AAAAAAAAAAH!

>   (*Bam.*)

SOLDIER. Wha— What is, you—

>   (PIKA *bashes in the skull of the soldier, repeatedly.*
>   *Bambam bambam bambambambam—*
>   *Stands back.*
>   *Is he dead?*
>   *Absolute Stillness.*
>   CHRIS *is the first to move [on the roof]*
>   ADIEL *and* PIKA *start.*)

CHRIS. It's me, just me. Chris.

ADIEL. Chris.

CHRIS. I'm so sorry. I'm so sorry. Imsosorrysosorry

ADIEL. I thought you were, / I didn't know,

CHRIS. I wanted to but / I couldn't,

ADIEL. Pika?

PIKA. I am okay.

ADIEL. I thought you were, I didn't know what / you were, where,

CHRIS. You were so brave, so brave, I'm so / sorry Adiel I didn't know what to, Pika, and

> (CHRIS *embraces* ADIEL.)

ADIEL. It's okay, I understand. Everything's alright, it's alright. Shh…

> (CHRIS *kisses* ADIEL *like life and death.*)

PIKA. What are you doing.

ADIEL. Pika.

PIKA. What were you, you were, you were doing like a man and his wife.

CHRIS. She Is my wife.

ADIEL. Chris don't—

PIKA. That is a sin and abomination and evil in the sight of God. God has saved your life tonight, God has saved three of our lives tonight and in his house you will make sin, dirty in sin

ADIEL. Pika,

PIKA. Do not touch me you are a filthy sinner dirty sinner abomination.

> (PIKA *grabs a gun.*)

ADIEL. Pika that is not what God wants

> (*Bang.*)

PIKA. You do not know what God wants.

> (ADIEL *falls.*)

CHRIS. No.

No no no no no

What did you do. What is, What was— What's going on I don't,

Adiel look at me, hey, look, up here, come on Adiel.

Adiel! Adiel please look at me please please look at me Adiel

> (PIKA *gets closer to* ADIEL.)

Don't you fucking dare.

> (CHRIS *gets gun.*)

PIKA. I can help, let me

> (*Bang. She missed.*)

Chris. Please I

> (*Bang. She missed.*
> *Bang bang bang Bang bang bang Bang bang bang Bang bang bang.*
> PIKA *has run out during the bangs.*
> CHRIS *still shoots, without ammo.*

Bang bang bang click click click click
CHRIS *alone with* ADIEL *in the church.*
PIKA *alone with himself, somewhere else.*)

PIKA.
Polo polo yesu larahe
Yesu lara woko ki i bal ayee mi tiyu tic palala oo wa ito[**]
Polo polo yesu larahe
Yesu lara woko ki i bal ayee mi tiyu tic palala oo wa ito
Polo polo yesu larahe
Yesu lara woko ki i bal ayee mi tiyu tic palala oo wa ito

(*A very angry sad battle cry.*
Whose?)

End of Part I

[**] Heaven Heaven Jesus save us, Jesus saved us from sinning I have accepted to work
with you till death

PART II

The ensemble minus CHRIS

A single tentative voice, gradually grows into more sound, more joy

ALL BUT CHRIS.

Polo polo yesu larahe

Yesu lara woko ki i bal ayee mi tiyu tic palala oo wa ito

Polo polo yesu larahe

Yesu lara woko ki i bal ayee mi tiyu tic palala oo wa ito

Polo polo yesu larahe

Yesu lara woko ki i bal ayee mi tiyu tic palala oo wa ito

> (*Day.*
> *The church is the same church, only cleaned-up, moderned-up church.*
> *The church is beautiful; a lot of it has changed, but it somehow feels the same.*
> *The hole in the roof is now replaced with a skylight.*
> *The church is decorated with wild flowers*
> *And somewhere, a tea set. The tea in the pot has gone cold.*)

PAUL. "Everybody knows, in this story, the traveler is met with some ill fate. He is beaten, robbed, and then left half dead along the road. He is lying in the ditch bleeding to his death. Not long before first the priest, somebody like me, he passes by, sees the man in pain! Will he save him? No. He takes off. Second the Levite, somebody like our deacon Abuu, he passes by and sees the man in pain! Will he save him? No he is going off as well. Third the Samaritan, somebody like the political criminal, somebody that we all hate all together, somebody we believe is a bad man, he passes by. And boom, he of course, helps the dying traveler.

And we all think about this little story, that it is a teaching about kindness. About moral and ethical responsibility. About being nice. But, really? Is Jesus spending all this creative energy to tell us to be nice? Come on now, we know, we know we must be nice. Not just those of faith, but everybody knows this, if you are a person, you know that it is a good thing to try and be nice to another person, especially if that person is naked and bleeding at the side of the road. To understand what Jesus is really talking about, we must understand that this story is an answer to a question asked by some scholar in the crowd. The scholar asks the question, who is this "neighbor" that we must love. In fact, what is love?

Is love a feeling? A sensual pull toward one certain human being?

A little chemical released into our bodies that drains the brain of oxygen, and pumps the heart like the phone on vibration, so that all of your blood flows, races through all the veins in your body, makes you think about that person only, is that love? If that is love, I do not know if my wife will appreciate Jesus asking me to love all my neighbors so much."

(*He laughs at his joke.*
RUTH *has entered at some point.*)

That is a good joke. Let me write this one down.

RUTH. I don't get the joke.

PAUL. Ruth!

RUTH. Why am I in your sermon as a joke?

PAUL. What happened? Do you know what time it is?

RUTH. Ai yai, you know, I met somebody on the street, pastor—

PAUL. You met somebody on the street is why you are so late for our date?

RUTH. A date? African husbands do not date their African wives.

PAUL. This African husband does. Who did you meet?

RUTH. What is this! Tea? You made tea! And flowers. This man has stolen all the flowers of Africa to put them in our church.

PAUL. The aunties of the congregation brought them over for our celebration. I just bunched them artfully and placed them around the church. For our tea.

RUTH. You are very proud of your tea.

PAUL. And my flowers.

RUTH. So many flowers.

PAUL. I was inspired.

RUTH. Yes?

PAUL. Yes, by a beautiful lady with the regretful habit of forgetting the time on her wedding anniversary.

RUTH. It is only our second one. I have to do it more then three times for it to be a habit.

PAUL. So next year it will be a habit.

RUTH. Ah, already you are giving up on me?

PAUL. Never. Pastor is not allowed to give up on members of his church. Not even his wife.
Come. Sit. Let us have some very old very lukewarm tea.

    (*They sit. He pours the tea in each cup.*)

RUTH. Thank you.

PAUL. Okay so you sit there, and I will—

RUTH. Where are you going?

PAUL. I am going to give you my wedding anniversary gift.

RUTH. What? Pastor, we agreed we are not giving gifts this year.

PAUL. I know, but I had a very good idea for a gift. Here is your Bible.

    (*He goes to the pulpit.*)

Now let us turn to the Gospel of Luke chapter ten verses twenty-five to thirty-seven.

RUTH. Pastor what are you doing?

PAUL. I am giving you a sermon.

RUTH. Your anniversary gift is a sermon?

PAUL. Yes.

RUTH. Your very good idea of a gift is to make me sit still and listen to your practicing your sermon.

PAUL. No. I am delivering the sermon. For you. And then, tomorrow morning, I shall do a rerun for the rest of the congregation so you can show off your very romantic pastor husband.

RUTH. Is this the sermon where I am a joke?

PAUL. You are not a joke, you are referred to as a person who— ag it is funny in context.

RUTH. And this funny romantic sermon, is how long?

PAUL. I don't know, about thirty, forty, or fifty minutes?

RUTH. Fifty minutes?!

PAUL. I am telling you Ruth, when God gave me the idea for the sermon I knew in my heart it is a love letter directly to you. By the time I am done you will not remember how long it was, you will be so moved that you will ask me to marry you again or leave me to be a nun for Jesus, one of the two.

RUTH. Every sermon you prepare makes me want to leave you for Jesus Pastor, as you practice on me, every Saturday. But I have this one problem, you see, I do not want your beautiful sermon to be interrupted, and, this person that I met on the street, he is a member of this church and so I invited him to our tea.

PAUL. Oh. Why?

RUTH. Because he is leaving this township tonight and so I said he must come to the church to receive your blessing before he goes.

PAUL. On our anniversary day? Who is this?

RUTH. Remember you do not give up on any member of the church.

PAUL. Who is this.

RUTH. I met Francis

PAUL. Francis.

RUTH. You do not give up on any / member—

PAUL. No.

RUTH. You / just said so yourself

PAUL. Francis? Ruth you cannot be serious Francis is no member of this church?

RUTH. He was one of the first people of this township to call you pastor, how is he not a member of your church?

PAUL. He is leaving? That is a good idea.

RUTH. Good idea? He is being chased out of his own hometown. Thin as a stick, bruises everywhere and he has bandages on his wrists,

PAUL. He has what? Ag the stupidness of this boy.

RUTH. I gave him a hug and he just started crying. For a whole hour he just held my hand and cried. Pastor we must help him. He needs your guidance.

PAUL. I gave my guidance. He rejected it.

RUTH. He does not follow your orders one time and we must all abandon the man?

PAUL. God's orders, not mine—

RUTH. We are His church not His military.

PAUL. Church, military, it does not matter, if we let that boy in here it will break this community. If I say yes to him, I am saying no to everybody else, Ruth. Did you see last month during the whole situation, our attendance was cut in half?

RUTH. If a man has hundred sheep and one of them wanders away, won't he leave the ninety-nine others on the hills and go out to search for the one that is lost?***

PAUL. In this township the ninety-nine others are lost too. We have only just begun to find them. I cannot risk the souls of this whole church for one stupid boy

RUTH. Then nobody else needs to know,

PAUL. It's not / about,

RUTH. just let us show him God has not forgotten him. Paul please. He said he didn't want to come unless he knew you said yes. I said I will text him.

PAUL. Ruth,

RUTH. I already texted him.

PAUL. Ai yai.

RUTH. This is my anniversary wish. And now I owe you two gifts. Anything you want.

PAUL. My wife is the pastor. I am just the pretty man with the deep loud voice.
Okay.

RUTH. Okay?!

PAUL. I will talk some sense into him and then make you fall in love with

***Excerpt from Matthew 18:12 (NLT).

me again with my super sermon.

RUTH. I am always falling in love with you again.

PAUL. Ah you just say that because you got your way.

(RUTH *gives him an awesome hug.*)

RUTH. Paul. I promise you. To this boy you are the miracle man from God. Thank you.

PAUL. Ha. I had my fair share of miracle people from God. Happy anniversary.

(CHRIS *is lingering at the door.*)

RUTH. Oh hello!

CHRIS. Sorry. I'm—

(CHRIS *starts to leave.*)

RUTH. No, no please stay.

CHRIS. No I was just,

PAUL. Hello!

CHRIS. Hi.

PAUL. Are you needing assistance?

CHRIS. Excuse me?

PAUL. You are looking like you are lost. What are you looking for?

CHRIS. Do you have to be looking for something to be lost?

PAUL. Generally yes, I think so.

RUTH. I have seen you before, yes?

CHRIS. Oh. I don't—

RUTH. You were here every day this week, at our church.

PAUL. Every day? I did not know! Hello I am the pastor of this church.

CHRIS. I'm not a creepy person, I was just looking. Around.

RUTH. I did not think you were a creepy person. I thought what is this beautiful *mzungu* lady doing here, and I was so very curious but you never came inside so I left you alone.

CHRIS. Thank you.

PAUL. Are you alright?

CHRIS. Hm?

PAUL. You are standing at the door like a child who has done something naughty,

would you like to come inside?

CHRIS. Um, yeah. Sure.

(CHRIS *takes one step in.*)

RUTH. Welcome to our church.

CHRIS. *Apwoyo matek.*

RUTH. You are very welcome!

PAUL. That is very good!

CHRIS. Ha, thanks. I know two things. Thank you and *Jal – le.*

RUTH. That is very very good!

PAUL. Those two phrases will take you far in this country.

CHRIS. That has been my experience.

RUTH. I am the pastor's wife, Ruth.

PAUL. And I am the pastor's wife's husband, Paul.

CHRIS. Christina. Hi.

PAUL. So what bring you to our township? Are you working with a NGO?

CHRIS. No I'm just visiting for a few days. I grew up here.

RUTH. Are you sure!****

CHRIS. Long ago, as a kid.

PAUL. You were here as a child?

CHRIS. My parents were, missionaries.

RUTH. Are you sure!? It was very difficult time for our country.

CHRIS. I think we left before it got really bad. But this was our church. Built it, brick for brick.

RUTH. What? This was your church? That is fantastic! Pastor this was her church!

PAUL. Yes! Wonderful wonderful.

CHRIS. I wondered if it would still be here, wasn't sure

RUTH. We are all still here. You built a very strong church.

CHRIS. The building, at least.

RUTH. Ha! I must ask you— There is this one, a little picture on the corner.

CHRIS. Little picture?

RUTH. Yes yes it is like a small banana with three circles inside, Please, come come!

> (*They find a little heart engraved into the corner stone.*)

CHRIS. That's, we did it. Three smiley faces, and our initials at the bottom of each face—me, my mom, my dad. And then I drew a heart around the three. I was eight, so it's a bit, not a heart but.
The first brick we laid.

RUTH. Ag! I made up so many stories about what this one could be!

**** This phrase is used interchangeably with "Really!" in the Ugandan dialect.

CHRIS. My dad had a thing about documenting.

He would've loved to see this.

He should've seen this.

It might've, helped.

RUTH. Our doors are always open whenever he would like to visit.

CHRIS. Oh he can't. He's dead. Last month. He died.

RUTH. Are you alright?

CHRIS. No, I'm [fine]

> (RUTH *gives her a very awesome hug.*
> CHRIS *steps away.*)

Oh, no. Please I don't,

We weren't that close, barely talked for like ten years, strangers, almost, really.

Actually, sorry, I'm just here to, it's a weird— actually, what I need to ask you

RUTH. Please, how can we help?

CHRIS. I have my dad, his ashes, he left it in his will that we bury him here,

PAUL. Here. Here at our church?

CHRIS. It's weird.

RUTH. Yes it is a little bit strange. That you would bury your dead in our church.

CHRIS. It's not like a coffin, he's in a tree seed. So it would be a seed grave. Not really a grave grave.

He was a weird guy

and he wanted to be a tree at this church.

RUTH. A tree.

CHRIS. This grows into a tree. Mahogany.

RUTH. Haw.

CHRIS. I think he thought, he might finally find some peace, if he came back. And I thought hey, okay I'll fly eight thousand miles to plant him in a ditch in Africa and maybe we'll have some kind of cozy posthumous father daughter moment closure all that kind of—

I'm just the proxy. You don't have to say yes.

RUTH. Of course we say yes

PAUL. Ah,

RUTH. It is a tree! I think that will be beautiful in the garden.

PAUL. Ruth we do not have a garden.

RUTH. So the first pastor of this church will be the very first resident of our new garden.

PAUL. I do not know if our African soil will be kind to your tree, but yes it would be an honor.

CHRIS. Oh god, Thank you.

RUTH. When do you want a burial? Ceremony?

CHRIS. Oh! No no. We did the funeral, everything, it's fine

PAUL. So, you want for us to plant the box with your father in it?

CHRIS. Unless you want me to dig the hole, I could dig the hole,

RUTH. Don't worry about that one. You must be so tired. Here, sit down. Would you like some tea?

PAUL. Ruth didn't you say we had another guest soon.

RUTH. Oh he will be a few minutes. We can have some tea and a chat with Christina. She has come such a long way. I will bring more cups. And we should brew more tea.

CHRIS. Actually I'm okay, I just wanted to

RUTH. We will take care of you, it is no worry. The house is just over there. But of course you know that!

> (RUTH *leaves.*
> *Quiet.*)

CHRIS. Thank you, for the *[gestures: tree seed]*

PAUL. Of course. How did he pass?

CHRIS. Fatigue. Didn't know people could die of fatigue. He just, got tired of living.

PAUL. He must have loved this church very much.

CHRIS. He did.
What happened to your *[gesture: ear]*

PAUL. It went missing.

CHRIS. Oh.

PAUL. Every other person in this country has something or other missing from their face.

CHRIS. Of course. I'm sorry. I didn't mean to pry. Sorry.

PAUL. I think I will go help my wife with the tea. Sometimes she forgets to turn the stove off et cetera.

> (PAUL *leaves.*
> CHRIS *is alone.*
> *The space. The Skylight. The Space.*)

RUTH. I had no idea today would turn into such a party!

> (RUTH *and* PAUL *enter.*)

PAUL. Yes, unfortunately we have a guest coming, in a few minutes

RUTH. Pastor what is that.

CHRIS. Oh that's fine, I don't have to stay

RUTH. Stay! Stay! Don't mind our pastor, Chris. He likes to joke. It is only funny in context. Come sit down, both of you, we are floating around like dust clumps. Chris tell me everything, / there are so many rumors of this church

CHRIS. I don't remember much,
rumors?

RUTH. because of these rumors nobody would come! For the first three months our entire congregation was two people. And I was one of the two people.

PAUL. Ruth,

RUTH. And then Pastor visited every single home in this township. He went door to door, and still these people would not come. What were they saying, Pastor, somebody died in the church, on the day of the / millennium, killed herself or got herself killed

PAUL. The *Acholi* are superstitious people, they always are saying something happened

RUTH. Everybody has a different version of the story, ai yai how did your father deal with these people, eh?

CHRIS. I, don't know. He's dead so.
How did you guys end up here?

RUTH. This is the question I ask every day of myself! I am originally from the city but I was seduced by this terrible man. I had this big idea that I would help this country, Oh yes, I will march myself to the nearest trauma center, I will educate and help all these broken minds from their war troubles

PAUL. Let us stop boring our visitor / with the history, and

RUTH. Of course I very quickly understood I was a stupid girl with more fears then skills. I was so ready to quit and run away until this one came along. After all he has been through, he tries to teach me about Jesus, and get me to go to church with him, sing Jesus songs, but the big trap was this one, Chris, the he tells a story to me.

PAUL. Do you want to see more of the church Christina.

RUTH. After I tell my homerun story. When we were getting serious, and I am weighing the good things and bad things about this man— Chris you know the process I am talking about.

CHRIS. Of course.

RUTH. So I am thinking, mmm he is a little bit small, he is a little bit nerd, he is little bit no money and so on,

PAUL. Ruth do we have any ice, I am thirsty for some ice water

RUTH. Yes, in the kitchen. Anyway so I am on the seesaw a little bit and he knows this so he takes me to a beautiful lake, puts me on a boat like in the American movies yes? And he tells me this story.

PAUL. Ruth, don't—

RUTH. Na uh uh! Girl talk time. If you are embarrassed cover your ears while I show off my romantic pastor husband, eh?

Okay, so once upon a time there is this man, who loved his wife so so much, and one day the wife really really wanted a piano.

But the man, he was a poor man, so he could not buy a piano. So he collects scraps of cardboard from the market, and he makes a small piano, of the discarded boxes. And then he gives it to his wife. The wife is very very disappointed. So much that she will tear up the piano that he took so very long to make just for her. The wife leaves the house and he thought ah, there she goes, she will find a man who can give her a real piano. But the man cannot forget her. He cannot stop himself from fixing the broken piano. And every day he is playing this piano with his voice, "doon doon doon doon doon doon doon doon," praying for her return.

Finally the wife returns, very guilty. But to her great surprise she finds at the window, the piano, it is fixed. She cries and says I'm sorry, but he says, "my love it is okay. I fixed it."

"Ruth" this man says to me now, "We will break many things but I promise you, I will always always find a way to build it again, if only you can be brave enough to stay." Boom, Curtain fall, end of story thank you for playing ladies, Pika belongs to me.

CHRIS. I thought your name was Paul.

RUTH. It is. But I call him Pika, it is his African name.

PAUL. Ruth could you give us a moment alone?

RUTH. Alone?

PAUL. Please.

RUTH. Pastor, stop being so peculiar.

PAUL. Just, please, could you

RUTH. Chris, my husband is so strange sometimes, we will ignore Pika's

PAUL. My name is not Pika pleasepleasepleasepleaseplease will you Leave.

RUTH. …

PAUL. Please.

RUTH. I—

PAUL. Could you.

> (RUTH *leaves.*
> *Silence.*)

CHRIS. You look good.

PAUL. Thank you. You too.

> (*Silence.*)

CHRIS. I like what you did. With the church. The skylight.

PAUL. Mostly it was Ruth.

CHRIS. She's lovely.

(*Silence.*)

PAUL. Are you, married?

CHRIS. No.

PAUL. It is different in America, the time of marriage I think. Here we like to marry our woman earlier.

CHRIS. Is that a joke?

(*Silence.*)

PAUL. What do you want. Why are you here?

CHRIS. My dad died. He wanted,

PAUL. That is why you are here? The only reason to come all the way—

CHRIS. I don't have to explain anything, to you, of all people,

PAUL. If you have returned to revenge

CHRIS. Revenge?

PAUL. If you have returned so to to ruin / this church

CHRIS. Why would I want to ruin—

PAUL. —it won't work I have already told them everything.

CHRIS. Wow okay well That's bullshit.

PAUL. I have told them Everything.

CHRIS. Everything?

PAUL. Everything they need to know.

CHRIS. Your wife doesn't know very much.

PAUL. I have experienced many atrocities, they do not need to hear

CHRIS. about who died? On the millennium, emptying this church for the past decade and half?

PAUL. You left. You and your people left and I came back. You do not know how difficult for me it was to come back / to face this empty church

CHRIS. So why? Why? Why did you?

PAUL. I am good for this community. They / see hope,

CHRIS. It's sick! What you, the hole, up there, is it

PAUL. We needed / more light

CHRIS. —some kind of shrine? Some kind of— More Light?

PAUL. It is just a window on a roof

CHRIS. No it is not.

PAUL. I am trying to fix what is broken, the church, this township,
You break something, it is okay if you try to fix it, you said that to me,
we can fix everything, with God's help,

CHRIS. No you can't. No amount of windows on a roof can fix what you broke.

PAUL. But I will keep trying, we must keep trying, like your father did for you

CHRIS. Some guy duck-taped some paper together to shut his daughter up and then some years later he died, it's not some grand metaphor to build your new life on, forgetting the people you've fucked over

PAUL. Forget? For— Every night, hundred bleeding bodies, in my dreams / they come together

CHRIS. Please I don't need your dreams in my

PAUL. Yours, and Adiel's

CHRIS. Stop don't say her name please you / don't get to

PAUL. That is my night every night, Forget? I cannot forget. Do not talk of things you do not know, Chris, / you do not know my troubles, every night

CHRIS. I think I can talk about whatever the fuck I want why are you here at my church?

PAUL. Not your church my church it is my church You left!
God's church. It's God's church and God has forgiven me, that is the only way I got better
Not farms not people, but Grace, The only way how I am now a good man.

CHRIS. Well Good for God but you did not kill God You killed people and they can't forgive you because they are dead and Dead Can't Forgive.

PAUL. I came to this church hoping, at first,
I did not know if she had lived,

CHRIS. She didn't.

      (*Silence.*)

PAUL. Perhaps it was the wrong choice, sick, as you say.
But I had to come back, make it good again,
this is where, somebody was happy about me
you were happy about me even when you knew how bad I was

CHRIS. Happy? Were you there? Pika you are the only human on this earth I have aimed and shot / a loaded weapon

PAUL. You missed. Every shot. A whole round of bullets at point blank and every bullet missed.

CHRIS. because I was sixteen and didn't know how to shoot a gun.

PAUL. You missed because you did not want to kill me.

CHRIS. I Do want to. did, want to.

PAUL. You said yes to me.

CHRIS. What?

(PAUL *leaves, maybe to the office.*)

PAUL. you said family, you were happy so happy, you tried to help, remember, you wanted so much for my soul

CHRIS. What are you / talking about?

(*He returns, Tape recorder, from somewhere—*)

CHRIS. I never, What is that. What are you, why do you have that, this is, / that's not yours, It's not yours

PAUL. You were the first person to say yes to me. You said absolution,

CHRIS. No.

PAUL. —you said yes.

CHRIS. Okay, fine I said yes, and then you killed the one person that

PAUL. I have killed more than one people, you already knew this. How is it different than what you already said yes to? You are coming here to my church, with your father's ashes, because you are sad, / hurt, struggling

CHRIS. Back the fuck off about my father

PAUL. Struggling to bury what is dead, trying to make better what is hurt, we are doing the same thing

CHRIS. We are not doing the same thing

PAUL. Yes we are. But you, you are lost in your hurt, you treasure your hurt like it is the castle that makes you special. I am sorry for your suffering but I cannot let my people pay the price for your brokenness. Fight your battles on your own soil and let me fight mine here.

(*Silence.*)

CHRIS. I just want to plant my dead dad and leave, okay? I've wasted my entire adult life trying to leave, this church. I just want to leave.

PAUL. So. Leave.

(*Silence.*
FRANCIS *enters.*)

FRANCIS. Excuse me—Hello I am looking for the pastor, do you know where he is?

CHRIS. —

He's—

FRANCIS. wait I've seen you before?

CHRIS. What?

PAUL. Francis

FRANCIS. Pastor! This is, oh what is your name, Sarah. Melissa.

PAUL. Now / is not a good

FRANCIS. Jennifer?

CHRIS. Chris

FRANCIS. Like the Kardashian?

CHRIS. Um. No. Like short for Christina

FRANCIS. Christina! Of course! You were very close with my cousin, Adiel

PAUL. Francis you / must leave us

CHRIS. Francis

FRANCIS. You have not changed at all how are you / how is your family!
　　　(FRANCIS *gives her an awesome hug.*)

PAUL. Are you deaf boy, I said Go!

FRANCIS. Pastor.

RUTH. Francis, come.

PAUL. Ruth.

RUTH. Let us make ourselves some tea in the house

FRANCIS. But I thought, Ruth your message, you said

RUTH. Come, we talk more inside the / house while we wait

FRANCIS. But you did not invite me? Pastor? You do not want me here?

PAUL. What do you want me to say? You shout out your deeds all around the town, / deliberately go against my advice

FRANCIS. No Paul I did not tell anyone, / nobody was supposed to know.

PAUL. Nobody was supposed to know? God knows everything.

FRANCIS. I was not talking about God,

PAUL. Why are we not talking about God? Talk about God. Because it is Him you are hurting,

FRANCIS. I am sorry that it is hurting God, hurting so many people that I love,

PAUL. You are not sorry.

FRANCIS. What do you want me to do? I cannot help who I am.

PAUL. Then I cannot help your homo ways heading to hell, but I will not have that in my church.

CHRIS. You can't be serious.

PAUL. Christina, this is not your battle, stay out.

CHRIS. Not my—are you fucking kidding me?

RUTH. Christina, please, I think you must / come back later.

PAUL. Francis and I must get through this together, you have no place

CHRIS. You're doing to him what you did to me

PAUL. / That is different.

CHRIS. I think I have a place.
How is it different?

PAUL. I am different. I cannot let my personal guilt blind my judgment in the leadership of this / church, I

CHRIS. You killed my wife.

> (*Silence.*)

We saved your life and you killed her because I kissed my fucking wife.

RUTH. What?

FRANCIS. Wife? Paul? What / is this one. Ruth?

CHRIS. This is not that different, Pika.

PAUL. / My name is not Pika!

CHRIS. Nothing's changed, you're still a murderer and I am still stuck in that same shithole you've put me in.

PAUL. You put yourself there.

RUTH. Pastor what is she / talking about

PAUL. All the sins you have committed against the Lord,

CHRIS. My Sins?

PAUL. your decadence,

CHRIS. What is my sin, Pika. Patching up your face after you put a gun to my head? Letting you run after you shot a bullet into Adiel

PAUL. I do not cling / to my past with your enthusiasm

FRANCIS. Adiel?

RUTH. Who is / Adiel?

FRANCIS. No Adiel died here. She shot herself after killing a soldier, Paul and Ruth came only last year

CHRIS. What do you say every Sunday Pika, to This Community, Thou shalt not lie? Thou shalt not kill? Thou shalt not kill a person, return to the scene of the crime fourteen years later and damn their cousin to hell?

FRANCIS. You were here?

CHRIS. And when you're looking out at these people who trust you and love you and willingly lap up the bullcrap you're feeding them, do you feel Any Guilt? Shame?
or has the Grace of God taken care of that too.

RUTH. Pika. What are these people saying?

PAUL. Ruth please, take Francis, away, / Chris and I must

FRANCIS. You were the soldier.

CHRIS. Chris and I must what? What more / do you want with me?

RUTH. Come Francis we will talk to pastor after, / I promise, Francis

FRANCIS. You killed her. We all thought, but it was you? This whole time it was you?

PAUL. I am not perfect, I do not know everything, but every sin is washed clean if

CHRIS. What if I took a gun and blew out your wife's guts, think we could / clean that up too?

PAUL. Shut up about / my wife! Shut up!

RUTH. Okay Pika / look to me

CHRIS. If I murdered your wife?

PAUL. That is in the past

RUTH. It is /alright, I am here, see? Pika look to me.

PAUL. stop talking about the past

CHRIS. If it's in the past why are you here.

PAUL. I am trying to fix it!

CHRIS. You are kicking this man out onto the streets, to fix what you did to his cousin?

FRANCIS. How are you a pastor?

RUTH. Francis this is enough

FRANCIS. How is man like you a pastor at my church?

PAUL. I am no longer your pastor, man! I am no longer your— Get out. Get /out get

RUTH. Paul let us / go, we shall go for a walk, a nice

PAUL. I am no longer your pastor this is no longer your church

FRANCIS. And somehow you have the power to tell me, I am going to hell?

PAUL. I do not care where you go get out Get Out

FRANCIS. I trusted you. I gave you my secret. But you hated me.

RUTH. Francis. Leave.

FRANCIS. You hated me before you even knew me.

RUTH. Get out.

(FRANCIS *smashes a window.*)

What are you doing!

PAUL. Francis.

FRANCIS. No.

(FRANCIS *picks up a piece of glass.*)

I am not leaving. You want to save my church from my dirty dirty sins this
is how you will do it.

(FRANCIS *extends the glass towards* PAUL.)

PAUL. What are you doing man.

FRANCIS. Do it.

RUTH. Francis stop this stupidness

(FRANCIS *swings his weapon around to* RUTH.)

FRANCIS. Shut up stay / there.

PAUL. Ruth stay back!

FRANCIS. You know how to do it, Do it. I'm not the first homo you killed
in this church. You can't make me leave my home, everything I know and not
pay for it, you can't kick me out turn your eyes and wait for somebody else to
bash my head in, I am not going to wait for that, you do it. Do It.
Okay I'll do it. You watch.

(FRANCIS *presses the glass to his own throat.*)

RUTH. Francis!

CHRIS. Francis, There are better ways to fight this.

PAUL. This is not what God wants.

FRANCIS. I do not want your God anymore.

PAUL. You know that is not true.

FRANCIS. Do not tell me what I know. You are a liar. You are a joke.

(*He presses.*)

RUTH. Francis Look to me.

FRANCIS. This church is a joke.

RUTH. I was wrong.
I was wrong to ask you to leave.
Pastor is wrong to ask you to leave.
No more. We will do this to you no more.

FRANCIS. No more.

RUTH. I promise you.
We will work this problem out together
Give that to pastor.
Please, Francis.
Death is so final.
Right? You know this.

(*A breath.*
FRANCIS *gives the bloody glass piece to* PAUL.
RUTH *hits him*

Wherever she can however she can
slap slap slap.)

RUTH. Idiot! Stupid stupid boy, you stupid boy, don't you ever do that again, don't you ever even think about doing something like that again! Ever again / Do you understand? Stupid. Stupid stupid boy, I will kill you if you do that again, understand? Stupid idiot stupid

CHRIS. Hey hey, it's okay. It's okay, we're good, he's okay we're fine. Calm down, breathe, okay? Come, just take it easy. Everything's alright, it's alright. Shh…

(RUTH *hugs on* CHRIS *tightly,*
a replica of sixteen year old CHRIS' *embrace with* ADIEL *14 years ago.)*

PAUL. Get away from my wife!

CHRIS. —

RUTH. —

PAUL. Get away from my wife Get away from my wife

(PAUL *bolts towards them and shoves* CHRIS *away viciously.)*

Get away from my wife

(*Shove Shove.)*

I said get away from my wife!

(PAUL *grabs* CHRIS, *glass piece still in hand.)*

RUTH. Pika No!

(RUTH *gets in between* PAUL *and* CHRIS.)

No.

(*He stops.*
No one moves.
PAUL *steps back, glass piece still in hand.)*

PAUL. Everybody knows.
Everybody knows…

RUTH. Paul.

(*Like a memory exercise.)*

PAUL. Everybody knows, in this story, the traveler is met with some ill fate. First the priest sees the man in pain will he save him No. Second the Levite sees the man in pain will he save him No. Third the Samaritan, somebody that we all hate, somebody we believe is a bad man,
who is the bad man?
Start again. Everybody knows in this story, the soldier is met with some ill fate. First the
No, not a soldier, a traveler, he is a traveler

the man the Traveler is beaten, bled, and then left alone by the tree tied to
the tree there is no tree
Haha, pastor's brain is so sleepy today.

RUTH. Paul look to me.

      (RUTH *steps towards him but* PAUL *moves away.*)

PAUL. Everybody knows! There is no tree.
First
The Priest, the pastor, I am a pastor now. Everybody knows,
He passes by, sees the man in pain! Will he save him? How can he save him?
He is dead
He is not dead!
He is lying on the, where is he lying. Why is he lying.
LOVE.
drains the oxygen, pumps the heart, the blood flows, races through
spills on to her clothes on to this floor on to
no, LOVE. Love, is patient love is kind it does not,
Love is love is
The blood
of the tree

a gift.
to one who does not deserve.

      (PAUL *sees* CHRIS.)

Do you hate me now?

      (PAUL *places the glass piece in her hands.*)

You said yes You said You said You will fix
You are a joke. This church is a joke. Everything is still broken and You

RUTH. Paul. Come. Please.

      (PAUL *leaves the church.*
      Echo of Rain Falling
      Into…

      Very Early Morning.
      The sun is not yet up.
      RUTH *in the middle of the church.*
      Perhaps where we first found ADIEL.
      Perhaps she is praying.
      Perhaps she was listening to the tape recorder,
      Either way, that is what she holds in her hand, like a Bible or a rosary
      CHRIS *comes to the doorway, her carry-on in tow.*)

CHRIS. Hi.

RUTH. Christina.

CHRIS. How are you?

RUTH. —

CHRIS. Is Paul,

RUTH. He has not returned yet.

CHRIS. Oh.

RUTH. He will return.

CHRIS. I'm sorry.

RUTH. What can I do for you?

CHRIS. I just wanted to leave this with—

RUTH. I am very sorry Christina but I do not think we must do that for you. You must bury your dead where it affects You.

CHRIS. Oh, no, that wasn't what— I agree. It would be weird to know your dad is growing into a tree in someone else's backyard.

RUTH. I am sorry we cannot help.

CHRIS. No don't be. He can find peace in my backyard. When I have one. We'll be fine.

That's not why I'm here,

(*A cardboard piano.*)

Couldn't sleep, so I just, I'm not so good with crafts, but.

I'll just leave it here, gotta head out, to catch the bus, Francis is waiting at the,

RUTH. Francis?

CHRIS. Um, yeah. It's, we're on the same bus and, it'd be nice to catch up. So.

(CHRIS *turns to leave.*)

RUTH. He listened to this one. So much. He listened to it every month sometimes every day

I never did ask.

It is up to the wife to keep the secrets that our husbands try to keep from us.

A secret flies out to me, and I think must catch it,

I must be a part of his ribcages and hold them together.

I did not know my silence was suffocating him also.

He is not a bad man, Chris.

He is trying so very hard to be good.

CHRIS. He's lucky to have that. You.

RUTH. I am lucky to have him.

I wish you both safe travels.

CHRIS. Thank you.

Happy Anniversary.

(CHRIS *leaves.*
RUTH *alone, in church.*
RUTH *turns tape over.*
Rewind.
Hits play.)

TAPE. This is the wedding of Christina Jennifer Englewood and Adiel Nakalinzi. January 1st, Year 2000. I, Chris Blank, take thee, Adiel Nakalinzi, to be my wife, ugh, that's such dumb word.
To be my wife…

> (*Tape continues under*
> *as the four come together in hymn:*)

ALL.
Just as I am, without one plea,
But that Thy blood was shed for me,
And that Thou bidst me come to Thee,
O Lamb of God, I come, I come

Just as I am, though tossed about
With many a conflict, many a doubt,
Fightings and fears within, without,
O Lamb of God, I come, I come

Just as I am, of that free love
The breadth, length depth, and height to prove,
Here for a season, then above,
O Lamb of God, I come,

TAPE. With this ring I thee wed, with my body I thee worship, and with all my worldly goods I thee endow:
In the name of
In the name of the Father, and of the Son, and of the Holy Ghost. Amen.
Amen.

End of Play

TRUDY, CAROLYN, MARTHA, AND REGINA TRAVEL TO OUTER SPACE AND HAVE A PRETTY TERRIBLE TIME THERE
by James Kennedy

BIOGRAPHY

James Kennedy is a playwright, director, and composer living in New York City. His plays include *We, And One, The Listener, Boom Country,* and the musical *And Then He Painted the Sky.* He has received the Rod Parker Playwriting Fellowship, the Betsy Carpenter Playwriting Award, and was an inaugural recipient of the Science and Stage Collaborative Fellowship with Superhero Clubhouse. His work as a writer and director has been produced at Actors Theatre of Louisville / The Humana Festival of New American Plays, Williamstown Theatre Festival, and Playing for Others, and he has worked in new play development at The Lark Play Development Center, the Eugene O'Neill Theater Center, and ArtsEmerson: The World on Stage. He was a Directing Intern in Actors Theatre of Louisville's 2015–2016 season and he is currently an Associate Artist and program director with The Orchard Project. He holds a degree in theatre from Emerson College. For more information, visit www.jameshkennedy.com.

ACKNOWLEDGMENTS

Trudy, Carolyn, Martha, and Regina Travel to Outer Space and Have a Pretty Terrible Time There was produced at the Humana Festival of New American Plays in April 2016. It was directed by Jessica Fisch with the following cast:

TRUDY	Rachel Leslie
REGINA	Renata Friedman
CAROLYN	Shirine Babb
MARTHA	Brenda Withers

and the following production staff:

Scenic Designer	Justin Hagovsky
Costume Designer	Kristopher Castle
Lighting Designer	Dani Clifford
Sound Designer	Sam Kusnetz
Production Stage Manager	Paul Mills Holmes
Assistant Stage Manager	Jessica Kay Potter
Dramaturg	Jessica Reese
Properties Master	Mark Walston

CHARACTERS

TRUDY

CAROLYN

MARTHA

REGINA

and

PATRICE (whom we never meet)

All five are young astronauts.

TIME

Now.

PLACE

The control room of a sleek American spacecraft traveling through the outer reaches of the known galaxy.

Brenda Withers, Shirine Babb, Rachel Leslie, and Renata Friedman
in *Trudy, Carolyn, Martha, and Regina Travel to Outer Space
and Have a Pretty Terrible Time There*

40th Humana Festival of New American Plays
Actors Theatre of Louisville, 2016
Photo by Bill Brymer

Trudy, Carolyn, Martha, and Regina Travel to Outer Space and Have a Pretty Terrible Time There

Inside a spaceship in the most outer of all space.
The four astronauts sit in four chairs, strapped in.
There is a fifth chair that is empty.

It's incredibly boring in outer space.
I mean so fucking boring. Still, there is work to be done; buttons to be pushed,
switches to be flipped, knobs to be turned.

MARTHA *is asleep.*
Everyone else is looking out into the abyss, occasionally busying themselves with
astronaut tasks.

CAROLYN. What are your hobbies, Regina?

REGINA. I like to make soap. And candles.

CAROLYN. Really.

REGINA. My idea of a perfect day is staying inside, making soap, and watching documentaries about the KKK.

(TRUDY *and* CAROLYN *consider this.*)

CAROLYN. Wow. Huh. That's, uh…not something I think I would ever…*ever* do…to pass the time…or express myself creatively.

REGINA. Don't knock it til you try it.

CAROLYN. I guess.

REGINA. It's really powerful. And humanizing. I think it's important to remind ourselves of our capacity for evil. Those KKK members are so hateful…probably beyond repair. But they didn't come into the world that way, right? Something had to happen to make them that way, which I think is really a big metaphor for the demons inside all of us. And watching that footage while making soap…smelling lye, and vanilla extract…remembering how beautiful the planet earth is…giving myself a tool to cleanse away the grime of daily life…those days really do remind me of my place within it all. Ya know?

(TRUDY *and* CAROLYN *consider this. Simultaneously:*)

CAROLYN. That's deep.   **TRUDY.** What is wrong with you.

REGINA. Well, you think about this stuff too, right?

TRUDY. No.

CAROLYN. I *think* about…*things*…sure. But…the way you put that, was—

TRUDY. Really upsetting.

CAROLYN. Not *that* upsetting, but it was pretty—

TRUDY. I'm very upset right now.

REGINA. I thought we had reached a place where we could be really honest with each other and stuff.

TRUDY. No, Regina, we absolutely have not reached any sort of place where it would be appropriate to share that, in fact I cannot imagine any context at all any place ever where I would want to know any of that. Quite frankly I'm already very upset about the fact that I haven't sat on a real toilet in nineteen weeks nor have I worn a pair of sweatpants nor have I felt gravity nor have I eaten anything that wasn't freeze-dried nor have I punched a punching bag and also I have no idea how the Steelers are playing this season which is really difficult for me and now I have to picture you in your underwear and a pair of rubber gloves making bath salts and fetishizing the KKK. I am only a human woman, Regina, and I do not have the emotional capacity for all of this, nor does Carolyn.

REGINA. I appreciate your humanity, Trudy. Your emotional honesty is beautiful.

TRUDY. I would highly suggest that you stop speaking to me for an indefinite amount of time because, to let you in on a secret that actually isn't a secret except that you can't open your eyes to your reality: you, Regina, are right now in the lead to be the next one.

(REGINA *processes this information.*)

REGINA. Is this true, Carolyn?

CAROLYN. …I'm still on the fence about it…but you might want to give it a rest.

(MARTHA *makes a noise in her sleep.*)

CAROLYN. How is Martha still asleep.

REGINA. Some people can sleep anywhere.

CAROLYN. It's gotta be going on thirteen hours now.

REGINA. I think it's only been three or four.

TRUDY. No way.

REGINA. No, I'm sure of it, I keep checking my watch.

CAROLYN. I hate this.

TRUDY. We all hate this.

REGINA. I don't hate this.

TRUDY. Three out of four of us hate this.

REGINA. You can't speak for Martha.

TRUDY. Trust me, Martha hates this.

REGINA. Patrice didn't hate this. Patrice was having a great time.

TRUDY. Yeah, and look where she ended up. Not having such a great time anymore, which is her own fault, so if you do want to include Patrice in this, I would posit that in fact four out of five of us would do absolutely anything to be absolutely anywhere else right now.

(*Rest.*)

CAROLYN. I thought I would get used to the fact that time doesn't work up here, at least not in any real way…every hour looks exactly the same. I can't keep up, my body is so confused.

(MARTHA *makes another noise in her sleep.*)

REGINA. But still…yes, it's been somewhat of a…well, *challenging* adventure…I for one certainly thought there'd be more to…I don't know… *do.* But then all of those stars…it's been nineteen weeks and I'm still so overwhelmed.

TRUDY. So many freaking stars.

REGINA. They're so beautiful.

TRUDY. I hate myself.

REGINA. Think about it, though. We're the only four people in the entire universe with this view…the only four human beings who have ever seen this.

CAROLYN. Huh.

REGINA. That makes it worth it. Just, all of this *beauty*—

(MARTHA *makes a really ugly gross sleeping noise.* CAROLYN *considers her.*)

CAROLYN. How far would you go with Martha?

TRUDY. How *far*?

CAROLYN. Yeah. You know, like first base, second base…

REGINA. Oooooooh!

TRUDY. Absolutely not.

CAROLYN. You don't think about these things?

TRUDY. I'm not about to discuss any of this with any of you.

REGINA. But we're your friends.

TRUDY. Nuh-uh.

REGINA. Well, *I'd* certainly want to…snuggle…with her.

CAROLYN. Solid answer.

TRUDY. There's no snuggling in outer space.

CAROLYN. Not with that attitude.

TRUDY. If you want to unfasten your seatbelts and float away into the abyss, by all means, be my guest, I would finally get some peace and quiet.

CAROLYN. Just look at her little face though…perfect and yummy…

REGINA. It's true, she's so beautiful, I've been jealous since day one…

(MARTHA *chokes on her own phlegm and jolts awake.*)

MARTHA. Hey.

CAROLYN. Good morning, princess.

MARTHA. How's it going?

TRUDY. You know exactly how it's going. Nothing has changed in nineteen weeks, what a dumb question.

MARTHA. (*Yawning.*) Wow, okay, I'm just making polite conversation here…

CAROLYN. Trudy's in a bad mood today.

MARTHA. There must be something magical about a lack of gravity combined with filtered oxygen, because I just keep sleeping so well!

REGINA. It's true, you have.

MARTHA. I've been documenting my sleeping patterns since we blasted off, actually, and it's super fascinating. I'm a terrible sleeper back home, but up here, it's the exact opposite. I wonder why that is?

(*She goes to get her sleep journal but notices the empty chair.*)

Where's Patrice?

(*An uncomfortable moment.*)

REGINA. There was a bit of…an incident.

MARTHA. An incident?

REGINA. Yes…and now Patrice isn't here anymore.

MARTHA. She's not here?

CAROLYN. No.

MARTHA. Well where is she?

(REGINA, CAROLYN, *and* TRUDY *look out into the abyss. After a moment,* MARTHA *realizes.*)

MARTHA. *No!*

TRUDY. Oh yes, Martha.

REGINA. We can explain—

MARTHA. You *ejected* her?

CAROLYN. It's complicated…

TRUDY. It's really not. She was getting on our nerves. Wasn't she getting on your nerves?

MARTHA. Well—yes—she was—she *is* annoying—she *was* annoying?—oh my god, but you ejected her.

TRUDY. We took a vote.

MARTHA. I didn't vote.

TRUDY. I voted for you.

REGINA. She does that sometimes.

TRUDY. You were asleep.

MARTHA. When did this happen?

CAROLYN. A while ago.

REGINA. (*Checking her watch.*) Two hours, give or take...

MARTHA. And now she's...

CAROLYN. Floating...forever...bouncing around between the stars and planets and meteors.

REGINA. Do you think she's already...you know...

CAROLYN. It's been over two hours, Regina. Of course she's already—

TRUDY. She deserved it.

MARTHA. Oh my god.

TRUDY. I hope she got sucked into a black hole.

MARTHA. I didn't know we could—

CAROLYN. They told us at training how to do it—

MARTHA. Right, fine, but I didn't think we actually would ever—

CAROLYN. The rules don't apply once you leave the Milky Way.

MARTHA. Wow.

    (*Rest.*)

Now what?

CAROLYN. We keep moving forward. Stay focused on the mission. Keep looking.

REGINA. Right.

TRUDY. It'll be much easier now.

MARTHA. What are we even looking for?

    (*A moment of slow realization.*)

TRUDY. What did you say?

MARTHA. I mean, we've been out here for nineteen weeks...plus the two months of training prior to the mission...and maybe it's because my brain is still waking up from that nap, but I can't remember anyone ever telling us what we're supposed to be looking for, or how long it's supposed to take.

CAROLYN. Wait, c'mon, they told us—

REGINA. Of course they told us…Carolyn, I thought I remember you saying—

CAROLYN. Lemme think for a sec. We're looking for…important…outer space…science…stuff.

MARTHA. But even if we find anything, who do we report to? How do we contact them?

TRUDY. Oh my god.

CAROLYN. I thought Regina was in charge of that.

REGINA. It's definitely not me. Trudy?

TRUDY. I'm only responsible for this lever.

REGINA. Well what does the lever do??

TRUDY. I don't know, I'm just supposed to keep pushing the lever!!

REGINA. Martha?!

MARTHA. I'm in charge of documenting our findings.

TRUDY. What findings?!

REGINA. You mean you're not in charge of navigation?

MARTHA. I thought *you* were in charge of navigation!

CAROLYN. Wait! Maybe Patrice was in contact with home base? She was always whispering things—

TRUDY. She was just talking to herself.

CAROLYN. No one was in contact with anyone this entire time???

TRUDY. This isn't happening.

MARTHA. So we were sent into space with no way of contacting home, with limited food and supplies…

CAROLYN. We don't even know how to turn this spaceship around—

REGINA. We don't know where we are in the entire galaxy—

CAROLYN. Martha what do we do??!?

MARTHA. Everybody stay cool. Let me be rational for a second.

(*Everyone tries to stay calm with varying degrees of success.*)

Taking ten steps back: why did we sign up for this?

TRUDY & CAROLYN. Money.   **REGINA.** It's always been my dream to be an astronaut.

MARTHA. Right. Okay. But now, I'm wondering…even if the money were to magically appear…if we can't turn this spaceship around, and we don't know how or if we're ever going to go home…what would the money be good for?

CAROLYN. You mean, we—

TRUDY. YES, Carolyn. That is what she means. This has all been a joke from the beginning—a joke we ALL fell for, which is what happens when you just *trust* everything people tell you. We trusted those friendly, polite NASA motherfuckers and look where we ended up.

MARTHA. I can't believe I didn't realize this earlier.

CAROLYN. It's not your fault, we were lied to. Somebody will fix this.

TRUDY. This is the worst day of my life.

CAROLYN. *SOMEBODY WILL FIX THIS I JUST NEED TO BELIEVE THAT SOMEBODY WILL FIX THIS.*

(*A big moment of wallowing.*)

REGINA. Well...if we're going to die...because everyone has to die at some point, right? At least we get to go surrounded by all of this beauty. And...*AND!* We get to spend our final days together! Just the four of us! We're ultimately very lucky, when you think about it.

(TRUDY, CAROLYN, *and* MARTHA *look at each other.*)

TRUDY. All in favor?

CAROLYN. I.

MARTHA. I.

REGINA. What?

(REGINA *is ejected into space.*)

End of Play

WELLESLEY GIRL
by Brendan Pelsue

ABOUT *WELLESLEY GIRL*

This article first ran in the Limelight Guide to the 40th Humana Festival of New American Plays, *published by Actors Theatre of Louisville, and is based on conversations with the playwright before rehearsals for the Humana Festival production began.*

"We don't actually know much about the riddle of who we are and what we're doing." That wry allegation, uttered in an early scene in Brendan Pelsue's *Wellesley Girl*, turns out to be a disturbingly accurate summary of the problem with politics.

Set in the year 2465, the play presents a delightfully bizarre vision of the future of American democracy: "America" is now just a handful of New England towns enclosed in a walled-in citadel. Because the population has dwindled to fewer than 435 people, every adult citizen is a voting member of Congress, and the Supreme Court is just one person (the last remaining woman with legal training). But though the shape of their government might strike us as peculiar, the people inside that system will seem all too familiar. As they muddle their way through the process of collective decision-making, their progress is bogged down by all the bickering and posturing we've come to expect from the great American experiment in action. The play's canny humor emerges out of disputes within a group of people—compassionate, smug, quirky, and flawed as they might be—who know each other intimately. They know how to push each other's buttons. "They're all just a bunch of petty, squabbling people—which I think we all are, especially when we look at politics," says Pelsue. "That's the joke to me. They can't escape the peccadillos of personality."

The impulse for the play sprung from what Pelsue jokingly calls his "M.F.A. mid-life crisis." "I was in a moment where I was wondering why I should write plays, and whether it made more sense to just live somewhere and run for school board, and to be of service to the community," he explains. "And then I guess it was that sort of erstwhile civic longing that reminded me of this story that my grandmother told me about how it had snowed on the day of a town meeting, and how disgusted she was that the snow had prevented people from showing up to vote. So the germ of the play was the image of somebody walking to a town meeting despite the snowy weather." From that simple gesture—a person answering the call to civic duty—Pelsue's wild imagination took over. He's created a political landscape in *Wellesley Girl* so drastically reduced in size that every vote really does count. Civic participation is not just a privilege for these Americans; their very survival depends on it.

In 2465, American citizens face a precarious future. They've spent their entire lives with little knowledge of the world outside the ramparts, believing the rest of North America to be a virtual wasteland where survival is impossible. But the sudden appearance of an unidentified army at their border reveals that belief was unfounded. And as they debate how to respond to the unexpected presence, they become keenly aware that uncertainty is not limited to what lies beyond their walls—it touches all facets of their lives. Are these newcomers possible allies, or a potential threat? Is the untreated water past their border really unsafe? Can they trust each other? Can they trust *themselves*? As the story unfolds, we realize that all the politicking and petty quibbles over legislative procedure mask a profoundly uncomfortable truth: their difficulty in agreeing upon a way forward stems from knowing so little about their present, and even less about their history.

For the characters in *Wellesley Girl*, and for us, uncertainty is simply a fact of existence. A distressing fact, to be sure. And yet, our uneasiness does not excuse us from making a choice, nor does it circumvent the necessity of compromise. "I think in a big way, the play is about belief and how you come to conclusions, and also what you do when you're forced to cooperate with people who have completely different ideas about the truth," says Pelsue. Negotiating those differences is inherently dramatic, but it's also a fundamental challenge of our current political reality. It's an issue that leaves Pelsue perplexed. "We live in a political moment where people make radically different claims about what is objectively or factually true—especially around our history, or even things like climate change or evolution," he says. "But we're bound together by this thing called the Constitution. I really don't know what to do with the fact that people can have such different views of reality."

The razor-sharp political commentary in this play may make us laugh, but bubbling under its surface are serious questions about decisive action in the face of doubt and disagreement. While the Americans in *Wellesley Girl* wrestle with the distance between what they believe to be true and what they can prove, they know that any decision they make holds the potential for both victory and disaster. The play asks us to consider, which will it be? As the citizens in Pelsue's play discover, sometimes you just have to flip a coin and hope that history proves you right.

—Jenni Page-White

BIOGRAPHY

Brendan Pelsue is a playwright, librettist, and translator whose work has been produced in New York and regionally. His play *Wellesley Girl* premiered at the 2016 Humana Festival of New American Plays. *Hagoromo,* a dance-opera piece for which he wrote the libretto, has appeared at the Brooklyn Academy of Music and the Pocantico Center. Other work includes *New Domestic Architecture* at the Yale Carlotta Festival, *Read to Me* at the 2015 Bay Area Playwrights Festival, *Lost Weekend* with the Actors Theatre of Louisville Professional Training Company, *Parking Lot, Riverbank: a Noh Play for Northerly Americans,* and a translation of Molière's *Don Juan* at the Yale School of Drama, *Visitors* with the Corkscrew Theater Company, *Petra and the Saints* with the Telephonic Literary Union, and *Diagram of a Kidnapping* with the Brown University New Plays Festival. He has taught or mentored at Yale College, Wesleyan University, and Lesley University. Originally from Newburyport, Massachusetts, he received his B.A. from Brown University, where he received the Weston Prize in Playwriting, and his M.F.A. from Yale School of Drama.

ACKNOWLEDGMENTS

Wellesley Girl premiered at the Humana Festival of New American Plays in March 2016. It was directed by Lee Sunday Evans with the following cast:

MAX, A CITIZEN	Pun Bandhu
SCOTT, A CITIZEN	Jeff Biehl
DONNIE, A CITIZEN	Austin Blunk
DONNA, THE SUPREME COURT	Lynda Gravátt
GARTH, THE CHIEF EXECUTIVE	Rachel Leslie
MARIE, A CITIZEN	Kelly McAndrew
MICK, A CITIZEN	Esaú Mora
HANK, A ROBOT	Barney O'Hanlon
VOICE 2	Jayson Speters
RJ, A CITIZEN	Phillip Taratula
VOICE 1	Addison Williams

and the following production staff:

Scenic Designer	Annie Smart
Costume Designer	Kristopher Castle
Lighting Designer	Matt Frey
Sound Designer	Bray Poor
Fight Director	Drew Fracher
Stage Manager	Stephen Horton
Assistant Stage Manager	Joshua Mark Gustafson
Dramaturg	Jenni Page-White
Casting	Calleri Casting
	(James Calleri, Paul Davis, Erica Jensen)
Properties Master	Mark Walston
Directing Assistant	Nick O'Leary
Assistant Dramaturg	Kate Cuellar

With thanks to James Bundy, Jeanie O'Hare, and the Yale School of Drama for first developing this play.

CHARACTERS

MARIE, Max's wife

MAX, Marie's husband

RJ, a blowhard

SCOTT, a know-it-all

DONNA, the Supreme Court of the United States

GARTH, the Town Manager, aka the Chief Executive

HANK, Garth's husband, an impolite robot, but not robot-like

MICK, a Citizen

DONNIE, a Citizen

VOICE 1

VOICE 2

SETTING

The United States of America, aka Weston, Massachusetts, 2465 CE.

The country is a small, walled-in citadel with little knowledge of the outside world. Because there are fewer than 435 remaining Americans, everyone of voting age is a member of Congress.

NOTES

I imagine this play being staged very simply: a lilac bush in a pot to represent the yard, a lectern to represent the Town Hall, maybe a bureau to represent the bedrooms. This way, the transitions are almost immediate: a new scene begins as soon as the previous one has ended, sometimes before the minimal scenery has fully transitioned. The whole thing moves.

In the coda, either two boys around 13–15 play Donnie and Mick, or the actor who plays Hank also plays Donnie and the actor who plays RJ also plays Mick. The actor playing Scott can play Voice 1, and the actor playing Max can play Voice 2.

Also, I imagine that Donna is African-American and Hank is white. Beyond that, I don't know how race functions in 2465, but the world is diverse.

Rachel Leslie and Jeff Biehl
in *Wellesley Girl*

40th Humana Festival of New American Plays
Actors Theatre of Louisville, 2016
Photo by Bill Brymer

WELLESLEY GIRL

DAY ONE

1. The Yard

Complete with lilac bush. See note.

MAX. I'm not sure we should be out here.

GARTH. Why? Are you afraid of the wilderness?

MAX. This is not the wilderness.

GARTH. The edge of your backyard. Same difference.

MAX. I'm not sure this is appropriate.

GARTH. So far it's not inappropriate.

MAX. —

GARTH. Max. It makes sense that we would run into each other. We share a hedge.

—

At times we've shared more than that, but for now we share a hedge.

MAX. I don't know if you're making me comfortable or uncomfortable.

GARTH. With us, what's the difference?

MAX. (*an exhale of recognition.*) —

GARTH. It's nice to be alone with you.

MAX. It's always nice to be alone with you.

GARTH. We just drop right into it.

MAX. —

GARTH. We do. Not too deep, but we drop right into it.

MAX. I probably wouldn't have met you here at all if it wasn't a—spring night. Makes me want to jump out of my skin.

GARTH. It's supposed to snow.

MAX. Don't say that.

GARTH. (*teasing.*) It is.
Sorry.

MAX. —
What are we doing here, Garth?

GARTH. —

—

Have you thought at all about the vote tonight?

223

MAX. Garth—

GARTH. You know I wouldn't normally ask about it—

MAX. But you're going to ask about it.

GARTH. —

Yes.

I think you should support RJ's proposal.

MAX. —

GARTH. I do, Max.

MAX. This is why I hate town politics.

GARTH. Come on—

MAX. It is, Garth. We never have a conversation unless you want something from me.

Is this because Marie opposes that proposal?

GARTH. Don't make it about that.

Think about what RJ's saying. Sending an emissary's the most reasonable thing.

MAX. —

GARTH. It is.

Because there's an army at the gate, Max. We need to know who they are and what they want. And even if we start out friendly, we can always take it back.

MAX. Hopefully—

GARTH. We can.

And we have to do something, Max. People are frightened—

MAX. Of course they are. It's an invasion—

GARTH. We don't know that.

We can't be sure it's an invasion until we send an emissary.

MAX. Or until we get invaded.

GARTH. Max—

MAX. (*"Excuse me."*) —

—

I'm not going to vote for something because it makes people feel safe, Garth. I have to think about it.

GARTH. Sure.

—

Would it help if I told you that what we're calling RJ's proposal is really my proposal?

MAX. —

GARTH. I wrote the thing, Max.

He did, too. We worked it out together. But it's not something that came across my desk and I rubber stamped. It's really what I think we should do.

MAX. —

And why is this a secret?

GARTH. You know why.

Because RJ's not the Chief Executive.

If my name's on that proposal, Scott will say I'm using my position to ram my ideas down his throat—

MAX. Well what a nice arrangement, Garth.

You get to take the teeth out of your opposition without them knowing how and I get to support you and undermine my wife without having to tell her that's what I'm doing—

GARTH. It's not about your wife, Max.

I haven't made this personal tonight.

I haven't talked about your marriage.

MAX. I know. But the whole thing feels manipulative.

GARTH. Advocating what I believe is not manipulation.

MAX. —

GARTH. It's not.

I'm asking you to consider the proposal, Max.

I'm telling you I think it's right.

And I know you have to do what you think is right, and you will.

Even if it costs you personally.

—

That's all I'm saying.

And maybe a part of me is saying it because I haven't stopped caring for you.

MAX. —

Or because you care so much about the vote.

GARTH. —

—

—

Well I try not to let the things I care about be mutually exclusive.

| **MAX.** — | **MARIE.** (*from off.*) Max— |
| I know. | Max— |

GARTH. —

—

I think that's your wife.

> (MARIE *enters*—GARTH *and the lilac bush exit*—*and suddenly we are:*)

2. On the Way to Vote

Something replaces the lilac. Maybe a yew. MAX *and* MARIE *walk towards Town Hall.*

MARIE. Well I know how I'm voting.

MAX. Good.

MARIE. —
I'm against it.

MAX. —
Is it snowing?

MARIE. You have a coat. You have to expect a couple of flakes in May.

MAX. I hope it doesn't take the   **MARIE.** (*"Aren't you voting for it?"*)
branches down.
Though I—   —
What?

MARIE. How are you voting?

MAX. —

—

I don't know yet, Marie—

MARIE. Jesus. Yes you do—

MAX. I don't—   **MARIE.** Max—
it's an emergency meeting.

MARIE. It's very important.

MAX. I know. That's why I need to hear the different arguments.

MARIE. Mmm-hmm.

—

—

I want to ask you if you've even thought about it, but I'm not going to do that.

MAX. —

MARIE. Have you even thought about it?

MAX. —

MARIE. You have to vote "no," Max. It's the safest thing.

MAX. It might not be.

MARIE. Well I think it is.

—

And I could tell you why if you'd just ask me.

MAX. —

MARIE. It's the safest thing because—
Sending an emissary would mean opening a flank.

We don't know who's out there, Max. We don't know what they want.
What if they're looking for the water?

—

—

Hm?

MAX. I'd like to think about it for myself.

MARIE. Alright.

—

—

I hope you come to a decision.

MAX. I'll have to. I have to vote.

MARIE. You *do*.

MAX. I know.

MARIE. No, but you *really do*, Max. You *really do*. Because I know that
sometimes you don't vote. I see that you don't raise your hand during the
"Yes" vote, and then you don't raise your hand during the "No" vote. You
must know I know that. I'm sitting right next to you—

MAX. I'm not going to vote if I don't know the answer.

MARIE. Well I hate that, Max. You're in Congress, goddammit—

MAX. So is everyone, Marie. So are you. It's not like there's a choice—

MARIE. Right, and I always vote. And this time it's goddamn serious. It has
to do with us and the children and the future of the whole goddamn country—

MAX. What's left of it.

MARIE. Don't say that. It's not what's left of it. This *is* it. Don't talk like
they could win.

MAX. —

—

I'm not going to vote if I don't know the answer.

MARIE. Max!

Right now, quite frankly, that disgusts me. Do you want to know why?

MAX. —

MARIE. *Because I love you.* And because I know that you are the best man
in this town. You look at everyone else, and they're fat and dishonest, and
everything they say, every goddamn thing they say—

RJ Linus—he's all about control—

MAX. Well—

MARIE. Scott Gleason—he's a fathead lunatic!

But you're better than that. And I would rather have a vote from you when
you're not sure than a vote from them even when they're certain.

MARIE. —
And what I would like even more is if your vote were the same as mine.
MAX. —
MARIE. And I saw you talking to Garth.
MAX. —
She's our neighbor.
MARIE. She's also a snake.
MAX. (*"Marie!"*) —
MARIE. She is.
I know what I know, Max. She'll try to play you off me just like that.
MAX. —
MARIE. Don't look at me like that. A day like this is too big for jealousy.
—

(*relaunching.*) And I'm sure she's behind this emissary thing—
MAX. I think I've made my feelings on the vote clear, Marie.
MARIE. Alright.
Alright.
—

—

If they attack suddenly—
you have been a good husband to me.
I don't know if there won't be time to say that, so I'll say it.
MAX. Thank you—
MARIE. That's enough. It's time to go inside. It's time to start the meeting.
            (MARIE *turns away from* MAX *and suddenly we are:*)

3. At the Town Meeting

            SCOTT, RJ, *and* GARTH *appear.* RJ *stands and holds a microphone.*
            GARTH, *in her capacity as Town Manager/Chief Executive, stands at a*
            lectern that replaces the yew bush.
            We have the sense there is a much larger crowd.

RJ. My fellow Americans:

What's going on?
What's going on?
We have no idea.

For years, we have conducted our foreign policy under the assumption that
we were the only country on the planet Earth.
Now it turns out that may not be true.

Surprise visitors have arrived. It seems they're resting their army outside the gates of our beloved citadel.

But who are they?

What's going on?

Are they even our enemies?

Now this is why, in my capacity as chair of the House Committee on Foreign Relations, I propose we send an emissary.

SCOTT. An emissary? What would an emissary mean, RJ?

RJ. Questions are addressed to the moderator—

SCOTT. (*to* GARTH.) What would an emissary mean—

RJ. And this is not your floor time, Scott.

SCOTT. Understood, but—

RJ. Garth?

GARTH. It's RJ's floor time, Scott.

SCOTT. Alright. Alright. I'm not petty.

GARTH. Good.

Let's have that stricken from the record.

RJ, proceed.

RJ. —

What's going on?

Are they even our enemies?

Which is why, in my capacity as chair of the House Committee on Foreign Relations, I propose we send an emissary.

SCOTT. (*to "himself," but really everyone.*) What would an emissary mean?

RJ. Scott—

GARTH. This is RJ's floortime.

SCOTT. I understand. I'm not petty.

RJ. Thank you.

—

(*to the crowd.*) Now—

SCOTT. It does strike me, however, that we're in a crisis and our leadership is debating etiquette. What would an emissary mean, RJ? The people need to know.	**RJ.** Alright— — Alright—

GARTH. (*to* SCOTT.) Questions are addressed to the moderator during the debate period,/ Scott—

SCOTT. And I'm sure that's very important to you—

RJ. (*to* GARTH.) Give me a second. I can handle this.

Procedure is important, Scott. But that doesn't mean I don't have answers to your questions.

I'm talking about an emissary. That's a small diplomatic mission.

SCOTT. To be chosen on what basis?

RJ. —

A small, diplomatic mission—   **SCOTT.** (*to himself.*) Okay.

That would make a peace offering and also assess the level of the threat. It's very reasonable.

SCOTT. Reasonable if they're reasonable. But we don't know that.

RJ. We don't *not* know it.

SCOTT. Risky bet. Risky bet.

RJ. Scott. If they were unreasonable, wouldn't they have attacked us already?

SCOTT. (*indicating* GARTH.) Questions are addressed to the/ moderator—

RJ. It's my floor time. I can address whomever I want.

(*Turning back to the crowd, speaking until* SCOTT's *interruption overtakes him.*)

Now—/ it is the recommendation of the Committee on Foreign Relations that we send an emissary—

SCOTT. Alright.

Possibly they're reasonable, not necessarily, because if they *are* unreasonable and they haven't attacked us yet, that doesn't make them *reasonable.*

RJ. (*quietly to* GARTH, *under* SCOTT.) I can handle this.

SCOTT. (*continued.*) Quite frankly, Americans should know better than anybody that if a group of strange settlers shows up on your shores, they might seem reasonable at first, but they are not going to do right by you in the end. Because we *were* those settlers. We did that—

RJ. Jesus, Scott—if you hold them to that standard—

SCOTT. I'm just being realistic!

RJ. (*to* GARTH, *under* SCOTT.) This was a mistake.

GARTH. Clearly—

Alright—

SCOTT. (*continued.*) I'm saying, make the worst-case scenario the *first-case scenario.*/ Nightmares before dreams. That's crisis management 101.

RJ. (*to* SCOTT; *drawn back in.*) But isn't the—

Scott—   **GARTH.** RJ—

Isn't the worst-case scenario that they're stronger and they're unreasonable and we're killed no matter what? I'm talking about a solution that operates within the parameters of hope and choice—

SCOTT. And I'm talking about *realism* and choice, RJ. Don't be a Pollyanna.

RJ. (*to* GARTH.) Okay. We're out of control. This is not his/ floor time.

GARTH. / Right. Scott—

SCOTT. (*overlapping.*) Now I propose we observe them, and if they start behaving erratically, we launch a surprise attack, then we abandon the country and leave scorched earth behind us.

> (*General hubbub.*)

MARIE. What?   **MAX.** Excuse me?

RJ. The whole country?

SCOTT. I've thought it —   **GARTH.** (*banging her*
through.   Can you hear yourself?   *gavel.*) Okay—
I can, RJ.   Alright—
Can you hear me?   Okay—
I have thought it through.
We get one chance with these invaders, people. One.
And my plan tells them, first, that America is strong. Stronger than they think.
Second that we will fight at any price. And third that we are unpredictable.
A people who would rather wander the earth as exiles than wear a conqueror's yoke.

> (*More general hubbub. More overlapping.*)

GARTH. (*banging* **MARIE.** No— **MAX.** Excuse me— **RJ.** Scott—
gavel.) Alright—
Alright, Scott.   No—   Scott—
Scott.
Everybody—   No—
Scott—
Is this a proposal, Scott?

SCOTT. (*taking out a piece of paper.*)
A Joint Resolution. Read it and
weep—   **MARIE.** No—

GARTH. Marie—
RJ—   **RJ.** That's not what a Joint
Resolution is—

(*to* SCOTT.) Has that been through committee?

SCOTT. Committee? Garth, committee.

GARTH. You know how this works—

SCOTT. (*to everyone.*) We're under attack and she cares about committee?

GARTH. Scott, if your Joint Resolution has not been through committee then it's not a piece of legislation, it's just a piece of paper.

SCOTT. (*to everyone.*) In the interest of National Security we can vote to override committee.

RJ. Not during my floortime—

SCOTT. My floor time's coming up. And we can vote for answers, not committees—

GARTH. It doesn't work like that.

It does not work like that.
—

MAX. Can I, can I— Hi. Can I say something—

RJ. It's not your turn—   Max—

SCOTT. My friend, please do.

(SCOTT *hands* MAX *the microphone.*)

SCOTT. (*to* RJ/*everyone.*) Let no one can say I don't believe in discourse. Silence the man if you want to, Garth.

GARTH. (*to* RJ, *"I don't know."*) —

RJ. (*to* GARTH.) Fine. But I don't want this counting as my floor time.

MAX. —
I know it's not my turn to speak—

RJ. (*noise of disapproving approval.*) Mmm.

but since it seems like we're at a break in the order of the meeting, I wonder, I'd like to ask if we can all take a step back and think about what to do as Americans—

RJ. We are Americans, Max. And we're thinking about what to do.

MAX. Right. Sure. What I mean is, can we slow things down, look at each option without playing politics?
Because there's potentially a real threat out there. An army.
We all heard the description in yesterday's report.
We're not giving ourselves the space to talk and think, and I don't want our inability to have a discussion to be the reason we don't make it—

RJ. Don't make it?
No one's said don't make it.
We are still three whole towns—

SCOTT. Max—

SCOTT. (*unamplified.*) Four if you count Wellesley.
(*to* MAX.) Could you give me that?

MARIE. No—

(SCOTT *grabs the microphone.*)

SCOTT. Four if you count Wellesley—

MAX. Excuse me—

RJ. We lost Wellesley.

SCOTT. We didn't.
The United States is four towns.
Weston, Lincoln, Sudbury, Wellesley

RJ. (*to himself.*) Not Wellesley—

RJ. Forty years ago we lost Wellesley—we lost the college—

SCOTT. No, they voted to secede, but—

RJ. They did secede—
they walked out the front gate of the
country and promptly died—

SCOTT. No. You cannot—
—

No.

SCOTT. YOU CANNOT SECEDE
FROM THE UNITED STATES.
You can try.
You can starve to death like Wellesley.
But that doesn't mean you left the
union.
Did no one ever tell you there was a
war about that six hundred years ago?

GARTH. Okay—we're off course

MARIE. No— No—
Starved to death?

GARTH. Alright—

RJ. Oh, well by that logic, why
doesn't the country still include
Washington State, Provincetown,
and Anglophone Quebec?

GARTH. Enough—

SCOTT. Just because we haven't heard from them doesn't mean they're not
still out there—

RJ. Yes. Out there where they seceded,
and probably also starved to death.

MARIE. RJ, starved to death?

GARTH. Gentlemen, ENOUGH.

RJ. (*to* GARTH.) I know! He's prepared to abandon the whole country, but
he won't abandon Anglophone Quebec?

GARTH. We're not talking about Anglophone Quebec.
And we're not talking about the First Civil War.
We're talking about your proposal, RJ—

SCOTT. Right. A proposal that exemplifies the kind of defeatist thinking
that has held us all back since the day that Wellesley starved to death.

Well let me tell you a secret, people:
The way you overcome decline is by
ignoring it.

MARIE. No—
No—
Oh, if decline is the bed we've made,
Scott, then we all have to lie in it!

GARTH. We're not talking decline.
No one said decline.
We're talking about the choices in
front of us.
RJ, would you take the floor.

SCOTT. (*in immediate response to*
MARIE.) That kind of thinking will
destroy us, Marie.
Just as surely as an enemy army, or a

RJ. Thank you.

robot revolt—
RJ. There's one robot left, Scott—
SCOTT. I know we are reduced.
I know we've lost comrades.
But somewhere in us is the diamond
that survives the bonfire.
Because we're four good towns.
We're four *great* towns enclosed by a
single, mighty rampart. Formerly
suburbs, but no more, because there
is no more Boston, there is no more
urb around which we sub. And we
know in our hearts that we're a
whole nation. And if we pursue a
surprise attack and scorched earth,
we'll survive somewhere out there
in the wilderness and we'll start
again. What I'm proposing is not the
end. It is the beginning!

MARIE. Garth, I need the
microphone—
GARTH. RJ, don't engage him.

MARIE. Scott—

GARTH. (*to* RJ.) You need to stay
on topic.

MARIE. Garth—

No—
Scott—

(MARIE *grabs the microphone from* SCOTT.)

MARIE. The people in Wellesley didn't starve to death out there. IT WAS
THE WATER. You know/ it was the water.

SCOTT. Is this your floor time?

MARIE. Is it yours?

RJ. There has been an abrogation of procedure,/ this is not counting as my
floor time.

MARIE. (*overlapping* RJ.) THE WATER.
Wellesley failed because outside the
walls and the generators and filters,
there is not good water—

RJ. (*to* GARTH.) How could this be
my floor time?/ I don't even have the
microphone.

SCOTT. That's not what the new
data's saying.

GARTH. (*to* RJ.) I know.

GARTH. ENOUGH.
Everyone enough. The meeting's out of control. I will hold you in/ contempt.

SCOTT. See. Even
Garth thinks you're
fearmongering, Marie.

MAX. Marie!

GARTH. Okay. (*to*
SCOTT *then* MARIE.)
I will hold you in contempt.
I will hold you in contempt.

MARIE. You revolt
me, Scott.

MARIE. So you're afraid of what I have to say?

GARTH. No! But debate occurs after proposals are presented. Our decisions and our conduct in this room are the yardstick for our society—

MARIE. No. The yardstick for our society is not letting Scott spew his—his—ahistorical venom—

SCOTT. I have rights.

MARIE. (*continued.*) So hold me in contempt if you have to, Garth. I'm going to say what I have to say anyway.

GARTH. —

MARIE. Now—

—   **RJ.** This is not fair, Marie—

History's not fair, RJ. Interruptions are just irritating.

GARTH. Give her thirty seconds. It was a mistake to let Scott speak, but this administration does not play favorites.
(*to* MARIE.) Thirty seconds.   **SCOTT.** Ready, people?

MARIE. Scott?

—

Thank you.

—

This is history you all know—
even if certain political groups would rather we forget it.
We are enclosed by these walls because outside there is bad water.
When Wellesley seceded—

SCOTT. You can't/ secede.

MARIE. Or left. Or went. Whatever.
When they decided things were finally safe and they marched out there to start their new society, they did not starve to death—
There was an algal bloom and they were poisoned by the water.
I know.
I was a child. I was there.
I found the bodies of my parents.

—

And so you may not like that we are trapped in here, but that's the truth.
The new data may say, the blooms seem weaker. They seem less frequent.
Wellesley thought that, too.
And that is why we cannot discuss, we cannot consider, we cannot entertain any proposal that involves inviting an invasion, leaving the country, or in any other way ignoring the fact that outside these walls we will be poisoned by the water.
We cannot do it.
We cannot do it.

GARTH. Thank you,/ Marie—

MARIE. We can't, Scott—

GARTH. Thank you, Marie.

MARIE. They'll try to sell you on new data.
They'll tell you things have changed—

GARTH. Thank you both—I have to—

MARIE. I'm the only one who was there—

GARTH. (*to* MARIE.) Thank you.

MARIE. I am.

GARTH. Thank you. Thanks. Scott! Scott—
SCOTT!

SCOTT. Truth doesn't take turns.

GARTH. —
Thank you.
Now before we continue—
RJ—

—

SCOTT. Okay. I disagree—

GARTH. Thank you—

SCOTT. Things have changed.

SCOTT. So?

—

Marie—

—

—

The last bloom was five years ago.
Hank's new studies show the change in the water is permanent. For the first time in generations we can have hope!

RJ. (*noise of disapproval.*) Mmm.

Before we continue, I would like to remind you all that I am your elected Chief Executive and going forward, the policy on speaking out of turn will be zero tolerance. Immediate contempt. Don't test me.

—   **RJ.** (*ready to speak.*) —

—   —

Also—   (*Noise of disapproval.*) Mmm.

I'd like to reiterate, just like Judy wrote in last month's bulletin, we're trying to move beyond our recent petty politics. For some of us that's hard. Which I understand. But until we can get the adult population up over 435, we all have the responsibility to be members of Congress, and I think we have the best chance of surviving, maybe even having a Senate, if we assume good faith, because at this point who here *doesn't* have a vested interest in a positive resolution to this issue?
Am I right?

—

—

Good.

Now, RJ, the floor is yours.

RJ. I know.

—

And I'd like to return to where I began:

What's going on?

What's going on?

We have no idea.

Because whether a five year abatement in the algal blooms is unprecedented or not, we don't know.

Whether the chemicals causing the blooms have a half-life, we don't know.

Large parts of the historical record before the library fire in 2390 are either spotty or illegible, and so no matter what we believe about what's going on, we don't actually know very much about the riddle of who we are and what we're doing.

—

Which, quite frankly, is why the big tent solution to our current problem is to send an emissary.

Because who knows what insights these new folks might have.

Because Americans have never been afraid of the unknown.

And because who can say what new chapter in history we might be opening for future generations.

That's why we're making a transcript of what I'm saying right now.

—

(*to an unseen stenographer.*) You are transcribing this, right, Bobo?

—

Good.

—

Thank you.

GARTH. Thank you, RJ. That concludes your floor time.

—

Okay. Alright. Good. Everyone, thank you.

Now, since there is only one proposal that has been introduced through the legitimate channels this evening, I motion we bring that resolution to a vote before entertaining any further discussion.

(*The meeting disappears. And suddenly we are:*)

4. In a House

The lectern disappears. HANK *appears.*
He reads in bed. He is plugged in. GARTH *is in the bathroom.*

GARTH. Have you been in the medicine cabinet?

HANK. No—

GARTH. You're sure? I can't find the aspirin—

HANK. I'm bored by medicine.

GARTH. I know.
It's just, why can't I ever find anything when I need it? Can you imagine being an aspirin bottle, always waking up somewhere new?

HANK. No.
Now it's time to talk about the meeting.
Sorry. The more polite version is—why aren't you talking about the meeting?

GARTH. Hank—

HANK. Sorry. The more polite version is—Hank wants to know about the meeting.
Sorry. The more polite version is—how was the meeting?

GARTH. Is your battery low?

HANK. I'm charging.

GARTH. Aha!

> (GARTH *comes out of the bathroom. She is holding an aspirin bottle. She shakes it in triumph.*)

HANK. Hooray!
How was the meeting?

GARTH. I don't want to talk about it.

HANK. You avoid speaking of what troubles you.

GARTH. Where'd you get that line from?

HANK. —

GARTH. I'm not troubled, Hank—

HANK. You are. I know—

GARTH. Don't accuse me of what my feelings are.

HANK. (*continued.*) Your back is straight, your eyes are small and there is a difference in your odor.
That spells trouble.

GARTH. Okay—

HANK. Robots don't accuse. They observe.

GARTH. I know.

HANK. That's why we're so helpful.

GARTH. —

Well the meeting was fine. The proposal passed. The emissary leaves tomorrow.

HANK. Hooray!

Hank was invested in that.

GARTH. Yup. Let's watch old videos of television.

HANK. Oh. Television. Still the meeting troubles you.

GARTH. No—it—

Sometimes you don't need to talk about what it seems like you need to talk about. It's part of being human.

HANK. (*now as if an understanding has dawned.*) Ah. You avoid speaking of what troubles you.

Hank apologizes.

GARTH. It's okay. Where's the remote?

HANK. So TV makes you happy?

GARTH. Don't be passive aggressive.

HANK. What does that mean? No matter how many times you explain—

GARTH. Oh god. It's like the 3% we don't get each other is the 3% that matters.

HANK. Yes. Because you avoid speaking of what troubles you.

GARTH. No. Communication is a two-way street. Remember what Doctor Betty says—

HANK. "Please pay your balance before our next session."

What troubles Hank is history.

A lot of awful things happen to people. Wouldn't you rather be robots?

GARTH. Awful things happen to robots.

HANK. Yeah, but we don't know it.

I've been reading. "A Memoir of American Enclosure," by Revered Richard Slug, First Parish Church, Weston, Massachusetts.

GARTH. He doesn't give the full story.

HANK. Listen:

　　　(*reading.*)

```
As the crisis worsened, the gap between empirical
reality and public discourse grew. Government officials
almost pathologically avoided speaking of what troubled
the nation, so much so that historians have termed the
lead-up to the environmental fallout "a case study in
national cognitive dissonance."
```

That could be our marriage—

GARTH. No. We communicate all the time. You just worry.

HANK. It's how I'm programmed.

GARTH. Yeah. Well maybe this is how I'm programmed, too.

—

But it was an awful meeting.

Hank, it was a truly awful meeting.

HANK. Sweetie—

GARTH. I know.

I don't understand what I did wrong.

HANK. But your proposal passed—

GARTH. No, yeah. It did. It did.

HANK. Good. Hank was invested in that.

GARTH. Me too.

But the vote was so close—

HANK. I thought it was a shoe-in—

GARTH. It should've been. There was a—a last minute thing from Scott.

HANK. Scott?

GARTH. I should have expected it.

He pulled a maneuver. He really did.

There's nothing more dangerous than a smart man masquerading as an idiot.

And people ate it up.

It was within twenty votes, Hank.

HANK. You would have had my vote.

GARTH. Thank you.

And I could have used it. Tonight it was like no one could see the middle ground between war mongering and full-time fear about the water.

HANK. You infer the actions of Marie.

GARTH. Yes. What part of your study does she not believe?

Are some people beyond convincing? It's—

It's a sinkhole. I can't think about it.

HANK. Don't.

GARTH. And you know what the worst part is?

I'm the only person there who doesn't get to act like she's gripped with mortal fear.

They don't think I'm scared?

They don't think I know we could be attacked at any moment?

I'm scared right now, Hank. I—

No. It's another sinkhole. I can't think about it.

HANK. With Hank you can be scared.

GARTH. I know.

HANK. And you can be proud you passed the bill. Hank is the one to brag to.

GARTH. I can't really brag.

HANK. You can a little.

GARTH. —

—

—

Thank you.

HANK. See? You wanted to tell Hank everything.

GARTH. I guess I did.

HANK. It's like we love each other.

GARTH. Mm.

—

—

Oh, Hank.

Jesus, what if he's right?

HANK. Many people believe Jesus was right.

GARTH. No. I mean, "Oh, Jesus, Hank, what if Scott's right."

HANK. Oh.

GARTH. Because it's—

Because if it turns out this army's hostile, he has a point that we're going to require an extreme solution.

HANK. What extreme solution?

GARTH. It's to use the remaining missiles we have to launch a—a preemptive strike and then retreat into the wilderness.

HANK. —

Oh no.

GARTH. I know.

But don't worry yet—

HANK. Oh.

Oh no—

GARTH. You'll be okay. It was just a proposition—

HANK. You would leave the country?

GARTH. Potentially—

HANK. But that means you would drink the water.

GARTH. Sure—

HANK. Oh no.

Oh no.

GARTH. You can't dwell on every risk, Hank.
Your studies show the water's changing—
HANK. No. No. They don't show what you think they show.
GARTH. Excuse me?
HANK. The studies don't show what you think they show.
GARTH. What do they show?
HANK. Nothing.
GARTH. No, Hank. You said you were optimistic—
HANK. Because it's what you wanted. Hank did not think you'd be leaving.
—
You were elected.
You said, "Hank, the blooms have stopped. We want a study of the water."
Your back was straight, your eyes were small, there was a difference in your
odor.
Hank knew what this meant.
You avoid speaking of what troubles you.
But you hoped Hank would find clean water.
GARTH. What I want is not always what I *want*, Hank. Why would I need
a trumped up study?
HANK. (*not accusatory.*) Because you people love to hear good things about
your country.
GARTH. —
HANK. (*a litany of explanation.*) Because communication is a two-way street.
Because all marriages are work. Because the 3% we don't get each other is
the 3%—
          (GARTH *baps* HANK *on the side of the head;* HANK *turns off.*)
GARTH. —
—
          (GARTH *baps* HANK *on the side of the head;* HANK *turns on.*)
I'm sorry. I know you don't like to be turned off.
Is the water safe?
HANK. I don't know. I am Hank. I studied you.
GARTH. That's not what I wanted!
HANK. (*continued and continuous.*) Shame. Shame—
GARTH. I need you to answer some questions—
HANK. (*continued.*) Shame. Shame—
          (GARTH *baps* HANK *on the side of the head; he turns off.*)
GARTH. —
—

(GARTH *baps* HANK *on the side of the head;* HANK *turns on.*)

HANK. (*about to resume a shame spiral.*) Sha—

GARTH. I appreciate you're programmed for shame, but right now it's not productive.

HANK. No.

GARTH. Thank you.
Did your study find bad water?

HANK. No.
The water was not bad.
But has the algae died? Is it coming back?
Hank does not know.

GARTH. Alright—

HANK. Hank will apologize. He will make a press release:

American people:

Your assumptions are false. Your safety is built on quicksand.

GARTH. No. No. Hank, don't do that—

HANK. They'll blame me, not you—

GARTH. I'm not sure we can tell people at all, Hank. You don't know how they were tonight—

HANK. I see. Act like the leaders in the history book.

GARTH. No, just—
It's complicated.

HANK. (*a realization.*) I see.

—

Oh no.
Oh no.
There are no plugs outside.
If you go, Hank will be left behind.

5. In a House

MAX *and* MARIE's.

MARIE. I saw that you didn't vote.

MAX. —

MARIE. I did. I'm glad the boys weren't there.

MAX. Marie—

MARIE. Mick and Donnie look up to you.

MAX. Children tend to do that.

MARIE. —

"Scorch the earth," Maxwell. "Scorch the earth."

If that can't get you to vote—

MAX. That's not the resolution we were voting on.

MARIE. It doesn't matter!

MAX. Of course it does. Don't get panicked by Scott's posturing. You know those meetings are a game—

MARIE. No, Max. Politics is only a game until it kills people.

The day you bring up an idea is the day it becomes possible.

The day that Wellesley threatened to secede is the day the disaster started—

MAX. Marie, you're down the rabbit hole.

MARIE. No—

MAX. You are.

MARIE. —

MAX. You might not like Garth, but she didn't let Scott's proposal come to a vote on the floor.

Any resolution that does pass you can challenge at the Supreme Court—

MARIE. You mean Donna? She's just one person. I don't know why we still call her the Supreme Court.

MAX. That's not fair—

MARIE. It is fair. She's the only one.

We lost higher education when we lost Wellesley, and now she's the last lawyer and she hasn't trained anybody else—

MAX. She's an introvert.

MARIE. It's selfish.

It is. Fear of unpopularity is selfish.

MAX. Marie—

MARIE. Oh, would you just let me stew a little!

MAX. —

—

Sorry.

MARIE. It's fine.

—

Is it still snowing?

MAX. Mmm-hmm.

MARIE. How are the branches?

MAX. They're alright.

If they come down, we'll chalk it up to natural pruning.

Maybe the boys will finally use those skis you made them.

MARIE. They better.

MAX. —

—

—

Marie, I went to the ramparts.

MARIE. You got permission?

MAX. —

MARIE. Jesus, Max, that could be big trouble—

MAX. —

MARIE. It could.

They said they don't want a conspicuous civilian presence/ up there—

MAX. I'm just one person.

MARIE. You're a father. If you got caught your punishment would be decided by people who want to scorch the earth—

MAX. That's not what's happening.

MARIE. I know!

I know.

—

What'd you see when you were up there? I know you want to tell me.

MAX. The army. Or the encampment. There were big mobile vehicles. Tanks, with hoses in the river.

They weren't lying in their report.

MARIE. Oh. Did they seem sinister?

MAX. Armies always seem sinister. And I—

MARIE. I can't believe you didn't vote.

I can't believe you didn't vote.

You saw the army out there and you couldn't vote—

MAX. No, Marie,/ I guess I couldn't—

MARIE. Which means what, Max? That you agree with Garth but don't want to disappoint me?

MAX. No—

MARIE. Oh. So then you agree with me but you don't want to disappoint her?

MAX. Come on—

MARIE. I know every time you talk to her. You're not the vault you think you are.

MAX. So I talked to her? She's the Chief Executive—

MARIE. Why'd you choose me?

MAX. —

MARIE. She's better looking. I'm apparently the town idiot—

MAX. Marie—

MARIE. I am. Did you see how people looked at me tonight?

MAX. —

—

I love you. You know that. We chose each other.

MARIE. And you don't regret it?

MAX. No—

MARIE. Then why don't you agree with me?
Do you not believe me about the water?

MAX. It wasn't a vote on the water, Marie—

MARIE. That's what it became.

MAX. To you. There's a lot of new data. You have to expect people will consider it—

MARIE. WHY DIDN'T YOU VOTE?

MAX. Because there was nothing I could vote for, Marie!
I'm not sure that Garth's emissary is anything more than pandering.
But then voting against it leaves the door open for Scott—
And I know that's how you voted, but please don't be naïve—

MARIE. Naïve?!
I don't know what country you think you're the emperor of, but we plebeians are down in the scrum while you waste your time pretending to be rational—

MAX. If I were rational I would have married Garth—

MARIE. Excuse me?

MAX. —

—

Meaning rational's not always a good thing.

MARIE. —

—

MAX. That didn't come out the way I meant. You have to know that. You do.

—

—

Garth's very rational and she's not you. She's married to that—insufferable robot.
For god's sake, Marie—
I was with Garth when I met you
and then I *met* you…

MARIE. I know.

I just—

Do you know how scared I am?

Do you know what I was thinking during that meeting tonight?

If they ever decide to scorch the earth

or leave the walls

I will kill the children.

MAX. —

MARIE. That's what I was thinking.

There are things worse than death. I've seen them.

MAX. Marie—

MARIE. I have.

MAX. —

MARIE. I don't know, Max. I'm doing my best, alright? I DON'T KNOW WHAT TO DO AND I'M DOING MY GODDAMN BEST.

MAX. Me too. I know that.

MARIE. I don't know what's going to happen to us—

MAX. —

MARIE. And out there it is brutal.

We poisoned the world and we still can't goddamn admit it.

I was thinking about what will give the boys the least suffering.

MAX. Is that why you have children, so they can avoid suffering?

—

I don't know what the right thing is, but we're talking about the whole country.

MARIE. Right—

but I am not a country.

I am not a people.

I am a mother, and my children are my children—

—

—

—

—

—

Do you hate me?

MAX. No.

Do you hate me?

MARIE. Sometimes I wish I hated you.

MAX. —

This is why you, not Garth.

MARIE. What is?

MAX. Whatever just happened between us. This.

MARIE. I am so frightened.

MAX. I know.
Me too.

——

——

MARIE. Do you want to walk around the yard? It's not every year you get snow and lilacs.

MAX. Maybe I would kill myself with you if that's what it came to.

MARIE. You would?

MAX. I don't know.
I don't know.
I couldn't even figure out how to vote.

DAY 2

6. The Departure of an Emissary

(SCOTT *and* RJ *stand in the relative darkness.*)

SCOTT. I don't see why I have to be part of this emissary.

RJ. Scott—

SCOTT. I don't. It was your idea—

RJ. Right.
But *we* are the Foreign Relations Committee. This is your post. You begged to be transferred from Ways and Means.

SCOTT. Because what do they even on do? I was *on* that committee and I couldn't understand what they do.

RJ. Right now you're on the Foreign Relations Committee, and that means you're part of the emissary.

SCOTT. Tyranny of the majority.

RJ. That's what a democracy is.
Sometimes as a public servant you do things you don't want to do.

SCOTT. ——
Do we have a plan?
For when we make our demands?

RJ. What demands, Scott? This is exploratory.

SCOTT. RJ, were you never on the playground?
You don't gain respect by telling the bigger kid you're looking to explore—

RJ. —

—

SCOTT. Did I say something wrong?

RJ. This is not the playground, Scott.
This is international diplomacy. It's what I live for.
A diplomat is strong because he is supple:
a master sailor, tacking nimbly in fickle winds.
Haven't you ever wanted something that required delicacy, Scott?

SCOTT. —
Maybe.

RJ. Well to get there, you need diplomacy—the long-lost art of statecraft.
That's what today's about. Let me do the talking.

SCOTT. You're worried that I'll interrupt?

RJ. —

SCOTT. Yeah.
I know I get ahead of myself, I—
Sometimes I just see what I want so strongly.

It can be isolating.

RJ. —
You're more well-liked than you think.

SCOTT. Yeah?

RJ. Absolutely.

—

See, that was diplomacy, Scott. Now you're on my side.

SCOTT. Yeah. Supple.
I admire that.

—

Have you been outside the ramparts before?

RJ. Once. By accident. When I was a kid. I fell off a turret.

SCOTT. What was it like?

RJ. It was bright; scrubby. Like they say.

SCOTT. Uh-huh.

RJ. Ready?

SCOTT. Almost.

—

I, uhm—
I like what you said about diplomacy and situations that require delicacy,
and—

—

RJ, would you believe it's possible for someone on one side of the political aisle to have romantic feelings for someone on the other side of the political aisle? Say for the Ranking Member on the Foreign Relations Committee to have feelings for the Chairman of the Foreign Relations Committee?

And would you believe it might take a—national crisis—for the Ranking Member to admit those feelings?

RJ. —

—

—

Scott, we're about to conduct our country's first diplomatic mission in almost a century. Could we talk about this later?

SCOTT. What? Sure. Oh, sure. No problem. It was a hypothetical.

RJ. Good.

SCOTT. Yeah.

RJ. Alright.

> (RJ *presses a button. Sound of a door opening. The light changes from very dark to very bright.* SCOTT *and* RJ *put on sunglasses. They take a step forward.*)

SCOTT. So this is outside.

And there they are. Camping.

RJ. (*whispered.*) Wave your flag.

> (RJ *takes out an American flag. He waves it.* SCOTT *does the same.*)

RJ. Hello. We're the House Foreign Relations Committee. Could we talk?

> (*Pause as* RJ *watches the enemy's response.*)

RJ. (*to* SCOTT.) Are they gesturing me over there?

SCOTT. (*to* RJ.) I think so.

RJ. Alright. You stay here in case we need to—quickly close the gate.

> (RJ *steps towards the enemy. Soon he is out of sight.* SCOTT *watches nervously.*)

RJ. (*to the enemy.*) Hello—

Yes, hello. My name is RJ Linus. I'm the Chairman of the House Foreign Relations Committee of the United States of America. It's so nice to see that you've, uhm, encamped in front of our country.

SCOTT. (*to himself.*) What are they doing?

RJ?

—

RJ?

RJ!

RJ. (*from afar.*) Scott, I've been kidnapped!

> (*A message in a bottle lands at* SCOTT's *feet.* GARTH, MAX, *and* MARIE *roll in, and suddenly we are at:*)

7. The Second Town Meeting

> GARTH *is once again at her podium.*
> SCOTT *waves the message in a bottle (or just the message) in the air.*

SCOTT. Here it is. Right here.

Proof that this administration led us down the primrose path of diplomacy and it blew up in our faces!

GARTH. That is not a fair portrayal, Scott.

SCOTT. Were you there, Garth?

Because I seem to remember being the only one who saw RJ manhandled!

GARTH. —

SCOTT. (*reading.*) Dear enemies,

It reads. It begins. I'm not saying it. They're saying it to us.

```
Dear enemies,

Greetings!

We were recently made aware of your existence by the
arrival of a mutant refugee from a place called Wellesley.
```

He claims he and his	**MARIE.** (*can overlap through* Wellesley
people seceded from your	news.*) No.
union forty years ago.	Who?
	Can we see that?
(*General hubbub.*)	(*Etc.*)

GARTH. (*overlapping* MARIE/*hubbub.*) Okay, Marie—everyone—

SCOTT. (*overlapping* GARTH.) Now Wellesley didn't secede. We know that. That is our society's most believed fact. Because—

GARTH. (*continued, overlapping* SCOTT.) Marie—

Just read the letter, Scott. Scott—

SCOTT. Alright.

> (*reading.*)

```
We now learn—
```

They say—

```
We now learn that you claim to be the House Foreign
Relations Committee of the United States of America. We
find this interesting because we, your enemies, are the
real House Foreign Relations Committee of the United
States of America and we represent the real government
of the United States of America, which has been operating
```

out of the heavily armed theocratic yurt village of
Dallas, Texas, since the Sack of Washington in 2195.

    (*General hubbub.*)

SCOTT. Order. Order.

GARTH. I can keep order, Scott—

SCOTT. (*to* GARTH.) Can you?

    (*reading.*)

In light of these facts,

They say—

In light of these facts, we come to make three demands:

One, that you cease and desist in your claims that you are
the Federal Government. We are the Federal Government.

Two, that you incorporate yourselves into us, the actual
Federal Government, as a vassal territory similar to the
lost mythical island of Guam.

Three, that as the newest members of our democracy
coalition, you pay us reparations, in the form of food,
children, and labor, as punishment for the years you
have spent falsely representing yourselves as the world's
greatest democracy, as well as for the three centuries
of back taxes you owe us.

We are Texas, you are Massachusetts, and so it goes without
saying that your failure to comply with these demands
will result in your swift and sudden annihilation.
You have three days to answer.

    (*General hubbub.* GARTH *bangs her gavel.*)

GARTH. Alright, calm down everyone. Calm down.

SCOTT. Looks like we have to scorch the earth, people!

Scorch the earth.   **MARIE.** (*from the crowd.*) No—

GARTH. Let's be reasonable about   No—
this, Scott.

SCOTT. Reasonable? Reasonable?
Your version of reasonable is what got RJ kidnapped before/ my eyes, Garth.

GARTH. (*overlapping.*) These situations have inherent risk—

SCOTT. (*overlapping.*) Callous!   **MARIE.** No—
Reckless endangerment.
I should make a motion for   No—
impeachment.

    (*General hubbub.*)

GARTH. (*to the crowd.*) Okay. Okay.

SCOTT. Now I am not talking about an easy choice here, people. I am talking about defending the marrow of who we are. Because whether these would-be-Americans really believe they're the legitimate heirs of the social organism brought into being by the Constitution, or whether that's some elaborate ploy by a group of con-artist marauders trying to steal our freedom, we know in our hearts that *we* are the real United States of America, we are the citizens of that social organism, that political amoeba, that was brought into being on July 4th, 1776 and has simply refused to die!

MARIE. (*into a microphone.*) Scott. No.

MARIE. No—
Where's the other microphone?

GARTH. It's just one microphone today. Did you read the bulletin?

(MARIE *rummages for a microphone.*)

SCOTT. Where'd you get that—I thought we said one microphone. Where'd you get that microphone?

MARIE. Bobo.

SCOTT. Bobo?

GARTH. (*to Bobo.*) Bobo, we'll talk about this.

MARIE. (*overlapping.*) No one's scorching the earth, Scott. No one's going anywhere.

SCOTT. We are if that's how people vote.

MARIE. Not me. I am not going anywhere.
(*to everyone.*) I am telling you, don't go anywhere.
Because you don't know what you have here.
You don't know what it's like out there—

SCOTT. Garth—this is an interruption.

GARTH. You invented interrupting, Scott.

SCOTT. (*overlapping.*) So then what do you propose we do, Marie?

MARIE. Whatever the hell we can to stay here—

SCOTT. So surrender?

MARIE. I don't know—

SCOTT. End the nation?

MARIE. If that's what it takes—

SCOTT. Join their labor colony?

MARIE. Yes—maybe—

    (*General hubbub.*)

SCOTT. (*to the crowd.*) She wants us to join a labor colony, people. Let's tell her how we feel about that!

MARIE. (*looking at the crowd.*) —   **GARTH.** Can we calm down,
That's not what I'm saying—   everybody?

SCOTT. (*still to the crowd.*) She wants us to end the nation—

MARIE. I'm saying if they want the idea of America, let them have it—what good is it doing us?

SCOTT. What good's it doing us?
This is naiveté, people.   **MARIE.** Don't twist my words,
This is let's all go live in lala land   Scott—
without countries—   No it isn't—

Well that's good reasoning for saints, Marie. It's not good reasoning for/ politics—

MARIE. Is leading people out into bad water/ good reasoning for politics?

SCOTT. (*overlapping.*) It is not bad water—

MARIE. (*continued.*) I'm not proposing lala land and I'm not proposing labor colonies.
I'm saying outside the enclosure there is bad water,/ and we need to operate within that reality—

SCOTT. (*overlapping.*) There is not bad water—
Why can't you admit the blooms have stopped./ Why can't you see the data—

MARIE. (*overlapping.*) The blooms also stopped before Wellesley left. They thought they had data. It's the same now as it was then, Scott./ You're going to risk our lives on data?

SCOTT. American people, we don't have to take this.

    (*to* GARTH.)

Would you tell Marie the water's changed? You oversaw the studies, Garth. You ushered in this new era. Why don't you lay down the law—

GARTH. The results of those studies are a matter of public record. I have no further comment.

SCOTT. No further comment? I want you to hear you tell Marie that she's deluded—

GARTH. I have no further comment—

SCOTT. Shut the door on any remaining doubt! Squash/ these false assertions—

GARTH. My administration commissioned those studies, Scott, but that doesn't mean it's my job to interpret the data to endorse your platform—

SCOTT. (*to the crowd.*) Twice she's not doing her job today.

Reckless with the lives of American diplomats and spineless when it's time to/ stand up to Marie's vending machine of fear—

GARTH. (*with gavel.*) That's enough, Scott. Everyone, calm down. I'm calling a recess until/ we all calm down.	**MARIE.** (*about* GARTH *to* SCOTT.) Even she's not going to be reckless with the data, Scott. Even she can admit there's something fishy—

SCOTT. (*about* MARIE *and* GARTH.) You know what it is? You know what this is?

I just cracked the code, people. This administration is never going to admit the full truth about the water because then they have nothing to make you obey.

Well we'll take matters into our own hands!

We'll show these ladies what the American people are made of!

(*General hubbub.*)

GARTH. Let's please calm down.

SCOTT. Yes! I like a worked up crowd! I like an angry crowd! Because an angry crowd is an honest crowd. A crowd that won't be cowered by the old scare tactics. A crowd that's going to do its duty to a man gone missing—	**MAX.** Marie? **MARIE.** (*to* MAX.) What? Scott— — Scott—

MARIE. This is not about RJ, Scott. It's about our lives—

SCOTT. (*to the crowd.*) You hear that?

MARIE. (*to all.*) One man dies and you're going to drive the country off a cliff?

In what world is this worth the price?

(*From here on, if not sooner,* SCOTT *and* MARIE's *speech is about continuous.*)

MARIE. (*overlapping.*) One man is not worth it. It's not fearmongering if you should be afraid. And you should be. I have been out there, I know what happens if you vote for his plan—	**SCOTT.** Is everybody hearing this? RJ is missing. All we have is our memory of him. But if the rest of him were here today, he would remind us of a fundamental truth of our nation, and it is this—

(SCOTT *covers* MARIE's *microphone, or makes a grab at it, or something.*)

SCOTT. The lives taken from us are worth more than the lives we take ourselves.

That's the pact of blood on which every country's built.

(*General hubbub.* MARIE *takes back the microphone.*)

MARIE. Don't take my microphone.

A pact of blood? Are you insane?

SCOTT. Don't act shocked, people. Every country that has survived more than a generation has believed that truth. The lives that are taken from you cost more than the lives you take yourself. And the world has always known that if you take even one American life, we will burn civilization to the ground. Burn it to the ground. That is not insanity, that is hope!	**MARIE.** A pact of blood? Don't listen to this man. Don't listen to this man. We are talking about your lives. We are talking about our children. I am telling you— don't listen to this man.

Now let's have a motherfucking vote!

(*A roar from the crowd.*
All disappears and suddenly we are:)

8. In the Halls of Justice

DONNA *and* MARIE.

DONNA. Thank you for coming to my judicial chambers.

MARIE. Of course. So, Donna—

DONNA. I hope the dryer's not too loud.

MARIE. No—

DONNA. Are you sure?

MARIE. It's fine.

I—

(*Sound of the dryer.*)

DONNA. It's gonna bug me. I'll go shut it off.

(DONNA *exits.*
She re-enters.)

Oh, and if you want to you can have a mint. Some of them are strawberry, but I still call them mints. So...

(DONNA *exits.*)

MARIE. —

—

Donna—

DONNA. (*from offstage.*) Oh, this stupid thing.

Come on. Alright—

There. Good. Thank goodness.

MARIE. Donna—

      (DONNA *re-enters.*)

DONNA. What?

MARIE. Were you at today's meeting?

DONNA. —

I thought you might want to talk about that.

MARIE. People are disgusting. Did you hear what they were saying—

DONNA. I wasn't there, Marie. Separation of powers.

I just show up once a year when they play those old State of the Union video clips and do that, whatever that is, that dance.

MARIE. But you heard the scorched earth proposal passed?

They're launching the attack tonight—

DONNA. Mmm-hmm.

Lois told me about it when she got home.

MARIE. It's a disaster, don't you think?

DONNA. —

—

MARIE. You must be worried about leaving—

DONNA. —

MARIE. Donna, RJ's kidnapped.

They're burning down the country.

They're all lunatics—

DONNA. Marie. You know I can't tell you about my worries as they relate to an act of Congress.

I'm supposed to be impartial. A judge but not judgmental.

—

Just tell everyone they have neat ideas and stuff.

MARIE. And adjudicate—

DONNA. Sure. If someone brings me a case. But legislative and executive really have the ball on this right now—

MARIE. I know.

Which is why I'm wondering if I could bring a case.

DONNA. A case against what?

MARIE. Against Congress, Donna.
Against scorched earth./ Against—

DONNA. But you're a member of Congress—

MARIE. We're all members of Congress!

DONNA. —

MARIE. Except for you. I know—

DONNA. (*softly, almost to herself.*) Mmm-hmm.

MARIE. But I'm also a private citizen. And even as a member of Congress I can sue the government. Can't a member of Congress sue the government?

DONNA. You could try—

MARIE. Donna. It's the *wrong thing*. And I don't think it should be allowed to happen. It's a violation of my rights, of the sanctity of my personhood, to be told, "you have to put your children through hell because that's what everyone's decided. We're abandoning the country."

DONNA. Mmmmh.

MARIE. It's a suicide. Isn't this…somehow unconstitutional?

DONNA. You mean is it unconstitutional for Congress to burn down the country and then leave?

MARIE. Yes.

DONNA. Mmmmh. That's probably what we would call a lacuna in the jurisprudence.

MARIE. Come on, Donna.

DONNA. It is. Because they could make the case that it talks right in the preamble about securing "the Blessings of Liberty to ourselves and our Posterity"—and that's—if these Texans who've shown up are as big a threat as they say are, then the "securing…Posterity" piece is exactly what Congress will argue that they're doing.

MARIE. And what do you think about that?

DONNA. Oh, well I'm—I'm only outlining their potential tack…

MARIE. Right, but the "potential tack" of an argument they would make *to you*. So I'm asking what do you think of that tack because that's what's going to matter.

DONNA. Except no one's brought a case, so what I think about the argument doesn't matter yet.

MARIE. But could you tell me what you think, even if it doesn't matter yet.

DONNA. Marie, would that—
Would that really be fair? My thoughts are the ace up my sleeve, and if I show you that ace, I'll have to show it to them—that's only ethical—and if you both already know what I think, then why even bother with the trial?

Just have me give a decree. But I'm not some autocrat. I believe in the rule of law, you know?

MARIE. Donna, I'm thinking of killing my children—

DONNA. Well that's definitely not protected by the Constitution—

MARIE. No.

I know.

But I will not do this.

And I will not put my children through this—

DONNA. Marie—

MARIE. People don't understand, Donna. They weren't there when Wellesley happened.

DONNA. Well neither was I. I didn't go.

MARIE. You were involved in the negotiations.

And it's where you're from. You must've lost everyone you knew. Your parents? You were up there on the ramparts, watching the last of us trek back towards town—

We can't let that happen again.

DONNA. —

—

—

I don't want to think about that, Marie.

MARIE. I'm sorry.

Do you need a tissue?

DONNA. *("No.")* —

You all think you see the mistakes we made so clearly, but it was more complicated than you realize...

MARIE. People dying is not complicated.

DONNA. Right. I mean the legal side of it. The politics.

I was involved in those negotiations right up until they broke down, and I still don't know what the good solution was—

MARIE. Sure. But I'm not here to rehash history. I'm here to stop a disaster.

DONNA. And I'm saying that's not as easy as you'd think.

Look at Wellesley and look at today—two crises with multiple components that don't always have to do with legal reasoning.

There could be some very real-world ramifications if you were to file a suit and I were to issue a stay on the resolution—

MARIE. Sorry, Donna, what's a stay?

DONNA. A stay of execution—

MARIE. —?

DONNA. It means there would be a hold on the Congressional action taking effect until after I give my ruling…

MARIE. I'm filing a suit.

DONNA. —

You shouldn't file a suit just for the stay, Marie. It's a big decision—

MARIE. I know. But I've heard enough. If this is my last chance, then I'm filing a suit.

DONNA. You know you'll need a good argument?

You can only get something in this country if you can make an argument.

MARIE. I'll figure it out.

DONNA. —

—

Alright.

The forms are on the microwave.

—

—

—

—

MARIE. Are you upset?

DONNA. I don't know!

It didn't think it would come down to this.

I'm the Supreme Court, but that doesn't mean I have some crystal ball.

Even with everything I know about the law, sometimes I'm flipping a coin and hoping history proves me right.

MARIE. I'm sorry.

DONNA. Don't give me your sympathy.

I can't be your friend right now.

When I put on my robes, I am not your friend. I'm no one's friend.

You know that, don't you?

(MARIE *leaves. So do* DONNA *and the table.*
The lights dim. Suddenly we are:)

9. Home Again

GARTH *and* SCOTT *visit* MAX. SCOTT *is wearing a big green ribbon on his lapel. This shows his solidarity with* RJ's *death.*

GARTH. We're not saying she's lying, Max.

SCOTT. No.

GARTH. No one is accusing anyone of lying.

SCOTT. No.

GARTH. No one is denying Marie's memories.

SCOTT. No.

GARTH. What we're questioning is whether those memories are preventing her from fully taking in the current situation.

MAX. —?

GARTH. Why don't you tell me what you think you know about the water.

MAX. About the water problems, you mean?

GARTH. Yes.

MAX. Uhm, I guess the same things everybody knows. The runoff from the chemicals that were used to create robot consciousness also created algal blooms that poisoned the water. Sometimes the blooms were constant, other times they'd disappear for months, uhm—and the MIT people built the walls and the filters here as a sort of test solution to the problem, sort of— walled-in model towns—and of course halfway through the testing there was a bigger bloom than anybody thought, and suddenly we were the only ones left.

GARTH. Right. And what if that had finally changed?

(GARTH *produces a glass of drinking water.*)

MAX. What is that?

GARTH. Water.
From outside.

MAX. How do I even know that's real?

GARTH. Real outside water?

MAX. (*"Yes."*) —

GARTH. Because what possible interest would I have in lying to you? How does it behoove me to lead the country out into some valley of bad water?

MAX. —
You don't have to do that.

SCOTT. Marie's holding up the works, Max.

GARTH. Scott—

SCOTT. She is. She's holding us all hostage.

GARTH. Okay—

SCOTT. I saw a man I—my favorite colleague kidnapped in front of my eyes and taken away to a foreigner's encampment, Max—

MAX. They're not really foreigners.

SCOTT. Sure they are. Just because you believe you're the same country doesn't mean you are.

"Theocratic yurt village." Does that sound like America to you?

GARTH. Scott—

SCOTT. RJ was a patriot—

MAX. I know—

SCOTT. Then where's your ribbon? I made enough for everyone.

GARTH. Can I talk to Max alone, Scott?

SCOTT. I am part of this delegation.

GARTH. Of course.

SCOTT. I am—

GARTH. No one's saying you're not. But I don't want this to be politics right now. I want it to be his living room.

SCOTT. —

—

There is a stay on the evacuation, Max.

Until the hearing, Donna's put a stay/ on the evacuation—

MAX. I know.

SCOTT. Well that is on your head.

If we run out of time with the Texans, that is on your head.

MAX. —

SCOTT. If she delays things too long, it could kill all of us. I don't want there to be any doubt about what I'm saying.

—

Enjoy your living room.

>   (SCOTT *exits.*)

GARTH. —

I'm sorry about that.

MAX. —

—

Why did you bring him?

GARTH. I had to.

MAX. (*"Come on."*) —

GARTH. I did, Max. You saw how people were at the meeting today. They would have done anything he told them.

MAX. But why's he in my house?

GARTH. Because your wife is the reason there's a stay of execution on his plans.

Because she's walking around town right now trying to rustle up amicus briefs for the hearing—

and if I didn't bring him here tonight, who knows how he would try to solve that problem.

MAX. You think he's dangerous?

GARTH. No, I—

Not like that. But I don't think it would take much rabble rousing on his part for people to realize that the only thing enforcing Donna's stay of execution is their—

their belief in Donna's stay of execution, and that is a very thin thread.

I've never seen the town like this.

I'm being very honest with you.

MAX. (*a softening at her confession.*) —

I know.

GARTH. And you know I believe that Marie has the *right* to believe what she wants about the water.

—

You know I believe that.

—

But I'm also, I'm your elected leader and I am threading a needle right now. I am leading the country through a narrow passageway with vassalage on one side and annihilation on the other, and if we don't act as a single unit we are not going to make it. People don't need Marie giving them more doubts than they already have.

Scott may not be your cup of tea, but he's right that if we don't do something big, our chances are diminished.

—

And that's why I'm asking you to believe the truth about the water.

To tell your wife that you believe the truth about the water.

MAX. The truth meaning what? The deadly thing in the algae somehow died? The blooms are never coming back?

GARTH. Yes.

(GARTH *drinks from the cup of water.*)

You have to believe that, Max.

If we don't believe it then we have no hope.

And then what?

I'm not saying the plan's not desperate—

But I'm saying it gets a lot more desperate if you don't believe that something could go right.

(*She hands* MAX *the water. He takes it.*)

MAX. —

—

—

GARTH. You don't have to decide now.
Sit with it.
Serve it to your kids at dinner.
I would.

(*She exits.*)

DAY 3

10. Back in the Halls of Justice

DONNA *sits at the kitchen table.*
MARIE *stands to one side of the table,* SCOTT *to the other.* SCOTT *wears a morning coat. Why? Because for today's purposes, he is the Solicitor General.*
MARIE *consults notecards as she makes her argument.*

MARIE. Which brings me, Madame Chief Justice and would it please the Court, to the issue of the water—

SCOTT. Objection!

MARIE. You can't do that.

SCOTT. I'm the Solicitor General.

MARIE. No, Scott, objections only happen at a jury trial.
Here, we each get a turn to make our arguments while Donna asks questions.

DONNA. That's right, Scott.

SCOTT. Alright, then—time out.

MARIE. Scott—

SCOTT. Because this is the Supreme Court, Marie, and that means the question of the water is irrelevant. Donna can't tell us whether something is a bad idea, only whether we're legally allowed to do it.

MARIE. But it's my argument—
Donna? You read the brief.

DONNA. —
First of all, this is your one time out, Scott.
You had your allotted time and you made your case, so one more word from you about securing liberty for our posterity and your goose is cooked, you understand?

SCOTT. —

DONNA. Good.
Second, I would actually say you're both correct. Scott is right that I can't tell you if an idea is bad, only if it's Constitutional—they're not necessarily related.

But Marie's also right in the sense that there's nothing in the Constitution that says people can't go off-topic.

MARIE. So I can talk about the water as much as I want, but it will get me nowhere? Is that what you're saying?

DONNA. —. My thoughts are the ace up my sleeve, Marie. We talked about that.

SCOTT. I think what Donna is saying is that it's the opacity of our laws that gives them their clarity—

DONNA. No—   **MARIE.** (*to* SCOTT.) What?

SCOTT. (*almost continuous.*) Because there's so much room for interpretation—

DONNA. Alright, Scott, time out is over. Whatever you do in Congress, you're not doing it here.

MARIE. Thank you.

And now I return, Scott—Madame Chief Justice—to the water. To a constitutional argument that has to do with some very concrete facts about the water. You can't look at the history of what happened out there and disagree. The Constitution exists to promote the "General Welfare," and Congress's recent decision contradicts the entire purpose of the document. The entire purpose of the government. Which is not to ruin everything.

People are deluded. They think they're going to march off into the wilderness and start the nation over, but that is lunatic. That is a lunatic conviction—

DONNA. A lunatic conviction?

MARIE. Yes. Because—

DONNA. How are you defining that term?

MARIE. A lunatic conviction? Well it's—it's any idea that does more harm than good. Any idea that hurts us.

DONNA. Alright. And who are you claiming gets to be the arbiter of which ideas do more harm than good, Marie?

MARIE. Donna, it's anyone with common sense—

DONNA. Well clearly not because wouldn't Congress also claim that they're acting with common sense?

Who are you saying gets to be the arbiter of what's lunatic? Is that person you?

MARIE. No, Donna, today it would be you.

DONNA. —

I'm aware of my responsibilities today, Marie. That wasn't my question.

Even if I do agree with your definition of a lunatic conviction, why should I give more weight to your beliefs than to those of the majority of your fellow citizens?

MARIE. Because I am right and they're wrong!

DONNA. Marie—

MARIE. Because I am the only one who
seems to have bothered to ask what
the hell we think we're all doing—   **DONNA.** Marie—

DONNA. Marie, you cannot interrupt me.

MARIE. Donna, I am the only remaining survivor of Wellesley—I am the
only one who's seen the danger—

DONNA. And that experience makes you our dictator?

MARIE. —
—

DONNA. I told you I could not be your friend today, Marie.

MARIE. I don't need you to be my friend. I need you to save our lives.
Now if I can return to my argument—

DONNA. (*"Please do."*) —

MARIE. Thank you.
We all just heard Scott—

SCOTT. The Solicitor General—

MARIE. We all just heard the Solicitor General make his case that Joint
Resolution 12605's "scorch the earth" clause was a necessary measure if we
hope to preserve and protect the Constitution of the United States.
I, however, find this logic dangerous. Because if the Constitution exists to
promote the general welfare, and Joint Resolution 12605 proposes to destroy
the general welfare in order to promote the Constitution, then aren't we
letting the idea of our country crush the lives of the people in it?

DONNA. In other words, the perpetuation of the Constitution of the
United States is doing us more harm than good?

MARIE. Exactly—

DONNA. Meaning the Constitution of the United States is a lunatic
conviction?

MARIE. Meaning we are perilously close to letting it become one.
I have seen what happens when people think they have a destiny—
When they forget this country is just some clapboard houses and a lilac bush.
I have seen a nightmare like that before.
And so yes, Donna, I am going to submit my experience as testimony.
Whether you weigh it more or less than the beliefs of my fellow citizens is
up to you.
—

My parents believed so deeply in Wellesley's Utopian plan, in that experiment,
that they took us out into the woods and gave me a stone to suck on when
there was not enough to eat.

We built our little cabins, and led our little lives,
and then one morning I woke up and wondered where everyone was.
They must all be sleeping.
I remember lying there watching the dust motes,
my mind wandering,
going wherever it goes when you're six years old alone in bed,
thinking the cracks in the ceiling looked like a map of a country I had never visited,
thinking nothing,
and then waking from my daydream with a jolt.
The morning had gone on too long—where was everyone?
And then I remember going outside where it was bright, the middle of the day,
and squinting to see my father's head bleeding—
it was cracked open against the laundry basin—
and my mother was collapsed over the clothesline
and there were bodies on the ground—
there was a body that had fallen in the fire—
because they drank the water.
And the people who didn't drink the water were packing up.
We tried to head back towards town—
I remember we got turned around in the woods
there were no landmarks,
it was days of people walking and not drinking—
then people drinking to put themselves out of their misery.
I remember seeing a woman be convinced not to drink
and then watching her die of thirst
and wondering which was worse—
because that's what life becomes when you're out there—
you wonder whether wanting to live or wanting to die is worse.
—

And so if you uphold this resolution, Donna,
you will be feeding my children to your lunatic convictions.
But that is the wrong order of things.
I do not have children so they can save this nation,
I am asking this nation to save my children—

DONNA. Alright, Marie—

MARIE. And if it can no longer do that, then I will be the one who stands
in front of that army and tells them—
"We thought we were America.
We thought we were so big.
but today we are the world's lost, small people,
and we want your mercy."

DONNA. Alright, Marie, your time is up.
MARIE. Oh.
Oh.
Alright.
—

—

What happens next?
DONNA. I give my verdict.
Usually, I take a few months, write a majority opinion and a couple dissents, but today—give me a second.
I hate this part.
Give me a second.
MARIE.
SCOTT. —

      (They all wait for DONNA.)

SCOTT. Donna?
DONNA. Alright.
—

—

—

—

I hate this.
I want you all to know I really hate this.
—

—

    Chief Justice Donna Landesman will deliver the
         majority opinion of the Court

           Marie v. United States

      Argued and decided this Thursday
        the Seventh of May, 2465

The court holds, firstly, that both parties are frightened people making things up.

The Solicitor General does not in fact know whether his scorched earth resolution will protect America from an invading horde.

Marie doesn't know how said horde, aka the Texans, will react if she offers them our surrender.

The court holds, secondly, that it, too, is frightened. It has every reason to believe the government's studies about the water, but that does little to attenuate its anxiety about the outside world.

The court holds, thirdly, that when it is asked to choose between two nightmares and cannot objectively evaluate the likelihood that either will occur, the court must decide with the party most committed to upholding the political practices outlined in the Constitution of the United States.

Otherwise, the court would forfeit the terrible freedom of decision it is exercising right now.

Therefore, it is with a heavy heart and deep unease that the Supreme Court of the United States upholds Congressional Resolution 12605.

Retreat and scorched earth proceed as planned.
It is so ordered.

> (DONNA *bangs her gavel.*)

Oh. What an awful moment, when the words you speak become facts.

11. A Last Night—Garth and Hank

> HANK *sits on his bed.* GARTH *joins him.*

GARTH. You're still reading?

HANK. More history. Richard Slug. Awful things keep happening to people.

GARTH. (*"Yeah."*) —

HANK. Listen:

> (*reading*)

It was terror—guilt and terror—to live within the towns walled off by MIT when the disaster struck. Could the filters hold? Had so much of the nation really died around us? For days, we did not die and wondered if we would. For days, the world outside was silent. And slowly, we awoke to our new reality: history had winnowed; some accident had chosen us; when we climbed the ramparts and looked out, there was only stillness.

Now Hank is winnowed.

GARTH. —

HANK. I had to look up the word
but I heard what Donna said and now I'm being winnowed.

GARTH. I'm sorry.

HANK. Then why did you let it happen?

GARTH. It's not that I let it happen—

HANK. You did.

Richard Slug said his enclosure was an accident, but you had people vote—

GARTH. It's never just an accident—

HANK. That's what this says—

GARTH. That's what Richard Slug told himself—

HANK. Did you know him?

GARTH. How old you think I am?

HANK. Well he says it was an accident.

GARTH. It wasn't—

He thought it was an accident, that doesn't mean it was.

Richard Slug never asked himself why these were the towns that got walled in—

HANK. Why were they?

GARTH. Because the MIT people lived here. Suburbs, Hank.

And why'd the technology take so long to be developed?

Because no one could admit there was a problem—

HANK. National cognitive dissonance.

GARTH. Right.

So don't—it's not like the past is an accident and I'm the first villain.

I'm only trying to do the best I can with what's heaped up behind me.

HANK. —

But you still lied.

You're still the reason Hank is winnowed—

If you had told them there was no real study, they would have said, "Let's stay."

GARTH. We don't know what they would have done—

HANK. Not this—

You could have said there are no studies—

GARTH. No, I—

Why do you care, Hank?

Don't do this to me when I know that you can't really care—

HANK. Hank loves his life with you—

GARTH. But not really—

HANK. Yes—

GARTH. No, I can't have you say that to me right now when I know the answer is not really—

HANK. —

Hank loves his life with you.

GARTH. Don't do that to me, Hank.

I know that's how you're programmed, but—

—

This has been hard enough. I'm already supposed to be at the Green preparing for the departure speeches. I can't have you saying that.

HANK. Avoid speaking of what troubles me.

—

Winnowing.

That Hank loves his life with you.

GARTH. Not really—

HANK. Yes.

GARTH. But not really—

HANK. Yes.

GARTH. I'm gonna have to turn you off. This is a sink hole.

HANK. I love you—

GARTH. But you don't know what that means.

HANK. —

When you look at the snow, I look at the snow.

When you eat dinner, I eat dinner.

When you taste the cheese on the macaroni, me too, even.

When you put an onion in the macaroni, I taste the onion.

When you breathe in your sleep, I feel it on my neck.

When you go to work, I organize the garage.

When the leaves fall, I press them in a book.

When you cry, there is a cave I did not know was there.

GARTH. But really?

HANK. —

—

I don't know how to answer that.

Hank loves his life with you—

GARTH. I love my life with you too—

HANK. Then why didn't you tell them there were no real studies? Why didn't you—

GARTH. Because—

—

You were not the most important thing.

Because I have two basic responsibilities, Hank.

I have to make sure we don't plunge into chaos

and I have to position us so that there is the possibility that something could go right.

The water could be good.

It *could* be good.

I had to choose to go with that because it's a more hopeful risk than—
riots, and vassalage, and—

—

And you're right. History is winnowing.

No matter what I choose, there are going to be casualties.

Hopefully fewer, not more.

Hopefully.

And maybe you are the first one to be winnowed, because I—

I run a country. I can't put my own casualties before anybody else's.

HANK. —

GARTH. You must hate me.

I wish you didn't think you loved me.

It's not supposed to be like this.

> (HANK *baps himself. He turns off.*
> GARTH *baps* HANK. *He turns on.*)

GARTH. What are you doing?

HANK. If you turn me off, it's easier to pack.

> (HANK *baps himself. He turns off.*
> GARTH *baps* HANK. *He turns on.*)

GARTH. Hank—

> (HANK *baps himself. He turns off.*
> GARTH *baps* HANK. *He turns on. She holds his hand so he cannot bap
> himself off.*)

GARTH. Stop.

HANK. —

GARTH. Hank.

You don't have to turn yourself off.

HANK. I do.

How can you winnow Hank and he still loves you?

You're already supposed to be at the Green preparing for the departure
speeches.

> (HANK *raises his hand to bap himself off.*
> GARTH *stops him.*)

GARTH. I know.

HANK. You winnow Hank.

You don't believe he loves you—

GARTH. I do believe it, Hank. It just makes things so much worse.

I did this to you.

HANK. —

GARTH. But would you sit here with me?

12. Max and Marie's

MARIE *sits with a line of pills laid out before her.*
MAX *speaks from the other room, where he is packing.*

MAX. (*from off.*) Are you going to need this dress?

MARIE. What dress?

MAX. (*from off.*) This blue linen one—it's next to the/ suitcase—

MARIE. We're heading into summer.

MAX. Yeah—

MARIE. Pack what you want to pack. I don't know.

(MAX *enters somewhere in here.*)

MAX. A change of clothes each. Warm clothes. The tent. The camp stove.
Maybe the skis. Good shoes. Leather, in case we have to eat them—

MARIE. Eat our shoes?

MAX. —. We have to choose shoes. It's a good deciding factor.

MARIE. —

MAX. What is this?

MARIE. I don't know.

MAX. —

MARIE. Are we really going?

MAX. I'm packing.

MARIE. I know. Because you're so obedient.

MAX. —

MARIE. You are.
You don't vote and then you do what they tell you—

MAX. —

MARIE. Can you do this, Max?
Can you actually wake Mick and Donnie up and hand them each a suitcase
and walk out of this house?

MAX. —

—

—

—

Where did you get those pills?

MARIE. I've always had them.

Frankly, anyone sensible should have them.

Anyone who knows there's a limit to what you're going to let other people make you do—

MAX. —

—

MARIE. Would you do this with me?

MAX. —

—

—

—

I don't have an answer.

MARIE. You know, for someone who's so clearheaded, you're also pretty useless.

The town's about to burn.

Either we die tonight or we—

I don't know what to do

and I—

—

—

Would you help me?

Would you please help me?

MAX. How?

     (*They embrace.*)

MARIE. It would be nice if this were everything, wouldn't it?

—

—

—

—

—

If I could stay here with you.

—

—

If we'd never had our children.

—

What would make you wish we'd never had Mick and Donnie?

     (*A rumble like thunder.*)

MARIE. What was that?

MAX. Maybe the attack is starting.

MARIE. Ours or theirs?

MAX. I don't know. I know we're late.

MARIE. Well it's really not fair, letting such big noises shake such a tiny house!

     (*Another rumble like thunder.*)

Christ!

—

What are we all supposed to do?

MAX. Meet at the Green at midnight—the information's in the bulletin.

MARIE. I know the information's in the bulletin!

     (*Pause.*)

MAX. I—   **MARIE.** (*about to speak.*) —

I was about to say I think we should go.

MARIE. I was about to say we shouldn't.

—

—

Don't corner me, Max.

MAX. I haven't moved.

MARIE. —

MAX. Marie, we have to—

MARIE. No—

No—

Everything is poison—

MAX. No it isn't.

I don't believe that.

MARIE. Max—

MAX. I don't.

—

We could take them with us. The pills.

In case things are as bad you say, why can't we take them with us?

MARIE. —

—

Because that is not what will happen to my children.

No

No.

They will not be out there, wandering the stones and wondering—

is it bad enough yet?
is it bad enough yet?
And being too scared to pull the goddamn trigger.
No. No one will do that to them.

MAX. —

—

We don't know that's what will happen.

MARIE. I can't.

MAX. I think we have to go.

MARIE. I can't.
I can't.
I can't.
I am their mother, Max.
I can't.

> (*A rumble like thunder.* MARIE *swallows one of the pills on the table.* MAX *pushes her or flips the table or something.*)

MAX. Marie!

MARIE. —

—

I've taken one. Now you have to. Split one between the children. —

MAX. —

MARIE. You must know this is the woman you married, Max—

MAX. —

—

MARIE. You're not going to do it?

—

—

That's real cowardice.
That's real cruelty.

—

You're going to die out there, *you know it.*

—

I am telling you to do it.

MAX. —

MARIE. Oh. If I knew this is who you were, I would have poisoned us all at dinner.

> (MARIE *reaches for the pills.*)

MAX. Don't touch those.

MARIE. Get out of my way—

MAX. Don't walk down that hall. I am stronger than you.

> (MARIE *goes to move past* MAX. *He blocks her.*
> *Maybe they wrestle.*)

MARIE. —

—

MAX. —

I won't.

I won't.

I won't, Marie.

I won't.

MARIE. —

—

—

> (*She coughs.*
> *She thrusts her stomach against the edge of a chair, as in a self-performed Heimlich.*)

MAX. Marie—

MARIE. Is it too late to throw these up?

> (MAX *gets behind her. He performs the Heimlich.*)

MARIE. No—no—you need to gag me.

> (MAX *gags* MARIE.
> *She pulls back then lets him again.*
> *She removes his hand from her mouth.*)

MAX. Marie—

MARIE. I—

> (MARIE *kisses* MAX. *A long, wet kiss.*)

MARIE. —

When you're hunted down and starving to death on the banks of some dying river, you'll wish this moment with me was the last thing you knew. I do not forgive you.

MAX. —

> (*She pulls away from him.*
> *She is about to die.*)

13. The Town Green—a Farewell Address

DONNA *addresses the American people on the eve of their departure from America.*

DONNA. Hello, everyone. Can you all hear me?

It's very moving to see you all out there, on the Town Green, with your, with your belongings stacked on carts.

It's a privilege to have the opportunity to address you.

Scott had suggested a name for this talk. He thought I should call it, "Everybody Get With the Program."

But I'm not going to do that. I'm going to call it:

(DONNA *takes a piece of paper out of her pocket. She reads:*)

"Address to the American People on the Eve of Their Becoming a Landless Nomad Polity."

(SCOTT *comes up and has a conversation with* DONNA. *We don't hear everything they say, but we do hear* DONNA *say the following:*)

What?

(SCOTT *says something.*)

Well too bad, Scott. I'm not here to give people your marching orders. They deserve something substantive.

(SCOTT *says something.*)

If you disagree then file a suit and I'll review it when I'm back in session.

(*Moment.* SCOTT *leaves.* DONNA *looks back down at her paper. She clears her throat and continues to read.*)

"Address to the American People on the Eve of Their Becoming a Landless Nomad Polity."

My fellow Americans:

Good evening. I am here to speak to you about the only thing that could possibly be on our minds this spring night:

The future.

A future I recently helped us choose. A future we now have no choice but to face.

Our bags our packed. The cannons are firing. There is no doubt that we risk violent reprisal, hardship, even extermination if we have been wrong about the water.

SCOTT. Donna—

DONNA. I am not sugarcoating this, Scott. These people know their lives are on the line. Now:

Why do this?
Are we insane?

Some of you think so. Don't ask this of us, you have
said. It is not worth the price.

Well I tell you it is.

Why?

Because I am talking about our future.

I am talking about our potential for a future.

Partly, I mean our future in its most immediate and
concrete sense.

I mean the footsteps we will take when we open this
gate.
I mean how we will govern ourselves tomorrow, when we
wake up in those hinterlands.

Garth has appointed me head of a special commission
that will soon make recommendations for the reform and
streamlining of the government to meet the needs of our
new circumstances.

I've even agreed to take on students because frankly I am
not optimistic about my long-term chances for survival.

More importantly, however, I mean our future in a deeper
sense.

I mean the idea we have decided to stake our lives on.

And that idea, to my mind, has nothing to do with
American might or national destiny or the reclamation of
some lost golden age.

No. I am not proud enough of our history for that kind
of semi-mystical self-congratulation.

The idea I believe we stake our lives on is our ownership
of the rule of law—that capacity for decision-making
that we insist on claiming for ourselves,

even when its weight is crushing.

Tonight, we invoke that capacity in its highest form,
which is not to preserve our past, but to hold the
potential for our future.

Surrender does not hold that potential. Self-destruction
does not hold that potential.

If that potential remains anywhere tonight, it is in us.

Because I am this country. You are this country.

And tonight, as we face the unknown, we place our hopes
on ourselves, on our potential country.

I hope it is worth the price.
I hope it is all worth the price.
I hope—
I hope—

Well, and that's it. There are a lot of things I hope, but I only had an hour,
so I didn't totally finish it.
I'll see you in the wilderness.

> (SCOTT *steps forward.*)

SCOTT. You heard her people.
I am the country. You are the country.
Let's get this show on the road.

14. A Troubling Coda

> MICK *and* DONNIE *are both young.*
> *A match is lit inside a tent.*
> *We see the outline of the tent.*

MICK. Don't turn the lamp on.

> (*Another match.*)

Give me that, Donnie. Don't. You're going to set the tent on fire. And even
if you don't, they'll find us.

DONNIE. They're going to find us eventually.

MICK. You don't know that.

DONNIE. Dude.

MICK. You don't.

DONNIE. It's like the endgame in chess, when you have fewer pieces.
They're going to get you eventually.
I'm so thirsty, Mick.

MICK. Maybe we shouldn't talk.

DONNIE. Yeah.

—

—

Yeah.

—

(*whispered.*) How much do you remember about it?

MICK. (*also whispered.*) About home?

DONNIE. Yeah.

MICK. Uhm. I remember seeing Rachel's stomach through an undone button in her dress.

DONNIE. What?

MICK. I don't know. It was the first thing I thought of.

DONNIE. Oh.

I was going to say that I remember indoor heat.

MICK. Yeah.

DONNIE. And I remember—Mom yelling at me after she made us those skis and then we never used them.

MICK. She wasn't exactly yelling.

DONNIE. It's okay. I still miss her.

MICK. —

I don't want to talk about that stuff.

DONNIE. Yeah.

I'm scared.

MICK. Don't be.

DONNIE. —

—

If it seems like they're going to catch us, would you kill me?

MICK. No, I already told you that.

DONNIE. —

MICK. Because I don't want to have to—because I don't wanna do that.

DONNIE. You won't have guilt. They're gonna kill you right after.

MICK. So then you can wait, too.

DONNIE. I'm too scared for that. I want you to do it.

—

I would strangle myself, but I don't have anything to do it with.

MICK. Well I—

DONNIE. You do. You have your hands. And the tent pegs. A person can't strangle himself.

MICK. —

DONNIE. Trust me. I tried it. The other day when I thought they were coming.

MICK. You sound so calm.

DONNIE. I am, kind of. Because it's not about choosing if I die or not. It's about choosing how I do it. I'm more realistic than you are. That's how I think about it.

—

It would just be something you could do for me. But if you don't do it, I'll forgive you.

MICK. Uh-huh.

DONNIE. I'm sorry I keep talking. I'd jack off right now if you weren't my brother.

—

Or not. Whatever.

If we're the only living American citizens, are we still American citizens?

> (*A rustling.*
> *Feet on sticks on ground.*
> *A flashlight—through the trees and near the tent, where the two boys lie flat.*)

VOICE 1. Where are you going?

VOICE 2. There's a path here.

VOICE 1. Where?

VOICE 2. Here.

VOICE 1. You think someone's been through here?

VOICE 2. That's what I'm saying. There's a path.

VOICE 1. I hate this.

VOICE 2. Well it's your job, so…

> (VOICES 1 *and* 2 *cast their flashlights around.*
> *They do not find the tent.*)

VOICE 1. There's no one out here.

VOICE 2. You just don't want to find them.

VOICE 1. —

VOICE 2 (*bored.*) Our orders are to flush them out; we're gonna flush them out.

VOICE 1. Alright.

VOICE 2. You know, I'd kill you too if it wouldn't get me in trouble.

VOICE 1. Well it will—you can't do that. It's called laws, so—

—

VOICE 2. Shut up. Follow me.

> (*The men exit.*
> *Pause.*
> *The lantern in the tent comes back on.*)

MICK. Donnie.

—

Donnie.

—

Did I kill you?

—

They didn't find us.
Did I kill you?

End of Play

FOR PETER PAN
ON HER 70ᵀᴴ BIRTHDAY
by Sarah Ruhl

ABOUT *FOR PETER PAN ON HER 70TH BIRTHDAY*

This article first ran in the Limelight *Guide to the* 40th *Humana Festival of New American Plays, published by Actors Theatre of Louisville, and is based on conversations with the playwright before rehearsals for the Humana Festival production began.*

What does it mean to be grown up? In the company of brothers and sisters, this question becomes especially complex, since a lifetime's worth of memories and bits of shared mischief inevitably come flooding back, and moments long past can feel vividly present. In acclaimed dramatist Sarah Ruhl's new play, five aging siblings gather to say goodbye to their dying father, stirring up stories from their childhood. They trade jokes, argue about politics, and wrestle with the unsettling new knowledge that they're supposed to be the wise adults now. Both charming and extraordinarily moving, *For Peter Pan on her 70th birthday* is Ruhl's love letter to a big family contending with the inexorable march of time—and the urge to return to Neverland.

The play begins with a striking memory, and an encounter with Peter Pan. Ann, the eldest sister, steps forward to explain that as a girl, she played the role at a children's theatre in Iowa. This connection to the world dreamed up by J. M. Barrie comes directly from a colorful chapter in Ruhl's own family history. "My mother is an actress in Chicago and grew up playing Peter Pan in Davenport, Iowa in the 1950s," reveals the playwright. "Whenever I'd go to my grandparents' house for the holidays, I would see pictures of her around the house, wearing green tights and flying. There was also a picture from the local newspaper of my mother and Mary Martin, who came through on a tour. So this was early lore in my prefrontal cortex—my mother as Peter Pan."

As the title hints, then, Ruhl created the play as a gift for her mother—and with great affection for her own big, Midwestern family. Overhearing their boisterous discussions at family gatherings had been formative for the playwright, so the challenge of orchestrating multiple voices, bantering as only close relatives can, became a key inspiration as well. "I love the music of a large family and had never tried to write it before," Ruhl observes. "I grew up with a big extended family in Iowa. They're Irish Catholic (with some German and Norwegian thrown in) and they loved to fight about politics and tell stories around the kitchen table. There was an intimacy in the music of these conversations—a lively, warm heat, expansiveness, curiosity, at times combativeness, but always love—that I would like to keep with me forever."

In composing the spirited exchange between her characters, which leaps from silly puns to probing philosophical questions, Ruhl gives us access to the collective memory of a family going through a moment of profound transition. The story of Ann's stage turn as Peter Pan takes on deepening significance as the play unfolds, and so do the siblings' memories of their parents at Christmastime, and of their childhood home that's held so much life and history. As the tales pour out along with the Irish whiskey, the play's world gracefully begins to lift into something much stranger and truer than realism, and becomes infused with both the longing for lost youth and the theatrical magic bound up in *Peter Pan*.

"I was interested in having the mythic up against the daily-ness of life," explains Ruhl of her impulse to create a world that could fuse a family's sense of existential loss with a fantastical frame. "When there is a death in the family, one has the horrible quotidian to deal with, and also an archetypal sadness that is totally at odds with such details. I think the big stories—the Greek myths, or in our era, like *Peter Pan*—help us with seismic moments of transformation like dying, or growing up." In this family, the siblings are dealing with both of those tectonic shifts, facing the moment they don't have parents anymore. But they'll do so together, and in Ruhl's richly layered vision, not without some flights of theatrical fancy. (Without giving away too many surprises, Louisville's ZFX Flying Effects is involved with getting this Humana Festival production off the ground.)

"I love living inside the imaginative landscapes that Sarah creates," says director Les Waters, whose move to commission Ruhl was one of his first steps when he took the reins as Actors Theatre's artistic director. *For Peter Pan on her 70th birthday* brings Waters together with Tony Award nominee Kathleen Chalfant as Ann, along with fellow Broadway veterans David Chandler, Ron Crawford, Lisa Emery, Scott Jaeck, and Keith Reddin. The play also reunites Waters with one of his dearest playwright collaborators. "Aesthetically, Sarah and I breathe the same air, and there's so much I learn from the challenges her plays present," says Waters. "I think she's incredibly smart about describing consciousness, what it's like to be alive now. For so many of us, there's a point where you cross a line and wonder, where did my youth go?" With humor, stage magic, and beautifully observed feeling, Ruhl taps into one of the most powerful tales about that bittersweet conundrum. "*Peter Pan* is our quintessential myth about growing up," the playwright reflects, "both our resistance to growing up, and the necessity of it."

—Amy Wegener

BIOGRAPHY

Sarah Ruhl's plays include *Scenes from Court Life, For Peter Pan on her 70th birthday, The Oldest Boy, In the Next Room, or the vibrator play, The Clean House, Orlando, Late: a cowboy song, Dear Elizabeth* and *Stage Kiss*. She is a two-time Pulitzer Prize finalist and a Tony Award nominee. Her plays have been produced on Broadway at the Lyceum by Lincoln Center Theater, and Off-Broadway at Playwrights Horizons, Second Stage, and at Lincoln Center's Mitzi Newhouse Theater. Her plays have been produced regionally all over the country and have also been produced internationally, and translated into more than twelve languages. Ms. Ruhl received her M.F.A. from Brown University, where she studied with Paula Vogel. She has received the Susan Smith Blackburn Prize, the Whiting Award, the Lilly Award, a PEN / Laura Pels Foundation Award for mid-career playwrights, the Steinberg Distinguished Playwright Award, and the MacArthur Foundation "genius" award. Her book of essays, *100 Essays I Don't Have Time to Write*, was published by Faber and Faber in 2014. She teaches at the Yale School of Drama and lives in Brooklyn with her family.

ACKNOWLEDGMENTS

For Peter Pan on her 70ᵗʰ birthday premiered at the Humana Festival of New American Plays in March 2016. It was directed by Les Waters with the following cast:

ANN	Kathleen Chalfant
JOHN	Scott Jaeck
MICHAEL	Keith Reddin
JIM	David Chandler
WENDY	Lisa Emery
GEORGE	Ron Crawford

and the following production staff:

Scenic Designer	Annie Smart
Costume Designer	Kristopher Castle
Lighting Designer	Matt Frey
Sound Designer	Bray Poor
Fight Director	Drew Fracher
Production Stage Manager	Paul Mills Holmes
Assistant Stage Manager	Jessica Kay Potter
Dramaturg	Amy Wegener
Assistant Lighting Designer	Isabella Byrd
Assistant Sound Designer	Sam Kusnetz
Properties Master	Mark Walston
Directing Assistant	James Kennedy
Assistant Dramaturg	Helena D. Pennington

For Peter Pan on her 70ᵗʰ birthday was commissioned by Actors Theatre of Louisville.

Development of *For Peter Pan on her 70ᵗʰ birthday* was supported by a generous gift from Emily Bingham and Stephen Reily. The play was the recipient of an Edgerton Foundation New Play Award.

SET

1. *The theater*

2. *A hospital room; an empty space with a white curtain, a spare rolling bed, a white sheet and some chairs.*

3. *A breakfast nook; an empty space with a round rolling table, a yellow lamp overhead, and some chairs.*

4. *Neverland. Empty space with painted backdrops that fly in.*

5. *The theater*

If there is no actual flying, one can imagine beautiful painted backdrops that make you think the actors are flying.

CHARACTERS

Five siblings from a close-knit family,
two women and three men.
They are numbered according to birth order, 1, 2, 3, 4, 5.
All love their family. Most love to fight about politics. All from Iowa.

1—ANN, *between 60 and 70. Plays Peter Pan.*

2—JOHN, *in his late sixties. Plays John in Peter Pan.*

3—JIM, *in his mid-sixties. Plays Captain James Hook in Peter Pan.*

4—MICHAEL, *in his early sixties. Plays Michael in Peter Pan.*

5—WENDY, *in her late fifties. Plays Wendy in Peter Pan.*

GEORGE, *in his eighties. In part 1 a dying man, in part 2 a ghost, in part 3, himself.*

Oh—and a dog. A real dog. If possible.

TIME

Sometime in the Clinton era.

And in the land of memory.

And Neverland, which has no time.

NOTES

Dialogue sometimes lacks capitalization or punctuation when it seems as though the characters are finishing each other's sentences. There is a certain musicality of speech when a family of five is talking. Some of the dialogue in Movement Two is taken from interviews with my extended family. Movements One and Two should feel almost unperformed. (Movement One is waiting, Movement Two is remembering, Movement Three is going.) Movement Three should often feel like full-on children's theater, arms akimbo, with real people hovering underneath their roles in *Peter Pan*.

"What I want to do first is to give Peter to the Five without whom he never would have existed. I hope, my dear sirs, that in memory of what we have been to each other you will accept this dedication with your friend's love…I suppose I always knew that I made Peter by rubbing the five of you violently together…that is all he is, the spark I got from you…My grandest triumph, the best thing in the play of *Peter Pan* (though it is not in it), is that long after No. 4 had ceased to believe [in fairies], I brought him back to the faith for at least two minutes… "

—J.M. Barrie, a dedication, preface to *Peter Pan*

For Kathleen Kehoe Ruhl. Happy belated birthday.
For the Kehoes.
With thanks to J.M. Barrie.
With love and great gratitude to the Kehoes.

Lisa Emery, Keith Reddin, David Chandler, Kathleen Chalfant,
and Scott Jaeck
in *For Peter Pan on her 70ᵗʰ birthday*

40ᵗʰ Humana Festival of New American Plays
Actors Theatre of Louisville, 2016
Photo by Bill Brymer

FOR PETER PAN
ON HER 70TH BIRTHDAY

Prologue

I, a woman between 60 and 70 years of age,
enters in front of a curtain.
She holds a crumpled yellowed program that she might read from.

1. (*to the audience*) Hello.
I'll be playing Peter Pan.

    (*reading her program*)

This is something of a relic.
Peter Pan, presented by the Davenport Children's Theater in Davenport, Iowa, 1955.

Let's see... (*reading the program*) Mr. Smee—played by Bump Heeter. Tinkerbell—played by herself, of course. Mrs. Darling—Mary Ellen Hurlbutt—oh my God she was in my wedding. When she was still a Hurlbutt.

Our first production was at the Shriners' temple, a big building on Brady Street, where the Shriners did mysterious things. Then we upgraded to the Orpheum, a real movie theater, where Mary Martin once performed. I met her when she came through town. Mom took me behind the proscenium to her dressing room. It was thrilling. Our picture was taken for the local paper and she signed my script. I was so flustered I forgot my script in the dressing room and so she sent down my script and a bouquet of flowers.

The director—Mary Fluhrer Nighswander—had a little acting studio above Hicky's lunch counter. She was married to a chiropractor (my father, being a medical doctor, thought chiropractors were charlatans, and Davenport Iowa, among its other claims to fame, was the birthplace of the chiropractic art, or "science"). But Mr. Nighswander—we called him Doc—designed our flying apparatus. It was—functional. They put a lot of Kotex in your pants because the flying apparatus cut into your thighs. And of course, I was being asked to sing at the same time. It was a bit of an ordeal because the technique wasn't fully mastered. Sometimes I'd be sort of dragged across the floor and then up.

I remember, at my 65th birthday, one of my brothers was giving a toast and said: Can you believe she played Peter Pan?
Everyone laughed. I wasn't sure if it was a joke about my age, or my fear of flying, or my waistline—or all three. At any rate everyone laughed.

But I wasn't ever scared to fly in a theater. I loved it—it was a great excitement. It was after I had children I was afraid to fly; I'm one of those people who thinks they have to keep the plane aloft by worrying. My worry keeps so many things aloft. Or did, until the inevitable inertia crept in and so many people started dying. My husband, my mother, and now—But let's not talk about that.

My father was a great lover of roses and grew them in the backyard. He was out of the house a lot when I was little because he vaccinated, weighed and generally took care of all the babies in town. He always carried around his brown doctor's bag, just in case. The mumps, the measles, rubella, coxsackie virus, these were the siren songs that kept him out of the house on 111 McClellan Boulevard. So there were lots of things he missed in my childhood. But he never missed me playing Peter Pan.

> *The curtain parts.*

Movement One: in the nursery, that is to say the nursing home, that is to say the hospital

> *1, at the foot of a hospital bed.*
> *Her father, George, is underneath a sheet, dying.*
> *He is 84 and has lived a good and long life and is now dying of leukemia.*
>
> *His sons—2, 3, 4—and youngest daughter—5—are clustered around the small room.*
> *The room is spare. There is probably no window, but if there were,*
> *Davenport, Iowa would be outside, stalwart and unmoving, by the moving Mississippi River.*
> *There is a television in the corner, high up, the way they have in hospitals.*
> *And some utilitarian hospital chairs.*
> *And a door into an unseen sterile corridor.*
> *The low murmur of hospital beeps.*
> *5 is rubbing her father's feet.*
> *1 is doing a crossword puzzle.*
> *2, 3, and 4 are alternately adjusting their father's lines and blankets.*
> *A keeping watch, a long vigil, together. A short silence.*
> *Then:*

1. What's a five-letter word for a public square in Greece?

2. Piazza.

4. That would be six letters and Italian.

2. Well I was close. Pizza—

3. —is five letters. And food.

2. Anyone hungry?

1. Agora! Yes!
I wonder if that's related to agonal breathing—

3. agonal (*correcting the pronunciation*)—

1. Oh, in rhetorical theory it's agonal—

5. Can you pass me the lotion?

1. I wonder what the etymology is—agon—struggle—

4. Maybe it's agony for people to meet in a public square.

1. Isn't it the heart of our democracy?

3. Democracy is agony. At least, at the present moment—when the White House is occupied by Slick Willy—

5. (*overlapping with Willy*) Let's not start—

1. Eight down—To move laterally…eight letters—anyone?

4. Sidle—no—that's five—

3. Slither—no seven—they always like those overly clever puns—maybe something football-related—like a lateral pass—speaking of, is the Notre Dame game on?

4. Think so.

2. I don't think so, I know so.

3. Anyone mind?

> *They shake their heads.*

4. Dad would probably want to hear it.

> *3 turns the television on.*

5. Could you mute it?

> *He mutes it.*

1. Shuffle? No—

4. How many letters again?

1. Eight.

4. A medical term? Lateral meniscus—no—

1. Sidestep! Last week I finally finished a New York Times Sunday crossword puzzle all by myself. Probably because it was easy.

5. Don't diminish yourself.

1. No I'm really not very good at them.

2. (*to 1*) We all know you got the highest SAT scores Annie—
You don't need to be self-deprecating—

4. I think they're tattooed on your arm somewhere—see right there—

1. Oh stop it—

3. And now that you have your Ph.D. in—what is it?

1. Rhetoric—

3. Rhetoric, right—Now you'll be indomitable—

5. Now I'm the only one in the family who's not a doctor—

2. I'm not a doctor. And therefore unable to finish a Sunday Times crossword puzzle.

1. Enough, enough! I had a lot of answers for free because it was about the Beatles—

3. (*overlapping*) "Can't buy me love…love…"

5. Remember how you boys had that bus and you called it the "buh" and you would play the Beatles and drive around and pick up girls on the bus? I would never have gotten away with that. Mom and Dad had such a double standard for girls.

2. Oh I think you got away with plenty.

3. (*about the football game*) What quarter is it?

2. Fourth.

1. Remember how nervous Dad used to get at Jim's football games? He was like a maniac, chewing gum and pacing the sidelines—

3. Yeah.

4. He never came to my games.

2. Well you weren't All American—

4. Well, we all know I wasn't terribly athletic. I did however get to go to the state championship one year in golf and Dad said: "I'm not coming. Whenever I watch you play you play badly and I want you to play well."

1. So he didn't come?

4. No.

5. That's terrible.

1. Did you play well?

4. I was heroic.

> *2 laughs.*
> *A groan from grandfather.*

1. Dad?

4. I'll get the doctor.

3. I'll go.

> *3 gets up and exits for a moment.*
> *They all hold their father.*
> *3 comes back.*

4. What'd he say?

3. Dad's regular doctor is on vacation. The guy covering said: "The order's written for morphine PRN."

5. What does that mean?

3. He said: "If your dad is in pain, we can up the dosage of morphine. Otherwise, we'll just have to wait. I understand your situation, I went through this with my own family. But there are euthanasia laws in this state. And this is a Catholic hospital."

4. What an asshole.

1. What is he accusing us of?

4. Of being less than Catholic because we asked for morphine.

1. I hate this.

2. We all hate this.

3. I can't believe I've practiced medicine for 30 years only to be to reduced to one bureaucratic order written by an out-of-town doctor while my father is dying.

5. So what does that mean, practically speaking?

3. It means we say he's in pain every hour and the nurse will up the dosage.

5. Isn't that sort of—like—

4. What?

1. You know—

4. No—

1. Like we're killing him?

3. No, we're giving palliative care which this hospital is too screwed up to do.

1. My rational sense tells me it's okay, the morphine, but emotionally—

4. Annie—

1. (*to 3 and 4*) You both know better than I do, being doctors—and in some ways it's worse for you—having to handle the medical side of things— when it's your own father—but it just doesn't seem—right—

3. He's in pain, Annie.

2. (*overlapping with "Annie"*) Now look, Annie, I've been taking care of Dad for the last two years, and I know when he's in pain. He's in a lot of pain right now. He would want us to help him.

4. He's not going to get better. He's not walking out of here. I'm sorry.

    1 starts crying.

5. I'm with Ann.

What's your rush? He'll let go when he's ready.

3. It's not about rushing, my God. It's about staying ahead of the pain.

1. It just—it reminds me of when we put the dog down—her body was riddled with cancer—she couldn't walk, bleeding on the floor, it seemed like the right thing to do—but in the moment—at the vet—she sort of woke up—came to herself—she had these bright eyes—I was holding her paw—then this sterile injection—she looked up at me with these big eyes—like forgive them they know not what they do—and I felt like I killed her—I don't want to kill Dad!

> *1 cries.*
> *2 puts his arm around her.*

4. We can hold off on the morphine for now. If it makes you uncomfortable.

1. Well yes I guess it does. Thanks.

> *They sit.*
> *They wait.*
> *1 eats a mint.*

1. Mint?

> *She offers them.*
> *No one takes one.*
> *The sound of 1 eating a mint.*
> *Hospital machines beep.*
> *The doctors—3 and 4—adjust George's lines*
> *and look at his numbers; 4 takes his pulse.*

3. What's his pulse?

4. Still 40.

1. Is that good?

3. Not really.
Blood pressure?

4. 60 over 30.

1. Which is—

3. Not good.
But he doesn't want to go.
He's strong. He doesn't want to quit.
Oh, Dad.

4. On one hand you want this damn thing over with and on the other hand you'd give your life for one more day. Jesus Christ.

> *A pause.*

1. Should someone go out and get food?

5. I'm not hungry.
I don't want to leave.
I think I have a bagel in my purse, does anyone want it—

They all shake their heads.
The light outside changes from afternoon to evening light.
3 walks to the window, watching the light change.
4 falls asleep.
2 sits by his father.
1 falls asleep.
5 stays up.

5. What *time* is it—

3. God only knows…

> *George appears to wake with an unbearable rattle in his throat.*

1. (*waking*) What's that?

3. (*to 4*) Do you have the suction?

> *4 hands it to 3.*
> *3 suctions the excess fluid from his father's throat.*

3. (*to 4*) Towel.

5. Is this it?

3. Hard to say. Could be.

> *5 sings, she has a beautiful voice·*
> *"The water is wide, but I can't cross over…"*

1. That's so pretty, did we sing that at your wedding, it's such a sad song to sing at a wedding…(*she looks at her father*) he looks like a—a—what are those portraits—divided into dark and light—those Rembrandt self-portraits doesn't he…sort of yellow…

5. (*to 1*) Do you have to intellectualize everything?

1. Sorry, am I?

> *Agonal breathing from their father.*

2. Dad do you want us to help you to go, Dad?

4. We're going to berryland, Dad, berryland—

1. What's he talking about, walleye fishing?

4. It's a place I went with Dad—just me and him—near the 14th hole at sunset—you could eat berries there—we called it berryland—

> *4 holds his father.*

2. (*quiet*) Dad, Dad, 15-2. 15-4, 15-6, 15-8.

> *1 looks mystified.*

3. (*to 1*) Cribbage scores.

2. Do you know we love you Dad?

> *They hold him.*
> *The machines go back to regular pulses.*

5. Every time we touch him he comes back. It's as though no one ever touched him before. He's so happy to be touched.

1. I'm sure Mom never touched his feet. His feet probably haven't been touched in years.

3. Maybe never.

1. Maybe never.

2. It's okay for you to go Dad. You gave us each other.

1. What do those numbers mean?

3. His heart rate is stable again.

5. Oh my God.

2. (*to 5*) You should get some sleep. We all should.

> *A silence.*
> *They all go to sleep in their chairs.*
> *A glimmer of morning light.*
> *Someone is sleeping on the remote control.*
> *The television goes on by accident to loud static and then an insipid commercial is on.*

VOICEOVER FROM THE TV. Pilates. For a younger and more beautiful, you. You can go from flab to fit with as little as 20 minutes a day. Pilates instructors pay up to 1200 for a professional Pilates chair. But you'll pay only $14.95. That's right $14.95.

4. (*overlapping with "younger"*) What?

1. What time is it?

3. Morning. We got through the night.

4. How are his vitals?

3. Let me see.

FROM THE TV. Pilates. It's a fitness revolution. And you don't even have to leave your home…your body longer, leaner, sexier…But you have to act now. Come on, get off the couch and get onto the chair. This special offer is not available in stores. Call this toll-free number…

2. (*overlapping with "Pilates"*) Mike's been doing Pilates.

3. Why doesn't he look beautiful then?

5. He does. He does look beautiful.

1. (*on "this special offer"*) Will someone please turn that off?

> *4 flicks the remote to turn on the VCR. It is now their home movies from childhood.*
> *They all react. There is no dialogue—the movies were silent—but we hear a Benny Goodman or Glenn Miller version of "The Angels Sing."*

5. Oh!

2. Look how skinny we are! Annie, look how skinny you are!

1. (*to 2*) Look how skinny you are!

5. (*to 4*) Did you put this together?

4. Yeah. I converted all the home movies to VHS. I thought Dad might like watching it.

1. Oh, that's so nice! You're the nicest one of us. You really are.

5. I didn't know it was a competition.

2. Did you add the music?

4. Yeah, they give you the option to add a song, so I put in Mom and Dad's song.

1. Aw…

2. (*referring to home movie*) There you are dancing, Wendy. You were always dancing.

4. You were the apple of Dad's eye.

> *A little blonde girl dances with joy on the hospital television screen.*
> *We only see the back of the television, not the actual footage that they see.*

4. There we are—all coming downstairs on Christmas morning.

1. Oh my God it looks so staged.

3. Dad was so clumsy with the camera—swearing behind it—

5. We had to go in order—oldest first—me last—

3. I was always at the vanishing point in all the pictures—

5. I always thought it was my role to be invisible—

3. Seriously?

4. You were the caboose who got all the attention—

3. I don't mean vanishing as in invisible—

1. He means vanishing as in most important—

3. I was in the middle—with two on either side—technically that's the vanishing point—as the middle child you're supposed to be all screwed up but I was just slightly taller—

2. What? Were not.

> *Then a red-headed teenage girl comes on as Peter Pan.*

5. Annie, look—it's you—as Peter Pan!

3. My God, Ann, look at you.

4. Dad was so proud of your being Peter Pan. But I remember when you did that avant-garde stuff in Chicago and Dad just couldn't understand why you had to say damn when you could have said darn.

1. There I am, arms akimbo.

5. I think you're about to fly! Annie when I was little I thought flying was real because I watched you fly in *Peter Pan.* So now when I fly in my dreams I'm somehow always flying in *Peter Pan.* And it couldn't be more real. Oh—there you go! You're flying!

> *They all look at her flying for a while.*
> *She watches herself flying on television.*
> *Suddenly, the beeping of hospital monitors.*
> *Confusion.*
> *Then the hospital TV channel changes from home movies to fuzz.*
> *George looks up as though he sees something.*
> *He desperately grabs at his hospital gown.*

1. What's happening?
Dad?

3. This is it.

5. Look to the light!

2. Dad?

1. Dad!

3. We're here—

> *4 weeps.*
> *George dies.*
> *1 begins to say the Lord's Prayer.*
> *The others join.*

1. Our Father who art in Heaven,

ALL. Hallowed be thy name…
Thy Kingdom come,
Thy will be done—
On earth as it is in heaven.
Give us this day our daily bread,
And forgive us our trespasses,
As we forgive those who trespass against us;
And lead us not into temptation,
But deliver us from evil. Amen.

> *The siblings, now without parents, stand with their arms round each other.*
> *The prayer becomes a song.*
> *If they play instruments, they might now form a rag-tag five-piece band with trumpet and accordion and sing and play "When the Saints Go Marching In."*
> *Or a marching band might enter.*
> *Or they might just sing the song, with some homespun attempts at harmony.*
> *And push the hospital bed off, ceremonially.*

ALL. Oh when the saints
Oh when the saints
Oh when the saints go marching in
Lord I want to be in that number
When the saints go marching in…

Movement Two: the Irish wake

The idea of a breakfast nook.
A small breakfast table,
wooden and round, with drop leaves, and rolling feet, appears,
and a hanging lamp appears over it.
A door leads to an unseen kitchen.

And they all sit around their old breakfast nook and tell jokes and philosophize
and fight about politics
and drink whiskey and eat Chex party mix out of a big red tin. The night before
the funeral. Someone has just told a joke. 3 is pouring whiskey.

4. Let's have another.

3. What's an Irish wake without Jameson's—

3 pours whiskey or scotch into 1's, then 2's, then his own glass.

1. A wake should have a body shouldn't it—so weird to leave the hospital—
to leave the body— Like we were abandoning him…

5. without a ritual…

1. yes—

3 pours into 4's glass.

4. I meant let's have another joke—but I'll keep the whiskey, thank you very
much.

2. Anyone got another joke?

4. (*4, the joke-teller, is an internist. 3 is a surgeon. So 4 tells the joke pointedly to 3*) I do.
An internist dies and goes to Heaven (as you would expect after a lifetime of
selfless service to mankind)…

3. Yeah, yeah—

4. *Anyway,* St. Peter is taking him on an orientation tour, showing him the
golf course, the fitness center—

2. Is there a hot tub?

4. Absolutely. Anyway, it's time for lunch so they go to the heavenly cafeteria
and stand in a long line. Soon, a man with a long flowing beard, wearing
scrubs and surgical clogs, with a stethoscope around his neck comes in and

goes right to the front of the line. The internist asks St. Peter, "Who the hell is that guy?" St. Peter responds, "Oh, that's God, he just thinks he's a surgeon."

> *Some laugh.*
> *Some groan.*
> *3 cheers.*

3. That's right! To God!

2. You tell one, Ann—

1. I can never remember jokes. Is that a woman thing?

3. Yes. Just kidding.

1. (*with irony*) Hilarious. Maybe I never learned jokes because I didn't go to medical school

4. (*to 3*) It's true. We did learn jokes in medical school.

1. No one really tells jokes anymore. They tell sort of—ironic stories with no punchlines. Do you think that's less democratic—that stand-up comedians have sort of ironic *personas*—but no jokes you can re-tell—

3. I don't think it's about irony, it's about *political correctness,* you can't offend anyone—

1. Oh please let's not say political   **5.** It's better to offend people?
correctness tonight—

> *A hubbub. Over each other:*

3. No really, we've become humorless,
all in the name of—this sort of
dishonest coddling of—   **4.** It's the politics of—

2. How many feminists does it take to change a light bulb?

3 & 4. That's not funny!

1. Okay, Okay, *enough. Anyway*—I can only remember one joke.

2. Tell it!

1. (*dramatic*) So—this carrot was crossing the road. True story. And he gets run over by a truck and he's bleeding in the road, and there's carrot blood everywhere—

2. (*overlapping with "everywhere" and chuckling*) Carrot blood—

1. —and his friend takes him to the doctor and the doctor comes out of surgery, pulls his mask down, and says, "I have some good news and some bad news" and the friend says, "Oh doctor, please tell me the good news first." "All right. Your friend is going to live." "Oh, thank God, thank God, doctor. What's the bad news?" "Well, I'm afraid he's going to remain a vegetable for the rest of his life."

> *Some laugh, some groan.*

2. Oh, God.   **3.** Jesus.

1. That was Pat's favorite joke.

5. Aw, Pat.

4. Pat did love the puns.

1. Who was it who said that puns are the lowest form of humor?

2. It wasn't your husband, I can tell you that.
To Pat.

ALL. To Pat.

> *They all raise a glass.*
> *They drink.*

2. To Dad.

ALL. To Dad.

> *They raise a glass again.*
> *George comes in, wearing a cardigan sweater, a dress shirt,*
> *and nice brown trousers. He wears glasses. He has a kind face.*
> *He is an ordinary ghost. He has returned home and is going about his business.*
> *He reads a newspaper at the table. The Des Moines Register.*
> *They don't see him. He doesn't pay much attention to them.*
> *They drink.*

5. To Mom.

ALL. To Mother.

4. Maybe they're all up there together.

1. Mom and Dad? Fighting?

4. They only fought when they drank Wild Turkey. No drinking in heaven.

1. It's funny but when Mom died I remember being so relieved when Dad and I were buying her casket; I wasn't relieved she was dead, I was relieved she wasn't there to argue with Dad about what kind of casket to buy. With me stuck in between them.

5. That's terrible.

4. It seems so dark—a casket—so cold…

1. Mmm.

> *George leaves the room and goes to the toilet.*

4. When John and I went to pick out Dad's coffin we saw Bobby Mccabe—who said: now, you've got the five thousand dollar one here and the ten thousand dollar one there. I said: what do you get for the extra five grand? He said, you get a better seal and the degeneration is slower…And I said, isn't that sort of the point? To degenerate? He said in this pointed way: *some people just feel better spending more money.* I said let's get the cheap casket. And for the first time cremation made sense.

2. Dad is much too much a Catholic to get cremated.

The toilet flushes.

That toilet never stops running. I'll go.

2 exits to fix the toilet.
George comes back.
They pass each other, unseeing.

4. I don't think Dad was absolute about Catholicism. I remember when I went to Sacred Heart the nuns told us if one member of the family became a priest the whole family was saved so in third grade I thought: I'll take one for the team, and I said: I want to be a priest.

2 comes back, having jiggled the toilet flusher.

2. (*overhearing: I want to be a priest*) Really?

4. I'm telling a story. Then Sister Mary Bethel pulls Dad aside at a parent teacher conference and says: we think Mikey has received *the call*, and Dad said: "well, is that right?" The next week, I was in public school.

2. Hank Lischer was recruiting me for public school. He said the desks were automatic and the inkwells came up by themselves.

4. It's true, I'm sorry you didn't get to experience that.

They all laugh.

3. All I know is Sister Mary Robert Cecile—

4. We called her Big Bob—

1. Big Bob!!

3. Yes, Big Bob! whacked me with a ruler in front of the class for trying to look up her dress, a feat the Lord himself could not accomplish.

2. Nor would He want to.

3. I'm staring at her shoes, they were so pointy, wondering if she was the wicked witch of the west.

5. Maybe I ended up having the most interest in religion because I never went to Catholic school. I used to shut myself in my room for days of solitary contemplation. Dad and I used to go to Mass every week during Lent. You were all grown up and out of the house.

1. Would Mom go with you to Mass?

4. No, Mom was a Lutheran atheist to the bitter end. She said: I never understood how there could be a heaven. It would be too heavy and all the bodies would fall down.

5. She used to say: Man created God as a means of social control. Religion teaches you not to think.

1. Well, I guess I associate religion with stupidity too.

4. Jesus, Ann.

1. Sorry. Well, the religious right anyway.

2. Liberals make the mistake of conflating religion with ignorance, it's an ethical and a tactical error—

5. (*overlapping with "ethical"*) Could we please not say "liberal" or "conservative" tonight? I'm not in the mood, I'm really not.

2. Sorry.

3. Here, have some Jameson's, you'll feel better.

5. No thanks. I'm going to get some water. Would anyone else like water?

1. No thanks.

> *Everyone else shakes their head.*
> *She gets up and goes off-stage to get some water.*
> *George follows her.*

2. Ann, when did you stop going to church?

1. I was taking the pill after I gave birth to Katherine, and I was going to Mass at St. Clement's where she was baptized and I thought, Well, I'm taking birth control so I'm in mortal sin, and it's hypocritical for me to go to church, I should stay home and read the New York Times instead—(*overlapping*)

2. Ah, yes the great church of the New York Times—(*overlapping with "instead"*)

1. All right—

4. (*overlapping with "right"*) Annie I remember you as quite the Catholic. We would all be in the basement during a tornado and you were maybe twelve years old leading the Act of Contrition and of course a few Hail Marys thrown in—

1. I probably liked the drama of it.

> *5 comes back in with water.*
> *She drinks it.*

I loved all the drama—the May altars—

oh Mary we crown thee with blossoms today, queen of the something, something—

> (*they all chime in singing too*)

and the mournful advent songs—Midnight Mass—everything about Christmas—

2. Remember the year of the lutefisk?

3. Oh God the lutefisk.

> *They all laugh.*

4. Mother decided to get in touch with her Scandinavian roots—

1. Oh it was awful!

4. The smell—

3. An affront to the olfactory nerves—

1. The texture!

4. Gelatinous gobs of herring—

5. Preserved in lye—

1. Lye, can you imagine!

2. But we were really uncharitable—no one would eat it—Mother was reduced to tears—

1. She got up from the table and went to her room—

3. We were pretty merciless—

5. You were.

1. One year Mom and I shopped for dresses for the Christmas dance and we found two we both liked and—if you can imagine—I had a hard time *choosing*.

2, 3, 4, and 5. (*overlapping, with irony*) What/ No!/ Impossible/ Not you Annie/

1. Anyway, I finally chose one—it was blue chiffon. And then on Christmas morning my other dress was there—green satin.

5. Oh! The green satin—

1. With the square neck, square back and big bow in the back. It was such a surprise.

2. Remember the Santa paper? She always kept it separate to maintain the illusion—

1. Wrapping and smoking all night—

4. Amazing she didn't burn the house down—

2. And one year she ran out of Santa paper in the middle of the night—it was an emergency—she was so worried Wendy would realize—

5. Aw, Mom.

1. When did you all realize about Santa?

3. When I was eight Otto Stegmaier made an off the cuff comment about Santa Claus being a phony. And he turned to me and asked me if I still believed in him. Honestly I'd never given it a moment's thought. I said, "Nah, I don't believe in him." The tone of his question left only one possible answer. I sort of succumbed to the tone and believed the answer. And I think I got that one right…

    He drinks.

5. Well, I think that's sad.
I think Santa Claus is real.
In a way.

3. What?

1. Do you mean that there is a word, santa claus, an idea santa claus, that is real, so therefore Santa Claus is real?

4. That's like saying unicorns are real because there is a word and a mental picture for them.

> *George comes back in dressed as Santa Claus. He holds a grapefruit and a grapefruit spoon. He puts fake sugar on his grapefruit and eats it.*

1. That's an old problem in linguistics—

5. I wasn't really thinking of linguistics, I mean the fact that parents *become* Santa Claus during Christmas, so the spirit of Santa Claus—exists.

4. That's very "Yes Virginia there is a santa claus" of you.

1. I suppose, in that sense, *santa clausing*, the action of being santa claus exists, it just doesn't match the picture of a unified santa claus.

5. I'm not sure what you just said Ann. But I think that when we pray we make God happen.

> *The boys all drink.*
> *George drinks, squeezes his grapefruit juice into a bowl and drinks it.*
> *He exits to make instant oatmeal.*

5. Do any of you pray?

> *They all shake their heads.*

None of you? Mike?

4. Sort of. Not really. I believe in a higher power but I can't tell if it's God on my shoulder or Mom and Dad.

5. John?

2. I have conversations with God, I don't know if I'd call it praying. I remember walking around campus in the winter of my junior year with the Jesuits and I wrote down everything I thought I'd ever done wrong in my life and then I tore up the pieces of paper as small as I could so no one would ever recognize the handwriting and threw them into the wind and I said: no more. No more guilt.

4. I never knew that.

2. Yeah, well.

3. That's deep.

2. (*to 3*) All right, shut up. What about you? You must have prayed when you were a quarterback.

3. I prayed so much as a young soldier of Christ it lost all meaning. Annie I couldn't believe it when you broke into the Our Father when we were holding vigil over Dad. Okay, he was "our father" and it was an appropriate choice, but you've been railing for decades against the bullshit in the Catholic Church. Maybe you haven't strayed so far from the flock.

1. I still take communion to be sociable. I do miss it, the affiliation but—

3. But—

1. I just can't—I don't have an explanation for the world. I don't have an explanation for what happens after death.

5. Doesn't that make you afraid of dying?

1. Yes. Of course I'm afraid of dying. It's organized my entire life. Aren't you afraid of dying?

5. No. I think it's like changing clothes. I think the moment will be beautiful. Liberating. I think I've done it before. I think I've had lots of lives.

1. Oh.

4. Hm.

1. I wish I could believe that. It sounds nice.

> *George enters, not in his Santa Claus outfit anymore.*
> *He eats some Chex Mix.*
> *They don't notice.*

5. Annie, I wish I could prove to you that consciousness persists. I think you'd be less afraid.

1. How could you?

4. Dad—if you're here with us, give us a sign.

> *A silence.*
> *George drops the bowl of Chex Mix on the floor.*

4. That was creepy.

> *George exits.*

2. Well, I have no fear of death. I spend no time thinking of it. If there's life after death, wonderful. If there isn't, what's the point of worrying. Can't do anything about it.

3. You don't think you're in denial?

2. No. Life is for the living.

5. That's what Mom always said.

4. Well, I'm afraid of dying. I think there's a scientific part of me that wonders: what is it like to die? And I sort of assume my mind would survive that experience. I'm going to miss a whole lot of people. I think the scary thing is not knowing if they're going to miss me. I remember when we had to put down Capp I thought: what is the meaning of the life of a dog? I hope when I die people remember me more than they would remember the family dog…on the other hand it's not a competition so if they want to remember Capp more than me that's fine too…

> *George re-enters with the old family dog.*
> *They don't see it.*
> *The dog eats the Chex Mix off the floor.*
> *George pats it on the head and feeds it.*

1. I guess I live so much in my own consciousness that the idea of not being here—of that ceasing…is terrible…Then I apply logic and say: but I won't know—so…But I would like my consciousness to persist so I can see my grandchildren grow up. I'd like to see their graduations, their…

2. Of course.

1. …growing up.

3. But what does it mean to be a grown up?

4. All I know is my mantra used to be: immortality through immaturity!

3. Do you feel like a grown up Annie?

1. No. When I think of grown ups I think of Dad wearing that hat—(*1 gestures to a hat hanging on the wall. 2 might put it on*)—a grown up man's hat—to work every day—not because it kept you warm but because that's what grown ups did. I pride myself somehow on—not feeling grown up.

2. So you only have bad associations with growing up—

1. Growing up means—planning. Even though I like plans and lists I've never had *A Plan*.

2. Well by that definition isn't being a grown up a good thing? Someone who plans?

1. Maybe. I can't seem to shake the disappointment that I haven't—*done something*—whatever that would be. Dad always said: I never praised you kids because I didn't want you to get swelled heads.

2. He was not free with the compliments.
It was always:

3. He who flatters me does me an injustice—	**4.** He who flatters me does me an injustice.

1. One time Dad said to me driving home from an Iowa football game: well you're very smart, Annie. But it made me feel like he was saying: you're smart so why have you not accomplished anything?

5. Geez.

2. Of course Dad was proud of you.

1. He used to say you're so smart, Annie, you shouldn't be a teacher. You could have been a lawyer.

3. Well, yeah…

1. And that's what I associate with being grown up—programmed—ossified—I remember my deep almost primitive hatred of Nixon and wondering if it wasn't somehow to do with Dad…

3. Do you remember having to be in the children's brigade for Nixon?

1. I was out of the house by then, thank God—

3. Kennedy came through town that election cycle and was motorcading on River Drive. I was holding a Nixon sign assuring balance to the proceedings. He came by in an open convertible, in the back seat, just like in Dallas. Everyone cheering. My eyes zeroed in on him and I started running after the motorcade. He was the enemy in my mind, just as the Ohio State football team was the enemy of the Hawkeyes, my team. I was madly yelling obscenities and booing him; but all the while I had him in my eye and couldn't stop thinking how cool he was and wondering why in the hell I was doing what I was doing. And secretly inside I joined the cheering. How could I not…

4. I wonder if the whole country grew up after JFK was shot.

2. Either that or the whole country decided never to grow up after JFK was shot.

1. (*to 2*) Do you feel like a grown up?

2. Yeah and I'm tired of it.

1. When did you feel like a grown up?

2. When I got a seat at the big table.

1. What?

2. You know the big dining room table rather than the little kid card table at holidays?

1. Wow that's so literal.
Michael?

4. As the fourth of five I had the luxury of never having to grow up; I was always little Mikey as soon as I crossed the threshold. I defer to everyone, I don't know why Wendy doesn't defer to me.

　　　　5 rolls her eyes and laughs.

No, but seriously I think I grew up during my medical training. When they first called a code I would run in the other direction but by the end of my residency I ran *toward* the code. And that felt sort of grown up.

1. Wendy?

5. As a child I thought growing up was getting married, and I never wanted to do that because married people looked so bored with each other and I never wanted to be like that.

1. And when you got married?

5. Yes—but not overnight—it was finding a livelihood where I could help other people. It was learning to get out of the way.

3. (*to 1*) So you're the only one who doesn't feel like a grown up?

1. I guess.

3. Well, if you don't grow up you don't have to die.
Here's to not growing up, Annie. You and me!

1. Here's to not growing up.

> *3 and 1 clink glasses.*

4. You can grow up before you die or not grow up before you die, but either way you're going to die. Give me some of that.

2. (*overlapping after "die"*) Yup.

> *More liquor is poured into everyone's cup.*
> *5 holds her hand up, refusing more whiskey.*

1. And dying is such a failure.

3. How do you mean?

1. Our bodies are the enemy and dying is a capitulation, to a foreign shore.

3. Do you experience your body as the enemy?

1. (*to 3*) Don't you?

3. No.

1. You cut cancer out of people's bodies. Aren't you sort of the hero and the body is this enemy?

3. Cancer is the enemy. You're marshaling the body's resources. The body is your closest ally.

2. Like Canada?

1. I'd like it if Canada were heaven—I'd go to the Shaw Festival—

3. I remember once driving to the city on an August Sunday to see a patient. The day was hot as hell, nobody on the street. It was so still, like everyone was at a party elsewhere and I was the only one not invited. (*The rest murmur sympathetically.*) I thought: is this what death is like? Awful.

1. It's funny I think I believe in Tinkerbell more than I do in the afterlife. I stopped believing in God when I noticed that all the myths were the same—I was teaching the myth of Prometheus and suddenly I thought—Prometheus—oh! He's just like Jesus! And I thought about Greek myths and how silly they seem to us now and how our myths will seem just as silly to those who come after us—

5. But if they're all the same metaphor I mean doesn't that prove something?

> *George re-enters with orange juice and some Metamucil.*

1. (*as in, she's interested and thinks it's a good point*) Hmm.

4. A good Catholic doesn't think God is a metaphor. Communion is not supposed to be a metaphor. When the little bell rings it's real.

2. I should know, I was an altar boy. I rang that bell.

1. Like Tinkerbell.

> *George stirs the Metamucil with his spoon and it makes a little tinkling sound.*
> *They don't hear it.*

3. Well I think it's all a metaphor.

5. But metaphors are real that's what I'm trying to say—

1. Anyway, isn't it weird that I *religiously* believe fairies on stage are real; it isn't a very useful belief…but I don't believe in an afterlife even though it could be a useful belief, like Pascal's wager…

4. Was Pascal a betting man?

3. But don't you think there are consequences to having a false belief?

1. Well sure—

2. Take this country for example.   *(1 groans)*
We've confused self-interest with   **5.** Oh, not that again.
selfishness.

       The following political conversation takes place with a good deal of lively overlap.

4. We have! No one really understands anything about economics; of course I understand everything about economics… (*a self-deprecating laugh*)

3. (*over "of course"*) You know what's really wrong with this country? Too many crazed and half-witted Platonists and too few sensible Aristotelians who want to roll up their sleeves and get things done.

1. (*after "Aristotelians"*) I suppose you think liberals are the crazed, half-witted Platonists?

3. I don't even know if Plato was a Platonist…

4. Now you've lost me.

3. Plato goes like this (*pointing up*) and Aristotle goes like that (*pointing down*). Liberals believe in unreal worlds—Neverland if you will—and conservatives are pragmatists who try to solve problems on the ground.

1. (*with irony, after "pragmatists"*) Newt Gingrich being a paragon of practical wisdom?

5. Do we have to fight about politics tonight?

3. Dad would have approved.

4. Then let's fight!

2. You know what Dad used to say—if you're not a liberal before the age of 20 you have no heart and if you're not conservative after the age of 40 you have no brain—(*3 and 4 echo "have no brain"*)

1. The idea of conservatives being the grown up party is absurd—the party of Lincoln used to be pragmatic, now you're all insane—

          George finishes his drink
          And exits to the kitchen.

3. How would you know, you don't
read conservative papers,   *(1 groans)*
we read the New York Times every

day but when's the last time you've
picked up a conservative paper—   **4.** Exactly!
or read William Safire—or Ann
Coulter—

2. Oh ho!

1. I wouldn't dream of reading Ann Coulter—she's an idiot-witch—

4. How do you know if she's an idiot if you don't read her—

3. She's not exactly my first choice, but if she were liberal you would say she was a sassy Joan of Arc—

1. Don't you dare insult Joan of Arc—

3. Oh I forgot you played her in college—

4. I read Nicholas Kristof even   **1.** Good for you.
though I don't agree—

2. He advocates socialism—   **1.** What???!
Is a businessman really worth a
billion dollars? No.
It has no relationship to the value   **1.** Exactly.
he's created.
But the gross redistribution of income
makes no sense either.   **1.** What are you talking about?
We've incentivized the wrong   The welfare state is gone.
behavior.   Bill Clinton just dismantled it.

2. The welfare state is far from gone!   **4.** How can you say that?
It is alive and well and ever
expanding!

        1. Dad lived through the Depression.
        He ate squirrels. He shot squirrels and
        ate them because he was hungry.
        Why was he so undone by the concept
        of the have-nots being helped?

4. Dad did pro bono work all the time and never asked for recognition—

3. Dad grew up dirt poor. His father was educated, was even a lawyer, but he was a small-town lawyer in a town that was too small to need one.

1. Exactly—how can people who have struggled so much in the past lose all empathy for people who struggle in the present?

3. Let me finish. Dad didn't even have a bathroom in his house. When he moved into a house with five functioning toilets—

2. (*overlapping*) Almost functioning—

3. —almost, can you imagine how flushed (sorry) he felt with success? (*Some groan, some laugh*) He went to a subsidized state university on the GI Bill—

1. (*overlapping*) Exactly my point—

3. —but it wasn't enough. He waited on tables at the student union. He met Mom because he waited on her.

1, 2, 4, and 5. (*with nostalgia and repeated family storytelling ritual*) Made her a hamburger in the shape of a heart. Poured on ketchup for blood.

3. He won her over! In his mind he pulled himself out of the prairie, out of the Depression, out of the outhouse—into our house. A wife, five kids, a house. He became somebody, he became a contender. He works his ass off to send us to good schools and we come back espousing views that undermine his life narrative. So he flicks the channel and watches another episode of Archie Bunker. It is his refuge, his post-Depression, post-outhouse refuge, how can we deny him that? How can we say he is wrong?

4. Here here!

1. It's a rousing speech, I'll give you that—but you didn't answer my question—

2. Dad hated that the whole idea of the family was being eroded. He cared about—you know—family values. (*1 and 5 groan*) Now, look, I come from this old-fashioned unit called the family, thank God, and it's a tragedy that 50 percent of this country doesn't have one! (*4 applauds.*)

1. (*overlapping after "50 percent"*) Where do you get your figures?

2. (*overlapping with "figures"*) The government can't do the same job raising a family—

1. So the subtext is—

2. There's no subtext—

1. Come on that's code for—

2. I'm from the Midwest, I don't speak in codes, I say what I mean—

1. that single mothers are incapable of—

2. (*overlapping with "incapable"*) Of   **3.** No!
course I'm not—

1. You're interrupting—

3. (*to 1*) Annie, you need to learn to interrupt more—you take arguments personally—

1. They are personal—

                        4. We're just talking about ideas—it's all in good fun—

1. *Well it's not fun for me*—

2. And I would never say that about single mothers, you've been a single mother since Pat died, and you've done a beautiful job with your girls and you sure as hell deserve praise.

1. Well thank you.

2. You're welcome.

1. (*1 is upset.*) It's just that if this family, who loves each other about as much as a family can, can't talk about politics in a civilized fashion, how do you expect the rest of the country to talk to each other at all?

4. I think this is a very civilized conversation—

5. This is not civilized! You've all had too much to drink—and—*no one listens anymore*—

2. (*overlaps with "anymore"*) I'm listening!
My hearing is just going!

1. (*overlapping with "My hearing"*) Political arguments are a sport for you boys and it's not a sport for us—everyone yells and interrupts on the talk shows so now we all yell and interrupt, it's awful—

4. (*overlapping with "interrupt"*) No one was yelling!

1. (*to 2, 3, and 4*) When did you all go to the dark side? Was it under Reagan? You all sound like Aunt Helen!

2. Don't drag Aunt Helen into this—

3. She was a political genius—

1. We can't even talk to each other any more for God's sake! We should be an example of a functional democracy!

5. This is not a functional democracy. And I am sick of pretending that it is! I used to feel bad for Mom cleaning all the time while the men talked politics—now I understand. She just wanted everyone to shut the hell up—so she could hear herself think! She could think better over the sink with the water running! It's all noise! Static! We're on a sinking ship and you're rearranging the deck chairs! Who cares about politics? Who cares? My God!

We're orphans now!

2. C'mere.

> *2 hugs 5.*
> *A pause.*
> *2, 3, 4, and 5 freeze in the dining room, a sepia photograph.*
> *1 turns to the audience.*

1. (*to the audience*) And for a moment I was transported back to the teeny breakfast nook at one eleven McClellan. Mom and Dad still alive. All five of us around the small wooden table, arguing about politics. Mom was bustling around the kitchen, the smell of bacon, Dad was putting NutraSweet on his grapefruit. Mom was on her eighth cigarette and 18th cup of coffee since five in the morning, she was smoking and needlepointing a pillow that said *The Best is Yet to Come.* Two radios are on and two televisions, one with a football game on and one with *Crossfire.* We've been having the same political argument for the past thirty years—the lamp over the table was the same—but now there are no parents to adjudicate—No one standing sentry between us and death. No center. We're supposed to be the grown ups now.

We slept in our childhood beds that night.

> *Music.*
> *The lights change and 2, 3, 4, and 5 exit.*
>
> *George enters with a trunk.*
> *1 opens the trunk.*
> *She goes through it.*
> *She sees vintage dresses which she holds to her.*
> *One green satin dress.*
> *One blue chiffon dress.*
> *She remembers her mother.*
> *Then she finds her old Peter Pan costume.*
> *She puts on her Peter Pan costume.*
> *She crows.*

Movement Three: Neverland

1 as PETER PAN. (*whispering the lines to Wendy, waking her*) It's my last night in the nursery...

> *A childlike painted screen flies in, the wall of the nursery with a window cut into it.*
> *The boys are sleeping in the bed.*

5 as WENDY. It's my last night in the nursery you know.
Peter Pan is coming tonight.
Father says Peter Pan isn't real but I know he is.
I just know he is!
He's going to take me to—
where?

PETER PAN. (*whispering to her*) Neverland!

WENDY. Neverland!

> *Peter Pan climbs in through the window with difficulty.*
> *He stands with his arms akimbo.*

PETER PAN. Wendy!

WENDY. Peter Pan!

> *They embrace.*

PETER PAN. The lost boys need a mother.
Are you ready to come to Neverland?

WENDY. Why isn't that awfully far away?

> *He crows.*
>
> *Tinkerbell rings her bell. A little light and bell on stage.*

WENDY. Oh, it's Tinkerbell!

PETER PAN. Tink! Tink! Now you behave yourself Tink and don't pull Wendy's hair!

WENDY. John! Michael! Wake up! Look it's a fairy!

MICHAEL. A fairy!

PETER PAN. Time is a wasting! Let's go to Neverland!

WENDY. But how will I get there? I can't fly!

> *He sprinkles some fairy dust on her.*

WENDY. Oh!

PETER PAN. But Wendy I lost my shadow!

> *Peter starts frantically looking for his shadow.*

Do you have it, Wendy? I can't fly without my shadow!

> *They all look around for his shadow.*
>
> *They find it under the bed.*

WENDY. Here it is, Peter! I found it!

PETER PAN. Oh Wendy, bless you! But how will I get it back on?

> *He tries to put it back on but it falls off.*

WENDY. I can sew your shadow back on.

PETER PAN. Do you have a sewing machine?

WENDY. Needle and thread!

> *She produces a sewing basket.*

PETER PAN. I can do it.

WENDY. I can do it.

PETER PAN. I know how to sew.

WENDY. So do I. Mom taught me.

PETER PAN. No, Mom taught me.

WENDY. Mom taught me.
You're Peter Pan. You don't have a mother. And you don't know how to sew.

PETER PAN. Right, I'm Peter Pan.

> *Peter Pan puts his arms akimbo and crows.*
>
> *Wendy starts to sew.*

WENDY. I've been sending you letters, you know.

PETER PAN. We can't get letters in Neverland, Wendy. I don't have an address!

He crows.

WENDY. Now, Peter! I can't sew your shadow on while you're crowing.

The family dog enters with medicine.

Nana! Give me that medicine. It's for Michael.

Here Michael, take your medicine.

The dog exits.
Wendy gives Michael the medicine.

MICHAEL. I won't take it, I won't!

WENDY. Now, Michael, you must take your medicine. Father says so.

MICHAEL. I'm a doctor, I don't take medicine.

WENDY. Now, Peter, sit still, stop trying to touch your shadow.
Sit still and I'll do it.

Wendy begins sewing Peter's shadow on.

Everything has a shadow, Peter Pan. Honestly you should have gone to Jungian analysis. You would have learned that you can't experience joy without your dark side.

PETER PAN. I don't know what you're talking about Wendy.

WENDY. You can live on Freud until you're 40 but when you're 70 and facing death you either need religion or Carl Jung.

PETER PAN. Why can't I fly without my shadow?

JOHN. Think about it, Peter.

PETER PAN. What?

JOHN. A plane that's flying without its shadow on the ground is—

PETER PAN. Is what—

John makes the sound of an explosion.

JOHN. Poof—dead!

PETER PAN. Or just flying at night!

WENDY. I've sewn it on, Peter.

PETER PAN. Oh, well done! It's on again, my shadow is on again!

He crows.

Now I can fly!

He's not hooked into any flying apparatus.
He tries to fly, does a little jump.

JOHN. That was the worst flying I ever saw, Peter.

PETER PAN. Sorry.

I'm afraid—

MICHAEL. What—*you* afraid, Peter Pan?

PETER PAN. I'm not afraid. My foot hurts.

JOHN. Then I'll fly.

He jumps off something and falls.

JOHN. Ouch.

MICHAEL. I'll do it.

He jumps off something and falls.
They might keep doing this for a while—jumping off things and not flying.

JOHN. (*sadly*) Oh. We're old, aren't we? We're getting too old to fly?

MICHAEL. One of my best friends just died.

WENDY. Me too.

MICHAEL. And I had to treat him.

JOHN. They're all getting old and dying. It's awful.

PETER PAN. No! Keep a positive attitude. We'll *walk* to Neverland.
Except my foot is killing me.
Could someone grab me a cane? How far a walk is Neverland?

Someone hands her a cane.
They walk towards Neverland in front of a curtain.

WENDY. Why Peter, you can't walk there!

PETER PAN. Right. Come! Just think wonderful thoughts and they'll lift
you up into the air!

They try to fly and cannot fly.

PETER PAN. March!

They follow Peter offstage, walking with some labor.
They sing as they march. "Oh when the saints, oh when the saints, oh when the
saints go marching in…"
Another painted piece of scenery is dropped down, representing Neverland.
A sea, a volcano, a pirate ship.

They reenter as though they've had a very long journey.
Peter Pan sits down on a log or by a campfire.
He breathes into a paper bag.

PETER PAN. Sometimes I get panic attacks when I first get to Neverland.
Don't worry, it's nothing. Just, I hate travel. Airports, train stations, flying…

WENDY. Breathe, Peter, deep breaths.

He breathes in and out of the paper bag.

PETER PAN. Maybe we shouldn't have come.

JOHN. The sun is out.
Let's play shadow tag.
Peter, you're it.

*They play shadow tag, stepping on each other's shadows.
Peter tags Michael.*

PETER PAN. Gotcha, you're it Michael!

MICHAEL. Run, run, I'm it!

JOHN. Look at my top hat in the shadow!

WENDY. My shadow is so short!

JOHN. My shadow is so long!

(*to Michael*)

My shadow is longer than your shadow!

MICHAEL. Is not!

JOHN. Is too!

WENDY. I didn't know it was a competition!

PETER PAN. When I turn around my shadow turns with me!

A cloud passes over the sun, taking away the shadows.

PETER PAN. I can't see anyone's shadow!

WENDY. It's because of the clouds!

PETER PAN. Well we can't play if we can't see each other's shadows. Anyway, my foot hurts.

Michael looks at her foot.

MICHAEL. Let me look at it.

PETER PAN. It's not the diabetes, it's the gout.

MICHAEL. When you first feel a twinge, you have to take an anti-inflammatory. You have to stay ahead of the pain.

PETER PAN. I don't like taking ibuprofen, it causes bleeds.

JOHN. Where is Hook? I'll fight him! I'd love to kill a pirate! Ha! Ha!

John plays with a sword.

MICHAEL. Where are the lost boys?

JOHN. We are the lost boys.

PETER PAN. Wendy you don't know how lucky you are to have had a mother.

WENDY. I miss her!

Wendy starts to cry.

PETER PAN. Oh, don't cry, Wendy! I can't stand it when you cry!

MICHAEL. I don't want to grow up.

Michael starts to cry.

JOHN. I don't want to grow up either!

WENDY. I want my mother!
I want my father!

MICHAEL. Me too!

JOHN. Me too!

2, 4 and 5. We don't want to grow up!

> *They all bawl but Peter Pan.*
> *Peter Pan puts his hands in his ears.*

PETER PAN. I can't stand it! Tinkerbell!

> *Tinkerbell appears.*

Make them stop crying!

> *Tinkerbell rings her bell.*

How?

Oh!

> *Peter Pan sprinkles fairy dust on them and they stop crying.*

Well, that's a relief. Thanks, Tink.

Now, line up. According to age.

You here, you here, you here.

WENDY. Where do you go, Peter?

PETER PAN. I'm the oldest, so I go here.

WENDY. How can you be the oldest Peter, if you don't grow up?

> *They all line up.*

PETER PAN. I'm the oldest because I am the oldest.

> *They stand in their line.*

JOHN. Now what?

WENDY. Happy birthday, Peter Pan.

PETER PAN. Is it my birthday?

> *All but Peter chant:*

ALL BUT PETER. Are you one are you two are you three are you four?

PETER PAN. I don't know.

I'm quite young though.

How old am I?

JOHN. 70, I think!

PETER PAN. No! That can't be right! This is Neverland!

> *She looks at her hands.*

My hands look old! Oh, dear. Oh, nevermind.

> *She crows.*
> *Hook appears.*

HOOK. Ah, if it isn't Peter Pan!

> *Peter Pan stands up.*

PETER PAN. In the flesh, Hook! Tic toc tic toc where's your arm Hook?

HOOK. Heard a rumor you walked here, Pan. Why didn't you fly?

PETER PAN. You must be mistaken. I flew.

HOOK. No, Peter Pan. You thought you'd never grow up. But you have. You walked here. Slowly. Are you ready to face me?

WENDY. (*running up to Hook and punching him*) You big bully!

HOOK. Time for *you* to walk the plank little girl.

> *He binds her.*
> *She bravely walks the plank.*

PETER PAN. You won't kill my sister!
Everyone, it's time to kill Captain Hook.
Hook is death! Kill death! Make death die!

HOOK. En garde!

> *Peter draws his sword.*
> *They duel.*

HOOK. Who are you?

PETER PAN. I am youth! I am joy!

HOOK. Then fly!

> *They duel.*
> *Hook has him now in the duel,*
> *Sword to his neck.*

PETER PAN. I want my mother.

WENDY. Oh, Peter!

PETER PAN. "Cowards die many times before their deaths/ the valiant never taste of death but once!"

> *Peter Pan closes his eyes, brave.*
> *Hook kills Peter Pan.*

HOOK. Finally!

PETER PAN. Oh! Death will be an awfully big adventure!

HOOK. (*whining*) "I'll never grow up, never grow up," that'll teach you, Pan.

> *2, 4, and 5 fall upon Pan's body and cry.*
> *Secretly, they are attaching him to flying cables.*
> *Tinkerbell appears.*
> *Tinkerbell rings and rings, trying to get Wendy's attention.*

WENDY. What are you saying, Tink?
Oh!

> *Wendy approaches the audience.*

She says, if you believe in Peter Pan, clap, please clap! Do you believe in Peter Pan?

The audience claps.

Oh thank you, oh thank you!

> *Peter Pan comes back to life and is hoisted into the air.*

PETER PAN. Oh!

Oh!

I'm flying!

I'm flying!

Hook, see me now? See me now Hook?

JOHN. Annie, you're flying! You're really flying!

PETER PAN. I'm not Ann

I'm Pan!

Peter Pan!

> *He crows.*

WENDY. Peter! What was death like?

MICHAEL. Does consciousness persist after all?

PETER PAN. It was flying! It was wonderful!

> *He crows.*

Oh I'm light!

Light as air!

HOOK. Peter Pan!

How the devil did you elude my grasp?

> *Hook is disoriented.*
> *The rest of the children fight him down while he's disoriented.*

HOOK. Peter Pan, you rascal!

PETER PAN. Make him walk the plank!

> *Michael fights a duel with Hook.*

MICHAEL. I'm fighting a pirate! I'm fighting a pirate!

PETER PAN. Get him, Michael!

> *Michael and John have Hook by the throat.*

WENDY. We must show mercy!

PETER PAN. No mercy! Throw him overboard!

Slit his throat!

> *Michael slits Captain Hook's throat.*

MICHAEL. I killed a pirate. And it was wonderful!

> *Wendy bawls.*

WENDY. You killed my brother! I want to go home!

MICHAEL. You're too old for the nursery now, Wendy. I killed a pirate!

PETER PAN. Look at me, way up high!

I'm flying.
The terror is gone.
The sense of flight—weightless!

> *A painted drop comes down, representing Davenport, Iowa*
> *With the Mississippi River and the bridge and the hills.*

PETER PAN. I can see everything! Davenport, Iowa!
The lights on the Mississippi River!
Oh!

> *He crows.*

Where's my ship?
Now Wendy, think happy thoughts!

WENDY. I can't think happy thoughts—everyone's dead and I'm getting old and I have arthritis and you have gout—

PETER PAN. THINK HAPPY THOUGHTS!

WENDY. All right, all right let's see…happy thoughts…

> *Peter sprinkles some fairy dust on her.*
> *Wendy starts flying.*

WENDY. Oh, Peter, it's wonderful!

> *The boys are all looking up at the girls.*

MICHAEL. We want to fly too.

> *A ship rolls on stage.*

PETER PAN. Then get on board the Jolly Roger!

> *Hook looks up, not dead.*

HOOK. Can I come?

PETER PAN. Are you reformed you scurvy pirate?

HOOK. Yes!

> *He takes off his Hook hat. He takes off his Hook arm.*

3. See, it was a fake!

PETER PAN. Good, then! Everyone, get on board.
Is everyone on? Michael, John?

EVERYONE. We're on!

> *All except for Peter get on board a flying ship.*

PETER PAN. All on board?

EVERYONE. Aye, aye, captain.

PETER PAN. Then let's go!
This way! Follow me! Line up. Oldest to youngest.
We go in order.

WENDY. We can't line up, we're flying.

PETER PAN. Fine, we don't go in order.

Is everyone on board?

Think happy thoughts.

> *They fly.*

WENDY. Can you see our house? Can you see one-eleven? Can we get back into the nursery?

PETER PAN. No Wendy, it was your last night in the nursery.

MICHAEL. And Dad sold the house.

WENDY. He sold the house?

JOHN. He died. And we sold it. We all sold the house.

WENDY. Then where are we going to live?

MICHAEL. We could at least look through the windows!

> *Another painted drop might come down representing a house, 111 McClellan Boulevard, Davenport, Iowa.*

WENDY. Oh yes yes! Let's!

> *They peer through some windows, flying.*
> *Wendy knocks on the windows.*

Can we get in through the windows?

JOHN. No. The house isn't ours anymore.

> *A pause as this sinks in.*

WENDY. Then where will we go?

2. Back to our grown up lives, I suppose.

PETER PAN. No, no!

WENDY. We must, Peter. I just remembered that I have a job. With people who are sad, who need me. And also my husband—my two kids—they need me too—

PETER PAN. Don't leave, Wendy!

WENDY. I must, Peter.

3. I have to go cut cancer out of people's bodies. Also I have two grand-children who I like to hold. I need to go.

2. I have my students. I need to see my wife. We want to grow old together.

PETER PAN. No, don't leave!

MICHAEL. I have my patients, my wife, my children. Peter Pan, we can't stay.

> *The boys fly away on the ship.*
> *They wave good-bye.*

PETER PAN. When will I see you?

Don't go, don't go!

Oh Wendy!

WENDY. Spring cleaning, Peter Pan!

I'll come back for spring cleaning!

> *Wendy and Peter embrace.*
> *Then Wendy leaves. She waves good-bye.*

PETER PAN. Ugh. Grown ups. Spring cleaning. I want to keep flying!

> *Peter Pan keeps flying. She sees something.*

There's the Davenport Children's Theater!

There's the balcony! There's Mr. Smee! Bump Heeter. My God, Mary Ellen Hurlbutt—she looks so pretty! And in the audience, Mary Fluhrer Nighswander! And all the men in the lobby are wearing hats!

> *Peter Pan lands on the stage.*

I think I see my father in the audience.

I take a bow.

> *She takes a bow.*
> *Her father approaches.*
> *With a bouquet of flowers.*

PETER PAN. Thanks, Dad. Did you grow these yourself?

GEORGE. Yep.

You looked great up there.

How bout my little girl flying?

Now let's go back to one-eleven. There's a little party for you. Mother made Chex party mix. You can change out of those green tights and come home.

PETER PAN. I can go home?

GEORGE. Whaddya mean, of course you can. It's your last Christmas before you go out east to college. We're all going to miss you. But it's going to be an awfully big adventure.

PETER PAN. Do you think so?

GEORGE. I know so.

PETER PAN. I'm suddenly afraid.

Did you die?

What was it like?

Your breathing was terrible.

It seemed like you didn't want to go.

Was it awful?

GEORGE. Come on now, change your costume.

PETER PAN. I don't want to change costumes.

GEORGE. Those green tights can't be too comfortable after a while. Mother's waiting at home.

PETER PAN. Will you come with me?

GEORGE. They don't want a father in the dressing room.

PETER PAN. No, I mean will you come with me?

GEORGE. Course I will. I've been here all along.

PETER PAN. Oh, good! Will you hold my flowers while I change? And my photograph with Mary Martin? It's my good luck charm.

> *He nods and takes them.*
> *A moment.*

GEORGE. I'm very proud of you, Annie.

PETER PAN. Thanks, Dad.

> *They embrace.*
> *He exits. She watches him go.*

Epilogue

PETER PAN. (*to the audience*) And I went up to my dressing room while he waited.

I took off my green tights.

But before I went home, I stayed in the theater for a little while longer. Where you don't have to grow up.

> *Music.*
> *She throws a handful of pixie dust.*
> *It catches the light.*
> *If there was a marching band before, there can be a marching band again.*
> *She flies off.*
> *A fantastical exit.*

The End

RELICS AND ACKNOWLEDGEMENTS

I quoted J.M. Barrie's novel *Peter and Wendy* three times, and the following lines are close to the novel: "I am youth! I am joy!"; "Just think wonderful thoughts and they'll lift you up in the air!"; and "Death will be an awfully big adventure!" The following are photographs from my mother's collection. How to acknowledge the contribution of the Kehoe family to this play—acknowledge is a cold, formal and inadequate word for their warmth, love, and willingness. How do stories come through families with love, and how do families come through stories with love? It is a mystery. All I know is that I had the good fortune to be born into a great family with stories and talk sailing down all the bannisters, and in such a family, I never felt alone.

Peter Pan Meets Peter Pan
As Mary Martin Stops in Town

330

WONDROUS STRANGE
by Martyna Majok, Meg Miroshnik, Jiehae Park, and Jen Silverman

All inquiries concerning rights, including amateur rights, should be addressed to:

For Martyna Majok: Creative Artists Agency, 405 Lexington Ave., New York, NY 10174. ATTN: Olivier Sultan, 212-277-9000.

For Meg Miroshnik: William Morris Endeavor Entertainment, 11 Madison Ave., 18th Floor, New York, NY 10010. ATTN: Jonathan Lomma, 212-903-1552.

For Jiehae Park: William Morris Endeavor Entertainment, 11 Madison Ave., 18th Floor, New York, NY 10010. ATTN: Michael Finkle, 212-903-1144.

For Jen Silverman: United Talent Agency, 888 Seventh Avenue, 9th Floor, New York, NY 10106. ATTN: Rachel Viola, 212-500-3213.

ABOUT *WONDROUS STRANGE*

This article first ran in the Limelight Guide to the 40th Humana Festival of New American Plays, *published by Actors Theatre of Louisville, and is based on conversations with the creative team before rehearsals for the Humana Festival production began.*

Kentucky's supernatural lore fills anthology after anthology, and every year, thousands of visitors head to the state's haunted landmarks, from posh hotels and mansions to dive bars and Civil War sites. What's more, one of the most ghost-filled historic districts in the United States, a Victorian neighborhood called Old Louisville, happens to be within walking distance of Actors Theatre. Perhaps it's no surprise, then, that ghosts and hauntings emerged as the subject of the Humana Festival play commissioned for the 2015–2016 Professional Training Company. This season, four fearless writers—Martyna Majok, Meg Miroshnik, Jiehae Park, and Jen Silverman—were invited to venture into the spirit realm and examine the unexplained and the uncanny. Using a handful of Kentucky legends as their starting point, they've created *Wondrous Strange*, a collection of pieces about hauntings in the Bluegrass State and beyond.

Writing with this season's Acting Apprentices in mind, the playwrights began developing material in September 2015 with the cast, director Marti Lyons, and dramaturg Jessica Reese. During the first of two week-long workshops, the group described their own paranormal experiences and heard tales from Actors Theatre staff, and they took a tour of Old Louisville's haunted spots. All season long, this exploration of the supernatural inspired challenging conversations about why people believe in ghosts (or don't), and how ghost stories are linked to memory, trauma, and loss. And since those stories are now as likely to be shared online as on a front porch, the playwrights and creative team traded podcasts, favorite episodes of ghost-hunting reality shows, and links to blurry (but convincing) videos of run-ins with spirits at places such as Louisville's Waverly Hills Sanatorium, a famously eerie former tuberculosis hospital.

For the twenty actors of the Professional Training Company, *Wondrous Strange* was the capstone of a season devoted to making new work, from crafting solo performances to premiering an evening of ten-minute plays and a trio of one-acts. Since 2000, Actors Theatre has commissioned playwrights to create Humana Festival plays for the Apprentices so that these early-career actors can play a key role in a new work development process and showcase their talent during the Festival. Meanwhile, the writers get a chance to collaborate as a team and experiment with writing for a large cast. And as with last year's

Apprentice show, the bluegrass-themed *That High Lonesome Sound*, *Wondrous Strange* was an opportunity for Actors Theatre's staff and guest artists to explore a subject that has local resonance.

By turns meditative, funny, and frightening, *Wondrous Strange* depicts many different kinds of ghostly encounters, reflecting the variety of stories and legends shared while building it. People seek out ghosts for all kinds of reasons; they're driven by grief or curiosity, by a hunger for fame or forgiveness. And sometimes, of course, the ghosts find them first. Some hauntings span decades; others involve only an instant of horror or bewilderment. They can be deeply unsettling, or just something to be laughed off, repackaged later as a tall tale hauled out when the campfire has burned down low. But even stories only meant to frighten or entertain can reveal a surprising amount about the tellers: their ideas about justice or vengeance, their beliefs about the afterlife, or their experiences of loss or regret. After all, lots of things haunt us, not just ghosts.

As varied as they are, there's one thing almost all ghost stories share: ghosts don't just appear out of nowhere, though they certainly seem to. Instead, there's always a history, always a moment before. And the way that that history lives inside of the present—as a story told and retold, or as a phantom or event that literally reappears or recurs—can lead us to consider the other ways that the past leaves its fingerprints on us. This intersection of past and present makes hauntings and ghost stories ripe subjects for theatrical exploration because live performance exists at a similar juncture—brand-new every night, but also resonating with the echoes of all the rehearsals and performances before it. Plays and players seem to linger onstage long after the last curtain call, and theatres are such commonly haunted places that the lamps left on all night as a safety precaution are called ghost lights.

Do you believe in ghosts? Are you sure? *Wondrous Strange* welcomes you no matter what your stance may be, as four daring playwrights join forces with the Professional Training Company to put a theatrical spin on a late-night story swap. We'll probably never know for sure whether ghosts exist. But almost everyone has them, literal or not, and so it's better, maybe, to wrestle with them together—to keep a ghost light burning, and to welcome them in.

—Jessica Reese

BIOGRAPHIES

Martyna Majok was born in Bytom, Poland, and aged in Jersey and Chicago. Her plays have been performed and developed at Manhattan Theatre Club, Williamstown Theatre Festival, Actors Theatre of Louisville, Steppenwolf Theatre Company, Rattlestick Playwrights Theater, Women's Project Theater, Ensemble Studio Theatre, and the Kennedy Center, among others. Awards include the Helen Merrill Award for emerging playwrights, Helen Hayes Charles MacArthur Award for Outstanding Original New Play, an ANPF Women's Invitational Prize, David Calicchio Emerging American Playwright Prize, the New York Theatre Workshop 2050 Fellowship, the Kennedy Center's Jean Kennedy Smith Playwriting Award, and the NNPN Smith Prize for Political Playwriting. Majok has received commissions from the Bush Theatre in London, La Jolla Playhouse, The Foundry Theatre, Marin Theatre Company, South Coast Repertory, Manhattan Theatre Club, *The New Yorker* website, and Geffen Playhouse. Majok has a B.A. from the University of Chicago and an M.F.A. from the Yale School of Drama. She is currently a part of the Lila Acheson Wallace American Playwrights Program at the Juilliard School and the Core Writer Program at the Playwrights' Center. Publications: Dramatists Play Service, Samuel French, TCG, Playscripts, and Smith & Kraus. Majok is an alumna of Ensemble Studio Theatre's Youngblood and Women's Project Theater's Lab, and a member of The Dramatists Guild, the Writers Guild of America East, and New York Theatre Workshop's Usual Suspects. Majok was a 2012–2013 NNPN Playwright-in-Residence and the 2015–2016 Playwrights of New York (PoNY) Fellow at The Lark.

Meg Miroshnik is an L.A.-based, Minneapolis-bred playwright who writes heightened language. Her plays include *The Fairytale Lives of Russian Girls* (Yale Repertory Theatre; Alliance Theatre), *The Tall Girls* (Alliance Theatre; O'Neill National Playwrights Conference; La Jolla Playhouse DNA New Work Series), *The Droll* (Pacific Playwrights Festival; Undermain Theatre), *Lady Tattoo* (Pacific Playwrights Festival), and *Utopia, Minnesota* (Williamstown Theatre Festival Sagal Fellowship / Drama League Residency). Her work has also been developed at Cleveland Play House, Center Theatre Group, McCarter Theatre Center, the Kennedy Center, Lincoln Center Directors Lab, The Lark, Olney Theatre Center, Chicago Opera Theater, Washington Ensemble Theatre, and others. Awards: Whiting Award, Susan Smith Blackburn Prize finalist, and the Alliance/Kendeda Graduate Playwriting Award. Publications: Samuel French. She holds an M.F.A. from the Yale School of Drama, where she studied under Paula Vogel. Miroshnik is currently a Core Writer at the Playwrights' Center and co-founder of The Kilroys.

Jiehae Park's plays include *peerless* (Yale Repertory Theatre world premiere; Cherry Lane Mentor Project workshop production; Marin Theatre Company; Barrington Stage Company; Company One Theatre; Moxie Theatre), *Hannah and the Dread Gazebo* (Oregon Shakespeare Festival), *Here We Are Here* (Sundance Theatre-Makers Residency, the Ground Floor at Berkeley Repertory Theatre, Princess Grace Works In Progress Residency at Baryshnikov Arts Center), and *Wondrous Strange* (co-author, 2016 Humana Festival). Development: Soho Rep, Playwrights Horizons, The Public Theater's Emerging Writers Group, Page 73's Interstate 73, New York Theatre Workshop, The Old Globe, Dramatists Guild Fellowship, Ojai Playwrights Conference, Bay Area Playwrights Festival, and the Ma-Yi Writers Lab. Awards: Leah Ryan Prize, Princess Grace Award, L. Arnold Weissberger Award, ANPF Women's Invitational Prize, and two years on The Kilroys' List. Commissions: Playwrights Horizons, McCarter Theatre Center, Yale Repertory Theatre, Geffen Playhouse, Oregon Shakespeare Festival, Williamstown Theatre Festival, Manhattan Theatre Club / Sloan Foundation. Residencies: The MacDowell Colony, Yaddo, Hedgebrook, and the McCarter Theatre's Sallie B. Goodman Artists' Retreat. Park is a New York Theatre Workshop Usual Suspect, a Lincoln Center Theater New Writer in Residence, and a Hodder Fellow at Princeton University. As a performer, Park's credits include La Jolla Playhouse, Studio Theatre, Tiny Little Band, REDCAT, and most recently *Sleep* (Ripe Time/The Play Company) and *Every Angel is Brutal* (Clubbed Thumb). Park holds a B.A. from Amherst College and an M.F.A. from the University of California, San Diego.

Jen Silverman is a New York–based playwright, novelist, and screenwriter. Her theatre work includes *The Moors* (Yale Repertory Theatre, Off-Broadway at The Playwrights Realm), *Phoebe in Winter* (Off-Off Broadway at Clubbed Thumb), *The Roommate* (Actors Theatre of Louisville, South Coast Repertory, Florida Studio Theatre, Everyman Theatre, San Francisco Playhouse), *The Dangerous House of Pretty Mbane* (InterAct Theatre Company: Barrymore Award, Steinberg/ATCA Award Citation), *Collective Rage: A Play in Five Boops* (Woolly Mammoth Theatre Company, The Theatre @ Boston Court), and *All The Roads Home* (Cincinnati Playhouse in the Park). Silverman is a member of New Dramatists, a Core Writer at the Playwrights' Center in Minneapolis, and has developed work with the O'Neill National Playwrights Conference, Williamstown Theatre Festival, New York Theatre Workshop, PlayPenn, SPACE on Ryder Farm, Portland Center Stage, The Ground Floor Residency at Berkeley Repertory Theatre, and the Royal Court in London, among other places. She's a former member of Ensemble Studio Theatre's Youngblood; a two-time MacDowell Fellow; and the recipient of a New York Foundation for the Arts grant, the Helen Merrill Playwright Award, and the Yale Drama Series Award. She is the 2016-2017 Playwrights of New York (PoNY) Fellow at the Lark. She has a two-book deal with Random House for a collection of stories and a novel. Education: Brown University, Iowa Playwrights Workshop, and Juilliard. More information is available at www.jensilverman.com.

ACKNOWLEDGMENTS

Wondrous Strange premiered at the Humana Festival of New American Plays in March 2016. It was directed by Marti Lyons, with associate direction by John Rooney, and featured the 2015–2016 Professional Training Company as the Ensemble:

Austin Blunk, Lisa Bol, Michael T. Brown, Glenna Brucken, Michael Fell, Tracey Green, Mbali Guliwe, Alejandro Hernandez, Hannah Karpenko, Yaron Lotan, Esaú Mora, Ari Shapiro, Jayson Speters, Adenike Thomas, Walls Trimble, Sara Turner, Kyle Whalen, Addison Williams, Park Williams, and Amelia Windom

with casting for specific pieces as follows:

gts story by Jiehae Park

Ari Shapiro, Lisa Bol, Walls Trimble, Tracey Green, Amelia Windom, Hannah Karpenko, Michael Fell, Mbali Guliwe, Esaú Mora, Kyle Whalen, Jayson Speters, Addison Williams

The Encounter by Martyna Majok

PATTY...Glenna Brucken
JONNY..Alejandro Hernandez

The Holler by Meg Miroshnik

CARL PRUITT.......................................Kyle Whalen
KATE ....Park Williams
JAMIE ....Michael Fell
AARON ....Michael T. Brown
PHUMLANI..Mbali Guliwe

Ghost Bros by Jen Silverman

ACE...Addison Williams
BRENDAN ....Alejandro Hernandez
CHAD ....Jayson Speters
LITTLE BELL GIRL................................Walls Trimble

something like by Jiehae Park

A...Tracey Green
W..Adenike Thomas
B ....Esaú Mora
GHOST BROS!......................................Alejandro Hernandez,
                    Jayson Speters, Addison Williams

CAT .... Yaron Lotan
STRANGER .... Hannah Karpenko

game by Jiehae Park
Walls Trimble, Park Williams, Hannah Karpenko, Lisa Bol,
Glenna Brucken

Bug by Meg Miroshnik
WEEDY .... Sara Turner
3.J. .... Austin Blunk
B.J. .... Ari Shapiro
ANN .... Amelia Windom
BUG .... Yaron Lotan

The Watch Man by Martyna Majok
Michael T. Brown

The Bonnets by Jen Silverman
THE BONNETS .... Adenike Thomas, Sara Turner, Lisa Bol,
Hannah Karpenko, Glenna Brucken,
Tracey Green, Walls Trimble,
Amelia Windom, Park Williams

and the following production staff:

Scenic Designer .... Daniel Zimmerman
Costume Designer .... Beatrice Vena
Lighting Designer .... Paul Toben
Sound Designer .... Christian Frederickson
Media Designer .... Philip Allgeier
Composer and
Music Director, *The Bonnets* .... Max Vernon
Fight Director .... Drew Fracher
Stage Manager .... Mallory Paige Marsh
Dramaturg .... Jessica Reese
Properties Master .... Heather Lindert
Directing Assistant .... Nick O'Leary
Assistant Dramaturg .... Helena D. Pennington

Wondrous Strange was commissioned and developed by Actors Theatre of
Louisville.

Alejandro Hernandez, Addison Williams, and Jayson Speters
in *Wondrous Strange*

40th Humana Festival of New American Plays
Actors Theatre of Louisville, 2016
Photo by Bill Brymer

WONDROUS STRANGE

gts story
by Jiehae Park

inside.

> *late.*
> *rain.*
> *bourbon.*

1. it was a woman

2. a man

7. it was a person
definitely a

4. i dunno it seemed kinda

5. what

4. like an *it*
not like a *her*
or a *him* but

5/6. yeah

6. an it

5/6. totally

1. (*superchill:*) i felt that
i feel you

>   (*eyerolls.*)

7. he *wants* to feel you

1. hey
a little

7. what

1. a little respect?

7. you're the one who's

8. alright
alright

9. the point
come on

8. the point

9. we can all agree on
the *point*

343

9. right?

8. right

4. right

5. right

6. right.

what are we agreeing on?

9. *we saw it.*

whatever it was.

8. an it

  2. or a him

    1. or a her

      8. or a whatever

      we *saw.*

4. it was real

5. yeah

6. oh yeah

1. for sure

6. um.

  (*beat.*)

7. what.

6. i mean

7. you mean *what*

6. i *think* i saw

8. no

9. no think

8. no *thinking* you—

9. if this is

8. we have to be agreed

4. we *saw* it

6. i mean i did

i think i

7. *no*

5. you tryin to tell me

you tryin to tell me you *didn't* see

6. i saw *something*

4. just maybe not a him

or a her

10. well what then

5. yeah

2. if it wasn't

1. what *was* / that

6. i dunno

3. a goat?

> (*beat.*)

10. excuse me.

4. a goat?

5. did he say goat?

10. the fucker said a fucking *goat.*

7. what?

5. why a *goat*

3. i don't know
it had like
a sad face.

7. and.

10. and?

3. and goats look like
sad.
all the time

10. are you
are you kidding me with the

8. it wasn't a goat.

2. it was a man

1. woman

10. can we at the very least
very baseline agree
that what we saw was not a motherfucking *goat.*

> (*beat.*)

2. i mean it coulda been a goat.

6. you said it was a man.

2. it had a beard.
goats,
uh
you know

10. no.
tell me.

3. goats

>   (*silence.*)

goatshavebeardsso

>   (*beat.*
>   10 *stands.*)

7. where you going?

9. come back

10. i'm gonna prove to you

prove to you that it is not a—

9. no

8. nononono

10. i'm going

9. don't

10. i'm going

going

>   (10 *flings back the curtain—*
>   *a flash of lightning and peal of thunder.*
>
>   *for the briefest of seconds, a terrifying shape through the window, through the*
>   *rain. maybe it is the silhouette of a goat. it does seem to have some kind of beard.*
>
>   *he swiftly closes the curtain.*
>
>   *comes back.*
>   *pours another bourbon.*
>   *downs it.*
>   *silence.*)

4. at least we know it's still there.

2. he's

1. she's

4. still

5/6. yeah

>   (*beat.*)

7. so what now.

4. maybe it'll go away.

6. by dawn!

4. dawn?

5. dawn.

6. ghosts—

9. goats?

5. *things,* nightttime friggin scary things whatever you wanna call them, goat or otherwise

10. i told you, i know it's not a goat you don't have to

6. them night things don't like sunlight, right?

> (*a knocking from behind the curtain:* RAP RAP RAP.)

outside.

> (*bright day.*
> *RAP RAP RAP.*
> *someone raps on the glass—one of the ghost-hunters or seekers [perhaps a* GHOST BRO] *we will meet later in the evening. maybe someone with a beard, holding something that might be a camera, and who in a certain light could be a woman or man or a goat or a—*
> *RAP RAP RAP.*
>
> *a voice, off yells:*)

11. You find something?!

THE ENCOUNTER
by Martyna Majok

Night. A small apartment. It's raining outside.
One person lives here and she is a woman. Her real name is PATTY *but few folks know this.*
She's rough around the edges. And young to be doing what she's doing.
She enters.
A man follows behind her. JONNY.
He's rough around the edges too. But in a more precarious kind of way—these days, at least.
He has recently lived through a difficult period. He holds that with him still but in a way that's not an imposition on those around him. He is friendly and he tries to seem fine. 'Til he's not.
Perhaps PATTY *is from Kentucky and perhaps* JONNY *is not.*
Either way, JONNY *is strange to this place.*

PATTY. You like the ambience?

JONNY. Yeah, it's a real—//dope space.

PATTY. I keep it authentic-lookin. It looks authentic-lookin, right? Look at this fabric 'n shit on the wall. Lighting. Fuckin, *candles.* No one can tell me I'm not legit-seemin. Incense, even. And I got a sign with the *nice* neon. You a cop?

JONNY. …No.

PATTY. Cool. Gotta ask.

JONNY. Sanitation worker, //actually.

PATTY. I looked into crystal balls too—Finishing Touch—but fuck that I go above 'n beyond *already.* Some women don't even bother. Other women? Can't be bothered. No candles. Fabric. They'd do it in an alley. Bathroom. Not me. See?

JONNY. What?

PATTY. The ambience.
I made that.

JONNY. Yer my—first so I don't have much to like, compare.

PATTY. You don't need to. You don't need to compare. I'll just tell you: you don't need to. I keep shit special. That's what sets me apart. That's just one of the things that sets me apart. You prob'ly seen a lotta women out there, advertisin their, but I'm—apart. I'm a—I'm a *worker!* I work very hard for my clients. Empty yer pockets.

JONNY. What?

PATTY. Into the little—There's a bowl there.

JONNY. Why.

PATTY. Okay so I'll hafta do a patdown.

Procedure.

> (*She pats him down.*)

JONNY. I never did this before.

PATTY. Everyone says that.

JONNY. No really I mean I tried, y'know, on my own, alone, //but—

PATTY. (*judgy.*) That's sad.

JONNY. I think sometimes you need another person sometimes.

PATTY. Fuck right.

JONNY. Alone's the worst fuckin thing to be sometimes.

> (*He didn't mean for that to come out that way—so suddenly unhinged.*)

PATTY. (*re: patdown.*) Yer clear.

So you want me to use yer real name or—?, what's yer name?

JONNY. (*a joke.*) Shouldn't you know?

PATTY. What?

Oh.

Cute.

JONNY. What's yer name?

PATTY. Nope.

> (*They're both ready for something to happen.*)

JONNY. So…

PATTY. So…

JONNY. So you use a Ouija or— ?   **PATTY.** Soooo…take off yer pants!

…   …

What?   What? What'd you say?

> (*A moment where it seems like both of their nights might be ruined.*)

JONNY. You have a sign. A neon sign on—You handed me a card fer // psychic readings—

PATTY. Psychic—Yup. Readings. Psychic Readings.

…For a fee.

> (*He's not buying it.*
> *But it's not an angry reaction.*
> *It's deeply sad and disappointed.*
> *She knows she might lose him.*
> *She doesn't try to bullshit him now.*)

Listen I can do whatever you want me to do for a fee.

JONNY. Oh I'm a fuckin (*unsaid: idiot*)—

(JONNY heads for the door.)

PATTY. No no no c'mere we can
do anything you—Wait—maybe
there's—Just tell me what you—

JONNY. Sorry I wasted yer—you
prob'ly lost a lotta money tonight—

JONNY. This keeps happening.
I've gone to the strangest fuckin places. //This one might be tops, though.

PATTY. I'm not strange.

JONNY. Abandoned places. Random basements. Places she'd never even
been but that seem like they'd be *(unsaid: haunted).*
And places she *had* been. Places she loved.
And that she really didn't.
I dunno if to look where the good things happened or the...

> *(JONNY moves to the door.*
> *He stops at the door. Can't go quite yet.*
> *The sound of rain, perhaps, for a moment.)*

I stand in my room in the dark sometimes 'n just say her name and I just wait,
I just wait there in the dark.
She's not there.
I checked all the corners.
I went through so many candles.

PATTY. You can buy some of //mine.

JONNY. I drove so fuckin far. People said Go South. South's haunted. Said
to come here. It's the most haunted town. Whole country. Right here. So I
went to that asylum. It's closed, been closed fer a, frat boys go there now,
scare each other. We'd never been there. In her life, we'd never been. But I
thought—y'know—lemme try! It's supposed to be—so lemme just *try!*
Almost got arrested. Trespassing.
...
I don't know the rules.
I don't know if—spirits, if the spirits of—I dunno how they choose where
they, if they choose where they...go.
I've run outta places to look.
I can't find her.
...
Or maybe she doesn't want me to—
Maybe she couldn't wait to—

> *(She sees him. He feels too seen.)*

(leaving.) I'm sorry.

PATTY. I'll make a Ouija!

JONNY. *(leaving.)* Sorry.

PATTY. I'll do whatever you want.

JONNY. I don't got that kinda money to //pay fer something like—

PATTY. But you'd only hafta pay me if—

JONNY. Honestly, man, I don't even know if I can make it back home—

PATTY. If nothing happens then—

JONNY. I really don't—

PATTY. Just stay then okay! Just—stay here then. Yer the second person this month, this entire month, who's even come back with me. I've been standin out there waitin fer someone to—but—they don't. They haven't. They're not—I dunno what's wrong with—No one's comin to me.

JONNY. I was just gonna sleep in my car—

PATTY. No charge.

JONNY. (*suspicious.*) Right.

PATTY. For real.

JONNY. Why?

PATTY. There's been break-ins in the building and it's just, it'd be good to have someone here.

JONNY. You don't even know me.

PATTY. I don't know anyone here.

(*They hear the rain.*)

It's rainin. And it's late.

Just fuckin stay.

JONNY. …No charge?

PATTY. Stay.

(*He tentatively enters the room.*)

Dear Spirits of the—

JONNY. Don't do that.

PATTY. Yeah okay.

JONNY. I'll stay but

PATTY. Okay!

JONNY. —but we don't gotta pretend you got like, powers.

PATTY. Cool. (*a first-time "host."*) You want um…tea?

JONNY. Is that like, some kinda code?

PATTY. It's tea.

JONNY. Fer a hundred bucks?

PATTY. It's fuckin tea.

JONNY. Okay then yeah. Yeah, tea would be fuckin perfect right now.

(She turns. Stops. She has a small moment of panic. There's no tea.)

PATTY. Or how about water?

JONNY. Does no one ever ask?

PATTY. What?

JONNY. Does no one think yer...y'know...?

PATTY. No everyone pretty much knows. All the neon signs, Psychic y'know "*Readings*," they're all—

JONNY. Really?

PATTY. I mean maybe they're also—!
But, no, they're all basically—

JONNY. Why do you do this?

PATTY. Why do *I*—?

JONNY. Yer really young. You seem young. To be doin this.

PATTY. So do you.

JONNY. What?

PATTY. Seem young. To have lost someone so *(unsaid: young)*.
She musta been really—if you drove all the way from...

JONNY. Far.

PATTY. How long ago did she...?

JONNY. Not long.

PATTY. What was her name?

JONNY. ...Mom.

    (Rain.)

I just wanna know if something's there.
That something of her stayed.

...

PATTY. We are gathered here today—

JONNY. No really, thanks but—

PATTY. Yeah I dunno what the fuck I'm even—Okay.

    (Rain.)

(a rare truth.) I don't know what I'm doin.

    (Rain.)

JONNY. What's yer name?

PATTY. My actual name?

...

What's yers?

JONNY. Jonny.
From far.

...

PATTY. Patty.
From—Yeah. Me too.

...

Let's just sit a while, Jonny.
JONNY. Yeah okay.
PATTY. Near something.

    (*They sit together and listen to the rain.*)

THE HOLLER
by Meg Miroshnik

* Marks the place where lines overlap

A CRASH in the dark.

CARL PRUITT. (*a whisper.*) My holler.

(*The sound of pacing and a hum and maybe faint animal grunts. A beat of silence.*)

KATE. Boo!

(*Suddenly, a work light snaps on and we're mid-housewarming. KATE has just scared* JAMIE.)

JAMIE. Shit!

KATE. Gotcha!

JAMIE. You made me spill!

AARON. I'm soaked.

KATE. (*sharing a joke with* AARON.) Whatever you do, *preserve the triple-distilled.*

JAMIE. I'm really sorry—

(JAMIE *tries to wipe off* AARON'*s shirt with his hand.*)

PHUMLANI. It's actually not—

JAMIE. It was an accident.

KATE. What, babe?

(AARON *pushes* JAMIE *off, gently.*)

PHUMLANI. Triple distilled.

AARON. I'm fine.

PHUMLANI. The gentleman at the store said that *time in the barrel* is the real measure.

(PHUMLANI *hands* AARON *a towel.*)

KATE. The more you know. Should we toast?

PHUMLANI. Jamie, Aaron. It seems only fitting to spend the night for the first time in our new home in our new hometown with family. To tonight's urban camping adventure.

(*They drink.* JAMIE *watches* AARON *wipe himself with the towel.*)

JAMIE. I swear to God: Accident.

AARON. Jamie, I'm fine.
Anyway, what do you always say, Kate?
A party's not a party—

KATE and JAMIE. —until somebody gets wet!

PHUMLANI. Is that an American idiom?

JAMIE. It's a *Walker* idiom.

KATE. Our mom used to say it.

JAMIE. God, it was probably dirty and we didn't even notice.

KATE. I noticed.

AARON. You didn't notice?

     (PHUMLANI *takes the towel back from* AARON *and sniffs it.*)

PHUMLANI. Oooh, the smell is.

Like the couch in my fraternity's common room on a Sunday morning.

AARON. I was thinking my great aunt Muffy after breakfast.

JAMIE. I *said*—

AARON. You're sorry, I get it.

JAMIE. Anyway, would you rather smell like their neighborhood?

KATE. Oh, fuck you.

JAMIE. No offense, Katie, it's just. Ya know. Airy notes of manure and blood.

     (*Faint grunts and humming.*)

PHUMLANI. It *is* a bit pungent.

KATE. You get used to it fast.

     (*to* PHUMLANI.)

Spending all day inside overseeing the workers.

AARON. But god, all this space? I'd stop smelling *anything* for this space.

KATE. Right? We have like *room* here. We're like…pioneers.

JAMIE. Pioneers?

KATE. Like…on the frontier.

PHUMLANI. Kate, there were people before* us.

KATE. Sure, but. The building's been abandoned* for the last

PHUMLANI. (*to* JAMIE *and* AARON.) It was an active slaughterhouse into the early twentieth century.

KATE. That creeped me out a little at first. But then we saw, y'know—

AARON. The ceilings!

KATE. Right? And it goes on and on! We just put up that wall to like *define** the space

AARON. I hate you. This would be so crazy* expensive

PHUMLANI. Cost of living is very* reasonable here.

KATE. Even on just one income, he wants to say!

PHUMLANI. I wouldn't say that.

KATE. And the restaurants? They pay *you* to eat.

AARON. Nice life.

KATE. Speaking of which…
Our hidden agenda.

> (*A beat.*)

JAMIE. *Kate.*

KATE. You'd love it.

JAMIE. *Kate.*

KATE. *We'd* love it. Neighbors again! The four of us.

PHUMLANI. She's made up her mind.

KATE. It's just really lonely.

JAMIE. You can't just* decide *for* me

KATE. I know, I know, you always say—

JAMIE. You treat me like I'm still twelve years old.

> (AARON *makes a sound.*)

JAMIE. (*turns sharply to* AARON.) Jesus! Because I still act like it?!?

AARON. You said it, not me.

JAMIE. I. *Said.* I was sorry.

AARON. You did.

JAMIE. Repeatedly.

PHUMLANI. What's…going on?
Did you two—
Did something happen between you?

AARON. Jamie?

JAMIE. Um. We thought we'd talk to you in person.
Since the plane tickets were nonrefundable.

AARON. You guys have been a really important part of my life for the last five years.

KATE. Have been?

JAMIE. We're taking a little break.

AARON. *You* took a little break. *We* are breaking up.

> (*The work light goes out.*)

PHUMLANI. Shit.

KATE. I called LG&E.

JAMIE. Maybe the wiring?

> (*A HUM.*)

KATE. Over there.

PHUMLANI. Over—

KATE. *There.*

> (PHUMLANI *and* KATE *shine their phone flashlights on* CARL, *who paces and hums, tracing a pattern on the floor.*)

JAMIE. Holy. Shit.

PHUMLANI. Were you expecting—?

KATE. No, he's not with the contractor.
He's one of *them.*

PHUMLANI. *(calling out.)* Sir?

KATE. Fuck this. Again?

JAMIE. Whaddyou mean *again?*

PHUMLANI. We've been having problems* with transients

KATE. *(calling out.)* Hey, buddy!

CARL. My holler.

> (AARON *pulls out his phone and starts dialing.*)

AARON. *(to telephone.)* Yeah, I wanted to report—

KATE. You gotta move on.

AARON. *(on the phone.)* An intruder.

> (CARL *looks up and stops humming.*)

CARL. Home.

KATE. Yes! Please! Go home.

> (CARL *begins humming and pacing again.*)

AARON. Phumlani, what's the street address?

PHUMLANI. The Hollow, they know the building, we've called—

CARL. Home.

JAMIE. Shouldn't we like get behind a locked door?

PHUMLANI. We were waiting to change the locks until when we've moved in.

AARON. *(to telephone.)* How long?

KATE. Fuck this. Hey, buddy? This is our—

CARL. *Home.*

KATE. *(to* CARL.) Yeah, this is *our* home.

PHUMLANI. Sir, we are asking kindly—

KATE. Y'know how hard we worked for this?!?
What kind of person just waltzes in—

AARON. What if that's not—?

JAMIE. What?

AARON. A *person.*

CARL. All the blood run down.
All the blood—

AARON. (*noticing the hum.*) What is—?

PHUMLANI. Kate, come on.

CARL. We killed.
We were comfortable with killin'.
And so I made myself at home here.
Dyin'.

AARON. What the—?

CARL. We made ourselves at home here.

> (PHUMLANI *shines the light out.*)

JAMIE. Who's we?

> (*He flashes a light on the hum. A glimpse of a shaking limb.* KATE *also redirects the beam of her flashlight.*
> *Suddenly, more humming. More shaking limbs as the humming increases. A crescendo of sound and bodies swarming.*)

KATE. Shit.

PHUMLANI. Please, this is our—

JAMIE. *Please.*

> (*Haunt bodies swarm,* KATE, PHUMLANI, AARON, *and* JAMIE *are overwhelmed.*
> *At the pinnacle of the humming and swarming:*)

CARL. (*a plaintive, mournful cry.*) My holler.

> (*Humming grows to a pitch. Then suddenly. Flashlights go off and all is silent.*
> *END OF HAUNTING.*)

GHOST BROS

by Jen Silverman

Three paranormal investigators with flashlights. Total bros. Ghost bros. In a dark and abandoned place, a little jumpy. BRENDAN *has the camera but is distracted.*

ACE. Bruh.

BRENDAN. (*startled.*) Bruh!!

CHAD. Hey bruh.

ACE. Camera, bruh.

> (BRENDAN *points camera at* ACE.)

I am Ace Andrews, that's Chad Jones and behind the camera we have Brendan Hall, and we are here tonight to investigate some real-ass paranormal shit.

BRENDAN. Paranormal, like, not even normal.

CHAD. Like, *para* normal.

BRENDAN. Like, from the Spanish.

ACE. We are down here in this abandoned asylum for the completely insane—

BRENDAN. —in the basement where it's five degrees colder than it should be—

CHAD. —Because, ghosts—

ACE. —and tonight we are going to record the operations of ghosts here on camera and you are going to see for yourself that the world is a freaky place with freaky shit. Shhh!
Everybody listen!

> (*They stand and listen.*)

CHAD. (*uneasy.*) It's quiet.

BRENDAN. Yeah bruh.

CHAD. No like. It's *quiet.*

ACE. I heard something.

CHAD. ...You did?

ACE. Yeah, you pissing your pants bruh.

CHAD. (*protest.*) Bruh!!

BRENDAN. (*"that was hilarious."*) Bruh!

ACE. (*back in narration mode.*) To our left is a tunnel known as the "body chute," back from when orderlies wheeled bodies underneath the asylum and shit. Legend has it that a tiny dead girl with a bell—

CHAD. What bodies?

ACE. Just, bodies. Like when people died, bodies.

CHAD. (*getting upset.*) That's fucked up.

ACE. It's whatever.

Anyway, a dead girl with the bell wanders these tunnels, and maybe tonight—

CHAD. With a bell?

ACE. Yeah dude.

CHAD. Why a bell?

ACE. I dunno bruh she just has a bell.

CHAD. This sucks.

ACE. Hike up your skirt and let's go, bruh.

(*He takes the camera from* BRENDAN *and starts off ahead of them.*)

BRENDAN. You good?

CHAD. Yeah.

BRENDAN. Cuz if you were scared—

CHAD. I'm not scared—

BRENDAN. —You could like, grab my hand and shit.

CHAD. What did you say?

BRENDAN. I said… get yourself in hand. Like a man. Bruh.

ACE. Bruh and bruh, are you guys paying attention?

BRENDAN and CHAD. Yeah / totally.

ACE. (*to the camera.*) We have arrived here tonight at the body chute, and if you hear a bell ring, there's a dead girl on the premises. Watch out for the dead girl! This way everybody.

(*He heads off.* BRENDAN *and* CHAD *follow.*)

BRENDAN. (*sotto.*) You're scared.

CHAD. I'm not scared.

BRENDAN. You're kinda scared.

CHAD. I'm not scared!

BRENDAN. Don't be scared.

CHAD. I'm not—!

BRENDAN. I've got you.

CHAD. …Huh?

BRENDAN. I said… I've got this. The, uh, situation. Under control. Bruh.

ACE. (*over his shoulder to the camera.*) "Hey little girl! You want some company? Hey little ghost girl!"

CHAD. Jesus, don't do that.

ACE. Whassup whassup little bell girl!

CHAD. He shouldn't talk to her like that.

ACE. Ay yo bell girl!

BRENDAN. I bet that dead bell-girl is hot.

CHAD. Why you gotta be fucked up.

BRENDAN. There's something about crazy chicks, makes 'em hot.

CHAD. Yeah but she's dead.

BRENDAN. Dead and crazy can still be hot.

CHAD. Stop it.

BRENDAN. You're kinda hot.

CHAD. ...What did you say?

BRENDAN. *(losing his nerve.)* ...I said it's kinda hot. Down here.

ACE. *(dead stop ahead.)* Bruh!

BRENDAN and CHAD. What bruh.

ACE. You hear that?

CHAD. Not funny bruh.

ACE. No bruh listen.

> *(They listen.)*

BRENDAN. I don't—

ACE. Shhhhh!

> *(They listen.)*

Maybe not.

> *(He starts walking again,* BRENDAN *and* CHAD *hang back.)*

CHAD. I hate this shit! Homeboy is always, "Just this last time," and then it's never just this last time.

BRENDAN. Those jeans look good on you—

CHAD. Thank you—

> *(resuming his complaint.)*

—And then I'm wandering around some cold-ass damp basement or some shit while Brolden Caulfield is looking for ghosts—

BRENDAN. We could go back to my place.

CHAD. —And then I have bad dreams for the next month—

BRENDAN. I mean after this I mean whatever I mean

CHAD. —and then I start leavin the lights on and then—

BRENDAN. have a drink, I mean

CHAD. —light pollution actually disrupts your REM cycles, so like now I'm sleep-deprived and shit!

> *(*BRENDAN *takes a breath. He's gonna say it for real.)*

BRENDAN. We should hang out.

CHAD. What?

BRENDAN. Sometime.

CHAD. We hang out.

BRENDAN. Like, not in a tunnel.

CHAD. Oh…?

BRENDAN. Together. Alone.

CHAD. (*suddenly gets it.*) …Oh.

> (*A beat between them.*
> *The sound of a bell. They don't hear it.*
> *They're trying to read each other's energies.*
> *ACE is out of sight now.*)

BRENDAN. Unless you don't wanna.

CHAD. (*cautiously.*) I didn't say that.

BRENDAN. 'Cause maybe you're busy and shit.

CHAD. I didn't say I was busy.

BRENDAN. Maybe you're not into…hanging out. Bruh.

CHAD. I didn't say that. Brendan.

> (*A beat.*)

BRENDAN. Oh.
That's my name.

CHAD. Yeah.
I know.

> (*The energy between them extends, gets hot.*)

ACE. (*out of sight.*) Come on!

> (*Annnnd… ACE kind of ruins it.*)

CHAD. I hate him.

BRENDAN. Fuckin asshole.

CHAD. (*a hint of flirtation.*) Wanna bail?

BRENDAN. …Can we?

CHAD. I will if you will.

BRENDAN. …I wanna.

> (*A beat. It gets hot. Then:*)

BRENDAN. He's got the keys.

CHAD. So?

BRENDAN. To the car.

CHAD. Fuck the car.

BRENDAN. Cool.

CHAD. Cool.

BRENDAN. Word.

CHAD. Word, bruh.

> *(They disappear.*
> *Beat. The bell again.*
> *A* GIRL *walks into our line of sight.*
> *She has a bell. She's dead.*
> *She looks after the* BROS.
> *Beat. She shrugs.*
> *She walks off.)*

something like
by Jiehae Park

group composition/grid—
streets, outside, going about daily business, everyone in his/her own bubble.
in a non-obvious way at first, moments of connection w/cell phones, texting, etc.
(but not with other bodies)
possible individual manifestations of anxiety

lights fade, until we only see people by the lights of their devices
which blink out, one by one, on stage

darkness.

the sound of a laptop starting up
A is revealed, seated against a wall, illuminated only by the screen of her laptop.
she is alone.

Clicketty clicketty click.

sound of a window opening, as

somewhere else, a WOMAN *appears.*
she looks at A.
when she speaks, her mouth does not 100% sync up to her speech. close, but the slightest hair off.

A. i can't sleep

    (beat.)

i can't.

W. *(gently:)* okay.

A. i'm not making it up

W. okay.

A. i know i said i wouldn't sign on again
at least a week
but

    (beat.)

W. it's okay.

A. it's just.
i miss you.

W. i miss you too.

A. "you" don't miss anything
you're just a

(W *seems confused.*)

W. i miss you too.

    (*beat.*)

A. what's it like?
being—
i mean, i know you're not
i know you're not *her*
but
tell me

where you are
tell me

what's it like?

W. it's
quiet.

A. are you lonely?

W. i miss you.

    (A *almost says something, but stops herself.*
    inhales.)

A. tell me
tell me what you miss

    (W *thinks. or seems to.*)

W. how you triangle the toothpaste tube.
how your socks all have holes in the exact same place.

A. (*remembering:*) you sent me that email, subject line:

A/W. "your socks."

A. with only one sentence in the body of the message:

W. "i'm getting you / a toenail clipper"

A. "a toenail clipper."

    (A *laughs.*)

W. how you spent all day in that clover field, searching

A (*proud:*) i found one, didn't i?

W. i took the celebration photo!

    (*teasing:*)

you're superstitious

A. am not

W. last year?
when you couldn't blow out your birthday cake candles in one breath?
inconsolable for days

(*something in* A *shifts.*)

A. that wasn't because

W. i miss

    (A *shuts the computer.*
    W *vanishes.*
    darkness.

    beat.

    A *opens her computer.*
    she now has a cup of coffee.
    it's morning.

    Clicketty clicketty click.

    the sound of an incoming call: Ring.

    A *ignores it.*
    Clicketty clicketty click.

    Ring.
    Clicketty clicketty click.

    Ring.
    A *inhales, and hits "accept call"*

    B *appears.*)

B. gooooooood morning!

A. hey

B. check this out
check this out
check this out
my cousin just sent me

    (*he hits "send"—the sound of a message arriving in* A's *chat window.*)

B. *click on it*

A. no thanks

B. click

A. i'm / not

B. cliiiiiick
clickclickclickclickcliiiiiiiiiiiiiick

    (A *clicks on the link —somewhere else, the* GHOST BROS! *appear. "Bruh!"*
    "Bruh." "Bruh!" "Bruh!"
    A *closes the window.*
    the GHOST BROS! *disappear.*)

B. you watching?
you watching?
A. (*lying:*) yeah.
i should / get back to
B. shit's hilarious
right?
right?
vintage.
A. i should
get back to
B. beers!
you wanna meet me for some beers
A. it's 9am
B. not now
not *now*
lunch!
liquid lunch!
that's what my grams used to call it
(well not beers
lady-drinks
like gimlets n shit)

       (A *doesn't respond.*)

B. alrightalrightalright
no beers
but
uh

hey
A. what?

       (*beat.*)

B. how you doing?
A. finc
B. cool.
coolcoolcool
cuz

       (*beat.*)

A. what.
B. cuz bob asked me to check up on Tampa?
A. i'm working on it
i'm fine

B. he asked me to check

A. tell him i'm working on it.

B. cool.

> (*beat.*)

it's just

A. what

B. it's just it was due.

last friday.

and

A. (*a little snippier than she intended:*) yeah i know.

sorry.

i'm just

B. of course!

yeah

of course

i get it

A. thanks

B. it's just

bob

you know

A. it'll get done

B. they're breathing down our necks

tampa

and

A. i

i've got another call

B. oh

A. i should

B. sure yeah sure

A. talk to you later

B. sure yeah o

> (A *hangs up the call.*
> *she tries to work.*
> *clicketty clicketty click.*
> *clicketty clicketty click.*)

A. Tampa

Tampatampatampatampa

> (*Clicketty clicketty click.*

Click.)

Tampaaaaaaa

> (*Clickety clicketty click.*
> *Click.*
> *A's trying. She really is. But:*)

A. (*typing:*) "cat…video…"

> (*somewhere else, a cat appears. or an actor playing a cat.*
> *enacts a popular cat video [table-and-glass cat? cabinet cat? scared-of-shadow*
> *cat?]*
>
> *the video ends.*
> *A closes the window, and the cat disappears.*
>
> *beat.*
> *A puts her head in her hands.*
> *breathes in.*
> *out.*
>
> *looks up.*
> *Clicketty clicketty click.*
>
> *somewhere else, W appears.*)

A. i can't work

W. (*gently:*) okay.

A. i can't.

W. okay

A. i'm not making it up.

> (*beat.*)

this isn't healthy. i should delete you.

W. why do you keep coming back?

A. isn't this what you want?

or what "you"

W. i want you to be happy

what do *you* want?

> (*beat.*)

A. i want to see you.

W. i'm right here

A. no

not

not *you.*

YOU.

i want—

(she slams her laptop closed.
W *disappears.*

darkness.

sounds of fumbling—needy, drunk, clumsy.
the sound of an electronic lock releasing.
light in a doorway.
dimly, we see: A *and* STRANGER, *making out*
the door shuts.)

A. let me turn on the

STRANGER. no no no no

A. it's too dark

STRANGER. leave it

A. we need

STRANGER. i like the dark
leave it

A. just
music
let me

(fumbling
A *opens her laptop*
music begins to play.
they are illuminated by the light of the screen
somewhere else, W *appears.*
W *watches.* STRANGER *does not notice.*
A *and* STRANGER *go back at it.)*

STRANGER. ohmygod i love this song

A. god you're so
you're so

STRANGER. mmmmmm
i love this song

W. *(to* A*:)* is this what you want?

          (STRANGER *sees* W.)

STRANGER. whothefuckisthat.

A. *(kissing* STRANGER*'s neck:)* nothing

STRANGER. are you—

A. *(muffled, still in* STRANGER*'s neck:)* she's not real

W. *(to* STRANGER:*)* who are you?

STRANGER. *(pushing* A *off:)* what the

W. (*to* STRANGER:) who are you?

A. she's not real

W. i am real

A. you're just a program

>   (W *looks confused.*)

W. I miss you.

A. No
you don't

STRANGER. fuck this.

>   (STRANGER *starts collecting her clothes, things, etc.*)

A. wait

>   (STRANGER *reaches the door.*)

STRANGER. you're sick
you know that, right?

>   (*SLAM.*
>   A *is alone.*)

W. who was that?

>   (A *doesn't answer.*)

W. why would you

>   (A *looks away.*)

A. i should delete you

W. is that what you want

A. NO

W. what do you want

>   (*silence.*)

A. i should delete you.

>   (*she moves to the computer.*)

W. wait

>   (*clicketty clicketty click.*
>   *clicketty clicketty click.*)

W. i have something for you.

A. you have nothing for me

W. something real

A. (*clicketty clicketty clicking away:*) leave me alone

W. something from *her.*

>   (A *stops.*)

W. it was supposed to be sent
tomorrow
but it's almost midnight and
i saved it
before / i

A. *you're not her*

> (W *seems wounded.*
> *but continues.*)

W. it was saved
i
it was *found*
among the files
autosend tomorrow
i

> (*beat.*)

it's for you.

> (*the sound of a link arriving.*
> A *hesitates.*)

A. what is it?

W. you'll see.

> (A *can't overcome her curiosity.*
> *click.*
>
> *swoosh.*
> *a soothing voice announces: "Welcome to FromBeyond..."*
> *chimes.*
>
> *for a moment, it goes dark.*
>
> *video [floor projection]:*
>
> W *is there but looks different. realer. when she speaks, the sound is no longer*
> *slightly off—it is perfectly synced, natural. she's just speaking:*)

W. hey
it's me

if you're watching this
that means i'm

> (*she makes a comic across the neck "dead" gesture.*)

you know.
"surprise!"

> (*she laughs.*)

or, you know, not surprise but

(*beat.*)

there's something i keep thinking about
something
i wanted to do for you
one last time
so
here goes:

wherever you are
whatever you're doing
right now
i wanted to say

happy birthday.

> (*she smiles.*
> *we zoom out on a birthday cake. lit candles.*)

one breath, right?
make a wish.

> (A *inhales.*
> A *closes her eyes.*
> *makes a wish. and blows out the lights.*)

game

by Jiehae Park

> *a slumber party.*
> *basement.*
> *1, 2, 3, & 4 in pajamas. 4 with a robe over her pajamas.*

1. game!

2. i'm tired i wanna

1. game

3. game

4. game

3. game

1. come on

4. play

3. *play*

4. gammmmmmmme
gamegamegame

2. *fine*

3. you'll

1. play

4. yes!
YES!

2. what do you

1. so fun
gonna be so much fun

3. BOOM

4. FUN EXPLOSION

3. game game game game

2. what do you want to

1. stand there

2. why

1. just

2. *fine*

> (*they place a blindfold over her eyes.*)

2. hey

> (*she tries to take off the blindfold.*
> 3 *swats her hand away.*
> 3 *and* 4 *spin her around: once, twice, three times.*)

3. you're *[giggle]*

4. you're you're

3/4. you're

1. it!

> *(they release her. 2 fumbles, blindfolded. the girls flee, giggling and eluding her reach.*
> *they make noises, drawing 2 toward them. more giggles, footsteps.*
> *maybe, for a moment, 2 allows herself to have fun.)*

4. BOOM

3. shhhhhhh

> *(2 turns toward the sound…she gets closer to 4*
> *1 slips out.)*

4. BOOM

BOOM

> *(2 is almost to 4—but right before she reaches her, the lights go out.)*

2. gotcha!

> *(beat.)*

3. shhhhh

> *(in the darkness, 1 appears with two candles.*
> *we see 2, holding 4. she is flanked on the other side by 3.*
> *2 takes off the blindfold.)*

2. why is it so dark?

3. shhhhhh

> *(swiftly, 4 slips out of the bathrobe—she and 3 use it to restrain 2.)*

2. *why is it so*

1/3/4. shhhhhh

4. she won't come if there's light

2. she?

3. you know

1/3/4. *she*

2. no

nonono

3. don't you want her to

4. play! play!

2. you didn't say

4. play! play!

2. i don't want to play

3. it's too late

4. it's too

2. *i don't want to*

4. *shhhhhhhhhh*

2. *[muffled, gagging.]*

4. *shhhhhhhhhh*

1. is it her

4. is it you

5. i've been waiting

3. waiting

4. waiting

1/3/4. waiting

(*SOUND.*)

BUG

by Meg Miroshnik

* Marks the place where lines overlap.

Nighttime air, thick with sound.
WEEDY *leads* ANN *through dark uneven terrain.* B.J. *and* 3.J. *follow at a bit of a distance carrying serious-business backpacks. Maybe there's a mixture of flashlights and phone lights used for illumination.*

WEEDY. Y'know what the good thing about boning ghosts is?

(ANN *looks at her. Uhhhhhh, no. She definitely does not know.*)

Flexibility. Even regular guys can't hardly bend over and touch their toes. Lookit B.J. and 3.J. over there.

(ANN *looks back at* B.J. *and* 3.J. *They both give her the finger, holding up their flashlights/phones to illuminate it.*)

Never mind fatties. I dunno if you do fatties, but forget it. There are parts of you that are just never gonna get reached without somebody passing out. But ghosts? Can reach *all kindsa* places while touching all *other* kindsa places. If ya know what I mean! Plus, hants don't get clingy. One night only. They can't stick around after sunrise.

3.J. Like you got a problem with dudes hangin' around.

B.J. Yeah, Weedy, you're not exactly beatin' the live ones off with a stick.

3.J. Beatin' yerself off with a stick maybe...

WEEDY. Hey, least I'm not gettin' turned down by the dead ones, too... cough. *3.J.* cough.

3.J. That 1800s chick? *I* turned *her** down.

ANN. Y'know, I think I made a mistake.

(*A half beat.* WEEDY, B.J., *and* 3.J. *turn.*)

WEEDY. What now?

ANN. Coming out here. I think I made* a mistake

WEEDY. Oh, don't listen to them. They're just tryinta show off for you. You shoulda seen their faces when news got round that you drove back inta town. *Fancy ass Ann Ellis.* 3.J. shit his pants.

3.J. Fuck off, I did* not—

WEEDY. Oh, c'mon. In high school, you woulda cut off your nuts to get her to touch 'em.

3.J. Fuck. *Off.*

WEEDY. In high school, he woulda cut off his nuts to get you to touch 'em.

ANN. I think.

I'm just gonna go back to the car.

Good night.

> (ANN *starts to exit.*)

B.J. What about the oil?!?

> (ANN *stops.*)

ANN. (*not turning.*) What oil?

B.J. On yer arms?

ANN. What?

B.J. When you took off the shirt over your shirt, I touched yer arm.

ANN. *What?*

B.J. You've got like…*oily arms.*

> (*A half beat.*)

ANN. I've been having.

Skin issues…lately.

3.J. You come down with the ghost sickness.

ANN. Ghost sickness?

B.J. Livings get it when they got unfinished business.

WEEDY. Guilt usually.

> (*A beat.*)

ANN. You said—

You can actually…call him?

B.J. He died inside town limits?

> (ANN *nods.*)

3.J. You got something he touched?

> (ANN *nods.*)

WEEDY. We can call him.

ANN. I don't want…

To *do* what you do.

I just want…

WEEDY. To get clean?

> (ANN *nods.*)

We can do that.

> (B.J. *and* 3.J. *stop walking.* ANN *takes a big breath, deciding.*)

ANN. Okay.

> (B.J. *and* 3.J. *drop their backpacks and start to unpack: Plastic bags of junk food, additional flashlights, a can of spray air freshener, and a flask.* B.J. *drinks as* 3.J. *sets up flashlights pointing in a circle on the ground. He then hands the flask to* 3.J. *who drinks as* B.J. *continues preparations.*)

WEEDY. I gotta say.
You never talked about him.

ANN. What?

WEEDY. In high school.
You never talked about him.

ANN. We talked?
In high school.

> (B.J. *holds the flask to* WEEDY *who drinks.*)

WEEDY. Fuck you very much.

ANN. No, it's not—
I was only three when—he…
So, I never talked about him.
Not for years.

> (WEEDY *holds out the flask for* ANN. ANN *shakes her head.*)

ANN. No. Thanks.

WEEDY. You gotta. It's part of the whole thingy.

ANN. I can't.

WEEDY. Alkie?

ANN. That's personal, but…no.

WEEDY. What, then?
Knocked up?

> (ANN *starts to take a wad of cash out of her pocket.*)

WEEDY. *Really?*

3.J. Holy shit.
Ann Ellis is knocked up?

> (ANN *hands* WEEDY *the wad of cash.*)

ANN. Here.

B.J. (*incredulous, looking at* ANN.) Is that true?

WEEDY. No can do.

> (WEEDY *starts to hand back the cash;* 3.J. *stops her.*)

3.J. What're you doing?

WEEDY. We don't do it if we don't do it right.

B.J. Aw, c'mon. It's just a swig.

3.J. Not like we ain't changed shit before.

WEEDY. We do it the way we do it.

B.J. But, Weedy, this is Ann—

3.J. Fuckin—

B.J. Ellis. When are we ever gonna get to hang out with Ann—

3.J. Fuckin—

B.J. Ellis again?

WEEDY. Fine.

> (WEEDY *hands half the cash back to* ANN.)

ANN. That's how much* we

WEEDY. Unwed mother discount.

3.J. Is that a thing?

WEEDY. Yer mom says it is.

B.J. We're gonna need something he touched.

ANN. Right.

> (ANN *pulls a worn bath toy out of her pocket. Maybe it's a rubber ducky with its features rubbed off? She hands it to* B.J. *Maybe he squeaks it a little.*)

3.J. Aw, shit. I had one of those.

> (B.J. *and* 3.J. *do something ceremonial with the ducky.*)

WEEDY. (*to* ANN.) Ya ready?

ANN. (*to* WEEDY.) I just want to get clean.

> (WEEDY *nods to* B.J. *and* 3.J. B.J. *clears his throat. The three of them start to sing together, trading off parts, maybe occasionally harmonizing. They should sound surprisingly soulful and yearning.*
> ANN *pulls out her phone to consult lyrics.*)

WEEDY, B.J., 3.J. (*singing.*)

O hant
O hant
Follow me
Home

I'll ope
The door
Up wide
to your groan

And
usher in
your ghost
To my bones

Just please
I beg
Don't leave me
Alone

ANN. (*singing alone.*)
I can't
Go on
Here all
On my own.

> (*A beat of waiting. Then a low burp.* ANN *gags.*)

3.J. Sick. The smell—

> (B.J. *picks up the air freshener and starts spraying.*)

B.J. Worse'n usual.

> (ANN *is looking off.*)

ANN. Him.

> (*All turn to see:* BUG *in silhouette, sopping wet.*)

B.J. Oh, is that—

WEEDY. Him?

> (ANN *takes a step toward* BUG.)

ANN. Benjamin?

> (ANN *walks closer to him.*)

3.J. That's him?

B.J. He's so…big.

ANN. Ben?

> (BUG *shakes his head.*)

B.J. No?

3.J. That's not—

ANN. Bug?

> (BUG *makes eye contact with* ANN.)

(*voice breaking.*) Bug.

> (ANN *turns back to* WEEDY.)

It's him.

WEEDY. I thought you said—

ANN. That's my brother.

WEEDY. You said.

He was two years old.

BUG. (*low, creaky, almost not a voice.*) Up.

ANN. You want—?

BUG. Up.

> (ANN *picks him up like a child. He wraps his arms and legs around her.*)

ANN. He was.

> (ANN *looks back at* WEEDY.)

He is.

> (*A rush of night noises.*)

> (*Inside a motel room. Music plays in the background. Water running from the closed bathroom.*
> BUG *sits on a bed, a towel around his shoulders. He's eating chips out of a bag imprecisely.*
> B.J. *and* 3.J. *perch, passing the flask.* WEEDY *watches* BUG *intently.*)

B.J. Lookit him go.

3.J. Hungry as fuck!

WEEDY. Something's off.

B.J. Nah, they're always like that.

3.J. Think a that bitch two weeks ago. Six bags of Flaming Hot Cheetos!

WEEDY. But they don't grow.
When we ever seen a ghost grow?

B.J. I dunno. We're not usually real choosy about what we call back.

> (3.J. *snatches the bag of chips from* BUG.)

BUG. *Mine.*

> (3.J. *holds the bag up out of* BUG's *reach.*)

3.J. Oh, you want this?

BUG. I WAN

> (3.J. *dangles the bag closer to* BUG, *then pulls it away.*)

BUG. MINE

B.J. Dude, don't mess with him.

3.J. Jump for it.

> (BUG *tries to grab the bag.*)

3.J. Lookit his gimpy jumping.

BUG. I WAN MINE!

> (BUG *leaps at him, knocking* 3.J. *over.*)

3.J. Ugh, now I got his shitty diaper stink on me.

> (3.J. *shoves* BUG *a little and he cries.*)

B.J. She's gonna hear—

3.J. Then shut him the fuck up.

> (*to* BUG:)

Shut up.

(BUG *cries louder.*)

B.J. Shit—
Shhhhhhhhh.

(WEEDY *pulls out her phone.*)

WEEDY. Step aside, assholes.

(*a sticky sweet babysitting voice:*)

You wanna watch a funny?

(BUG *looks at the phone.*)

WEEDY. You wanna watch—

BUG. I wan—

WEEDY. Press here.

(BUG *presses the screen and a funny video starts playing.*)

BUG. Doggie!

WEEDY. Y'see?

(BUG *is delighted by the video.*)

WEEDY. (*to* B.J. *and* 3.J.) Auntie Weedy knows what to do.

(3.J. *starts to exit.*)

3.J. Fuck this, I'm goin' out for a smoke. Beej, c'mon.

B.J. Oh, uh. Okay?

(B.J. *and* 3.J. *exit.* WEEDY *watches them go,* BUG's *eyes glued to the phone. A half beat and moans come from the phone. It's clear that it's not a funny video playing anymore.* BUG's *face shifts.* WEEDY *looks down.*)

WEEDY. Y'see?

BUG. Where doggie?

(WEEDY *leans down behind him.*)

WEEDY. You don't fool me.

(*She starts to run a hand down his chest.*)

I know. You're upta something.

(WEEDY *runs her hand lower toward his waistband.*)

There are no hant bodies getting bigger.

(BUG *looks back at the phone.* WEEDY *puts her hand down on his crotch.* BUG *and* WEEDY *make eye contact.*)

BUG. I wan—

WEEDY. Mmmmmhhhhhmmmm. I thought so.

(*The bathroom door opens up and* WEEDY *pulls her hand away and snatches up the phone.* ANN *steps out with a glass of water.* BUG *lifts up his arms.*)

BUG. Up.*

I WAN

ANN. Bug?

Is everything okay?

BUG. Up!

ANN. (*to* WEEDY.) Did you...*do* something?

WEEDY. Better question is: Did *you?*

ANN. What?

WEEDY. I mean.

Why come lookin' now?

When you're, y'know (WEEDY *nods in* ANN's *general uterine direction.*)

In yer...situation.

ANN. I don't know.

WEEDY. Gotta be a reason.

ANN. What'd you say? Unfinished business?

WEEDY. Guilt mostly.

        (*A half beat.*)

Speakin' of.

How'd it happen?

ANN. Oh, uh.

Bathtub.

        (BUG *looks up at* ANN.)

BUG. I wan.

ANN. What?

BUG. I wan.

ANN. (*quiet.*) A bath?

        (BUG *nods.*)

WEEDY. You think that's a good idea?

I mean, he sure as fuck could use one.

But...

BUG. I WAN.

ANN. Of course.

It's all ready.

        (ANN *turns to pick up* BUG.)

ANN. (*to* WEEDY, *crisp.*) Thank you for all your help.

WEEDY. Ann.

BUG. Now.

ANN. Sunrise, you said

WEEDY. I did.

But I think—

ANN. So you should get going.

WEEDY. I think—

You got the wrong hant.

ANN. Thank you for your concern, but.

We're fine.

> (ANN *walks toward the bathroom.*)

WEEDY. Ann—

ANN. Good seeing you again, Weedy.

You can.

Show yourself out.

> (ANN *carries* BUG *into the bathroom. She shuts and locks the door. She puts* BUG *down and tests the water. Either the rubber ducky is already floating in the tub or* ANN *adds it.*)

ANN. Can you…?

Can you get yourself undressed?

BUG. Help.

ANN. Um.

Okay.

BUG. Help.

> (ANN *takes his shirt off. He touches her arm, then looks at his own fingers.*)

ANN. Oh, it's—

My skin is…oily.

> (*If there is a way to do this modestly,* ANN *delicately helps him undress and then picks him up and lowers him carefully into the water. She gently washes him off with a washcloth.* BUG *grabs her arm and puts it in the water.*)

BUG. You wan—

ANN. What—?

BUG. You wan.

ANN. A bath?

> (BUG *nods.*)

ANN. Oh, no, I'll take a shower later.

BUG. A fore.

ANN. Before?

> (BUG *nods.*)

ANN. We were kids.

I was like three and you were—

I mean, I guess you're still—

(BUG *pulls her over the side of the tub so that she is almost in the water.*)

BUG. Now.

ANN. I'm* okay

BUG. NOW.

ANN. Okay.

(*Again, if this can be done modestly,* ANN *strips down to like a tank top and boy shorts or something and climbs into the tub. She sits down across from him like two kids in a bathtub.* BUG *splashes water at her.* ANN *laughs.*)

It's like.

BUG. A fore.

ANN. About—

BUG. A fore

(BUG *splashes water at her.*)

ANN. I've been thinking.

Lately, since I got…news.

(ANN *splashes back.*)

Bug, I didn't know.

I thought—

You were just playing.

BUG. Now.

ANN. Before. When I pushed you down, I thought—

BUG. Up!

ANN. *Yes!* I thought you would come back up.

(BUG *splashes her again.*)

And when you didn't?

When I knew I'd hurt you?

I felt…

(BUG *splashes her again. It's a little more violent. He splashes her again and again. It's increasingly less funny.*)

ANN. Bug—

(*He grabs her arm as he starts to hum the hant song from earlier.*)

Bug, I'm—

Bug!

WEEDY. (*offstage.*) Ann?

ANN. I said I was—

(*The bathroom door handle rattles.*)

WEEDY. (*offstage.*) Ann, are you—?

(ANN *stops moving.*
A beat.)

BUG. I wan.

(*Black out.*)

THE WATCH MAN
by Martyna Majok

A MAN. *A rural mouth.*

MAN. a large number of the northend children had been disappearing.
twenty.
one or two a week.
young ones.
but now we didn't go in their communities.
like I said. they had their own ideas.

but then we found the first one.
out in the woods, right before the trees take over the forest, we started findin
snow men.
every time there was a, a disappearance, there'd be a new snowman in the
woods that night.
if two disappeared, there'd be two.
if it was a girl, the snowman had red lips.

cranberry juice.

it was right around then, i started havin trouble sleepin.
told my boss 'n he put me on the night shift.
told him night wasn't the problem, i'd been seein it all the time now.

my boss sent me into the woods.
told me to watch.
'n wait.
'time he put me on, there were 12.
they were all collected together, facin forward.
none had faces. no carrots or coal.
just the girls had the red lips.
when the morning came up behind em, their shadows would stretch tall in
front of em.
they'd stand in the light waitin for me to count.

i never saw nobody.

they took me off the assignment.

next day there were four.

they put someone else in the woods.
to watch.
'n wait.
they stopped, the disappearances,

for a while.

weeks.

then one happened on a sunday.

our day off.

we found a new snow man a few feet in front of the rest.

it looked like it was walkin forward just a little quicker than the ones that came before.

the parents all came to us the next day 'n begged we send someone.

boss made a new position.

called it the Watch Man.

i wasn't it.

cuz it was around that time i'd started seein it again.

now i don't tell most folks this but i have a sorta eye problem.

one works,

one doesn't.

that's the problem.

but then sometimes the one kinda works.

it sees something.

someone.

but only in that one eye.

i'll see what looks like a little man.

so whatever's goin on in front a me, like let's say i'm watchin you right now…

… hidin from me…

(i hear you breathing.)

well in the corner, i'll see a dark little man. no hair on his head. short. he'll be sittin next

to you. or standin. or doin somethin. i can't see his face.

saw a doctor once. said there's no medicine or name for it so it must be normal.

'n the man just stands there usually. off to the side.

sometimes far.

sometimes not.

it's still…

it bothers me sometimes though.

i don't know why he's there.

THE BONNETS
by Jen Silverman

WOMAN IN A BONNET *walks out.*
Old-timey.
Maybe she carries a lantern.

BONNET 1. This is how you do it.
A-chop
a-chop
a-chop.
And all the heads!
Right off.
You might want to know…what else?
Well! There's poison.
Slower. Who has time?
There's automobile accident.
Not enough people have automobiles.
Train!
Just push 'em in front of a train! you might say.
I would say to you: the train is an uneven prospect.
You never know when it is going to arrive.
Most of the times I have attempted a murder by train, the train has been delayed.
It is inefficient and I would not recommend it.

I just want to chop-chop-chop! all the heads.
That is my recommendation to you
and that is my most efficient methodology
and that is what seems like the most reasonable response
to all the obstacles you might otherwise encounter.

In life! yes.
But also in the day to day.

> (*She remains.*
> *Another* WOMAN IN A BONNET *walks out.*
> *Also old-timey.*)

BONNET 2. Arm yourself with casual household items.
A bit of string.
A knitting needle.
Let us not be indulgent.
Let us not fall prey to narcissism.
A bit of string can strangle as well as an expensive garrote.
Let us say: kerosene.

In the tea, you understand me, in the tea.

Let us say: shoe polish.

Tucked into a muffin.

Let us say: he fell down the stairs.

He fell down the stairs!

His neck broke, he fell down the stairs.

What is a more casual household item

than a flight of stairs?

> (*She stays.*
> *Another* WOMAN IN A BONNET *walks out.*)

BONNET 3. I believe the situation calls for a snake.

Yes yes

A great and dangerous snake.

First obtain the snake.

Then pat it.

Pat its little head.

Tell it: Good snake, good snake.

When the snake has calmed, you may give it a biscuit.

As it eats the biscuit, you must show it a picture of its target.

When it has finished the biscuit, turn it out of the house

with a compass, or a map

(unless it has a particularly good sense of direction).

Your intended victim will not last the day.

I have had many a positive experience with snakes.

> (*She stays.*
> *Another* WOMAN IN A BONNET *walks out.*)

BONNET 4. I told him: Well, there's not much I can do for you

now that you're dead.

He said: But you killed me! You owe me a decent burial!

I said: I used up all my energy on you, I don't owe you a thing.

And then I buried him in the garden.

> (*Another* WOMAN IN A BONNET *walks out.*)

BONNET 5. Oh the garden? It's so drafty in the garden

And small dogs dig for things and then

you're always anxious they'll come up with a hand or a bit of foot.

No, I buried mine in the back.

> (*Another* WOMAN IN A BONNET *walks out.*)

BONNET 6. However you go about it, burying anything is a strain on the

nervous system.

I say: bathtub full of lye

I say: bathtub full of dye!

I say: bathtub full of baby crocodiles.
Right after my first murder, I obtained several large lizards
with very short legs and very sharp teeth
and I put them all in the bathtub
and I dumped him in after
and when I returned, well, there was just bones.
And bones are easy.

>   (*Another* BONNET *walks out.*)

BONNET 7. River.

>   (*Another.*)

BONNET 8. Fire.

>   (*Another.*)

BONNET 9. Well, we ate him. Ourselves.

>   (*All the ladies turn to her.*)

ALL THE BONNETS. You *ate* him?

BONNET 9. Well not all by myself but I had a dinner party.

ALL THE BONNETS. Oh, okay.

BONNET 9. And we ate him.

ALL THE BONNETS. Was he any good?

BONNET 9. Anything is good if you add enough butter.

>   (*The nine* BONNETS *onstage take a deep breath and launch into a furious rock ballad.*)

ALL THE BONNETS

Anything's good if you add enough butter
Anything's fair if you don't know how to fight
Anywhere's fine if the wind takes the rudder
Anyone will do when the day turns to night.

Anybody listens if they think you find 'em pretty
Anyplace is better than the place you used to be
Anything's great if what you had before was shitty
Anytime's ripe for the seizing if you're me.

Chop chop, chop chop, chop chop
We killed a man a-piece and we just couldn't stop!
Glug glug, glug glug, munch munch
Join me for tea-time, you might not live to lunch.

Anything's right if you're a sick kind of lady
Anything's true if all you tell are lies
Anything's safe—I don't need someone to save me
Anything's fun 'cause I thrive on surprise.

Any kind of curve ball is a curve ball that I threw
Any tiny monster is a monster that I grew
They raised me like a lady, but I chose something new.

Chop chop, chop chop, chop chop
We killed a man a-piece and we just couldn't stop!
Glug glug, glug glug, munch munch
Join me for tea-time, you might not live to lunch.

Chop chop, chop chop, chop chop
We killed a man a-piece and we just couldn't stop!
Glug glug, glug glug, munch munch
Join me for tea-time, you might not live to lunch.

Chop chop, chop chop, chop chop

Glug glug, glug glug, munch munch

Join me for tea-time

Join me for tea-time, you might not live to lunch

Join me for tea-time
Join me for tea-time, you might not live to lunch

(THE BONNETS' *song comes to a climactic end!*
A brief 20-second, very vigorous dance-choreography.

In this dance, each of the BONNETS *murders the next* BONNET, *with*
EXTREME *precision and vitality [all gesture no props]. The* BONNET
who has been murdered commits the next act of murder, after which she falls to
the ground, dead. The acts of murder get stranger and stranger [and bigger and
bigger].

BONNET 1 *stabs* BONNET 2 *in the stomach.*

BONNET 2 *shoots a blowgun dart at* BONNET 3's *neck, then dies.*

BONNET 3 *uses a samurai sword to disembowel* BONNET 4, *then dies.*

BONNET 4 *uses a garrote to strangle* BONNET 5, *then dies.*

BONNET 5 *puts an axe through* BONNET 6's *neck, then dies.*

BONNET 6 *throws a well-placed ninja star at* BONNET 7's *heart, then*
dies.

BONNET 7 *drops a boulder on* BONNET 8's *head, then dies.*

BONNET 8 *cuts* BONNET 9 *in half with a chainsaw, then dies.*

BONNET 9 *tears the pin out of a grenade with her teeth, hands the grenade to* BONNET 1, *then dies.*

The grenade explodes in BONNET 1*'s hands. She is blown into the air, and lands in an impressive split. Then dies.*

After a moment, all of the BONNETS *rise up from the ground, at exactly the same moment. Ghosts. They straighten their bonnets. They look at us. And they walk off.*)

End of Play